CRISIS
in
Central
America

About the Book and Editors

In the early years of the recent Central American crisis, analysts often predicted a rapid, dramatic resolution—whether by revolutionary victory or through military intervention by the United States. The 1980s, however, have witnessed an intensification of conflicts with increasing U.S. involvement. Rather than standing at the brink of a sharp turning point, Central America is at an interim point in an evolving historical process. This text provides an assessment of this process and of its immediate and long-term implications for the region and for U.S.–Latin American relations. It focuses on the complex and contradictory effects of the Reagan administration's efforts to influence the Central American debate within the United States and to reestablish U.S. hegemony in the region itself.

The first part of the book examines the development of various aspects of U.S. policy toward Central America. In particular, contributors discuss the interaction between the executive and legislative branches in shaping U.S. strategy, the implications for constitutional democracy of presidential control over foreign policymaking, the treatment of Central American refugees, the counterinsurgency strategy of "low intensity warfare," and the effects of U.S. policy on regional peace initiatives put forward by Mexico and other Latin American countries. In the second part, contributors analyze external pressures on Central American countries and regional dynamics. They begin with a discussion of the economic crisis—aggravated by conflicts in the region—and regional integration. Other topics include the ambiguous position of the Catholic church, Guatemala's "hidden war," "demonstration elections," the changing balance of forces in El Salvador, and the obstacles Nicaragua faces in constructing a new economic development model.

Nora Hamilton is associate professor of political science and **Linda Fuller** is assistant professor of sociology at the University of Southern California. **Jeffry A. Frieden** is assistant professor of political science at the University of California, Los Angeles. **Manuel Pastor, Jr.,** is assistant professor of economics at Occidental College.

A PACCA Book

CRISIS

in

Central America

Regional Dynamics and U.S. Policy in the 1980s

edited by
Nora Hamilton, Jeffry A. Frieden,
Linda Fuller, and Manuel Pastor, Jr.

Westview Press / Boulder and London

Copyright © 1988 by Westview Press, Inc.

Published in 1988 in the United States of America by Westview Press, Inc.; Frederick A. Praeger, Publisher; 5500 Central Avenue, Boulder, Colorado 80301

Library of Congress Cataloging-in-Publication Data
Crisis in Central America.
  Includes index.
  1. Central America—Politics and government—
1979–   . 2. Central America—Foreign relations—
United States. 3. United States—Foreign relations—
Central America. 4. United States—Foreign relations—
1981–   . I. Hamilton, Nora, 1935–   .
F1439.5.C737 1988   327.73072   87-21020
ISBN 0-8133-7431-6
ISBN 0-8133-7432-4 (pbk.)

Printed and bound in the United States of America

The paper used in this publication meets the requirements of the American National Standard for Permanence of Paper for Printed Library Materials Z39.48-1984.

10   9   8   7   6   5   4   3   2   1

Stacks

Contents

Preface

This volume is the result of a conference entitled "The United States and Central America: A Five-Year Assessment" held at the University of Southern California in February 1986. The conference responded to a widespread concern with U.S. policy toward Central America and a recognition that the crises in the region would not be resolved in the near future. Its purpose was to undertake a comprehensive examination of developments over the previous five years and, where possible, to assess prospects for the future and develop policy recommendations.

Many people contributed to the planning of the conference and while it would be impossible to mention them all I would especially like to thank Joan Palevsky for her encouragement during the early stages of the planning and Bill Bollinger, Margaret Crahan, and Robert Stark for advice and suggestions as well as moral support throughout the planning process. I also want to acknowledge the assistance of Laurien Alexandre and Pat Hoffman, who brought a high degree of competence and commitment to the administrative tasks of the conference, and Jody Battles, who patiently and competently typed the voluminous correspondence.

The conference was made possible by a grant from the Ford Foundation and assistance from the University of Southern California, the Immaculate Heart College Center, the Campus Ministry of Loyola Marymount University, the Latin American Studies Committee of the Southern California Consortium for International Studies, and Stanley Sheinbaum. Sponsoring organizations were PACCA (Policy Alternatives for the Caribbean and Central America) and the Faculty for Human Rights in El Salvador and Central America.

The conference included two days of workshops, at which papers were presented and discussed, and a one-day public conference. Thirty specialists from the United States, Mexico, Central America, and Europe participated in the three-day session. In addition to the authors whose work is represented here, I would like to thank the other discussants, panelists, and commentators whose participation contributed immeasurably to the success of the workshops and conference: Robin Anderson, William Bollinger, Roger Burbach, E. Bradford Burns, Norma Chinchilla, Charles Clements, Martín de la Rosa, Paul Drake, Paul Espinosa, Murray Fromson, Timothy Harding, Nancy Hollander, Milton Jamail, Jane Jaquette, Saul Landau, Abraham Lowenthal, Carlos Rico, and Laurence Whitehead. All brought a high level of expertise and commitment to the sessions, and many of their ideas and recommendations have been incorporated in the following pages.

The transformation of the papers and discussions of the conference into the present volume was funded by the Rockefeller Foundation. I am indebted to Grace Stimson for her very proficient editing of the papers of this volume; to David Ayón, Richard Anzaldúa, and Maria Irene Alvarez for their skillful translations of Spanish language papers; and to Brad Barham for his excellent notes on the conference and his contributions on economic conditions in Central America. I also want to thank Terry Dye, Karen Pokraka, and Luisa Reyes for their competent typing of manuscripts.

It is of course only the willingness of the authors to take time from their numerous other commitments to revise and update their papers that has made this book possible. And the exceptional dedication and professionalism of my coeditors, Jeff Frieden, Linda Fuller, and Manuel Pastor, Jr., have made the work of editing and organizing this volume a genuinely collaborative effort and a very rewarding experience.

Nora Hamilton

CRISIS
in
Central
America

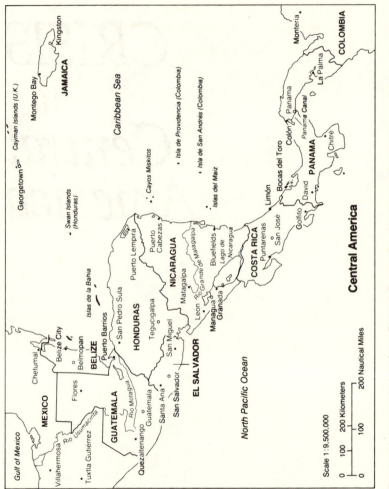

Central America

Scale 1:9,500,000

0	100	200 Kilometers
0	100	200 Nautical Miles

Reprinted, by permission, from Richard Fagen, *Forging Peace: The Challenge of Central America* (Basil Blackwell, Inc., 1987; copyright © PACCA 1987), p. xii.

Introduction

Nora Hamilton and Manuel Pastor, Jr.[1]

When the Reagan administration came into office in 1981 revolutionary movements appeared to be ascendent in Central America. The Nicaraguan government was attempting to reorder its society according to what it termed the logic of the majority. In El Salvador, guerrilla movements had united to form the FMLN (Farabundo Martí Front for National Liberation), and in both El Salvador and Guatemala revolutionary forces were threatening the status quo. These activities posed a sharp challenge to the oligarchic elites of Central America and to the regional control traditionally exercised by the United States. The Reagan administration attributed the developments in Central America to interference by foreign powers, specifically the Soviet Union and Cuba, and viewed them as a threat to U.S. security. Resolving to "draw the line" in Central America, it increased military aid to the Salvadoran government and began a process of organizing, training, and financing a counterrevolutionary force against the Sandinistas in Nicaragua.

As the second Reagan administration approaches its end under the cloud of the Iran-contra investigations, neither revolutionary movements nor U.S.-sponsored forces have achieved a victory in Central America. The conflicts in the region have not been resolved and the United States has become more deeply involved in these conflicts. Military aid to the contras has prolonged the conflict in Nicaragua without bringing it closer to resolution. The guerrilla forces have not achieved a victory in El Salvador but neither have they been defeated despite massive military aid to the Salvadoran armed forces. In Guatemala the military, though dealing a significant blow to the revolutionary movement, has not crushed it, and the conditions that gave rise to these movements in the past still exist.

As this volume goes to press, it is too soon to know whether acceptance of the Arias plan by the five Central American governments marks a long-awaited breakthrough toward the resolution of the Central American conflicts. The issues are difficult and complex, and their resolution will take time. In any case, events of the past seven years have shown that the conflicts in Central America, and U.S. reaction to those conflicts, are part of an

1

evolving historical process, with serious long-term implications for the relations between the United States and Latin America.

To assess this process and to determine the probable evolution and consequences of U.S. policy in the future, a conference of U.S., Mexican, Central American, and European specialists was held at the University of Southern California in February 1986. What emerged from the conference papers and discussion was the contradiction between the apparent success of the Reagan administration in achieving control over the U.S. debate on Central America, on the one hand, and on the other the failure—or the limited success—of U.S. efforts to assert hegemony over the region itself. Within the United States the Reagan administration has succeeded in narrowing the terms of the debate on Central America and in achieving a consensus with Congress over the nature of the Central American conflicts if not always on the means to resolve them. Whereas earlier assessments of the revolutionary movements had recognized the importance of internal factors in the affected countries—endemic poverty, inequality, and political repression—by the mid-1980s the debate on Central America had been recast in terms of the East-West conflict. Administration spokespersons have almost entirely succeeded in their efforts to portray the Sandinistas as totalitarian and Soviet-controlled, the Duarte administration as a democratic alternative for El Salvador, and U.S. domestic opposition to contra aid as naive and ill-informed. Even the Iran-contra investigations have failed to question U.S. policy in the region, focusing instead on whether the law was broken in implementing it. Debates have generally ceased to be concerned with policy objectives; rather they concentrate on the most effective tactics for containing communism.

At the same time, U.S. hegemony over the region itself—the ability to achieve the administration's objectives on the ground—has remained tenuous. In contrast with the 1950s, when the Central Intelligence Agency (CIA) overthrew Guatemala's elected president in a relatively small and inexpensive operation, today massive aid to El Salvador cannot defeat the guerrilla forces, which have demonstrated increased strategeic ability; the Sandinistas retain control despite years of U.S.-sponsored attacks; and U.S. policy initiatives, such as the elections in El Salvador, often have unintended consequences (e.g., the opening of political space for widespread opposition to the Duarte administration).

Both these assertions—that the Reagan administration has achieved control over the debate within the United States, but that U.S. hegemony over the region is limited—require qualification. Despite its failure to achieve a military victory in Central America, the administration can claim success in preventing an FMLN victory in El Salvador and in aggravating difficulties for the Sandinistas in Nicaragua, and in general it has evolved a working policy in the region which enables it to adjust to unanticipated outcomes. At the same time, a strong, articulate opposition to U.S. policy in Central America has emerged among the U.S. public and in Congress. Nonetheless, the contradiction between administration control over the policy debate and its lack of control over the effects of its policy is one of the outstanding phenomena of U.S.–Central American relations.

The following discussion examines these and related issues raised in the conference debate and developed in the resulting articles. Given the diversity of opinions expressed, the discussion should not be construed as a consensus among conference participants but rather as an effort to bring together elements of the debate for an analysis of the impact of U.S. policy toward Central America, in the United States and in the region.

U.S. Policy: The Quest for Hegemony

The revolutionary movements in Central America have been construed as evidence of a decline of U.S. hegemony in Latin America and throughout the world, and several explanations have been advanced for this decline. First, by the 1970s the dominant role of the United States was shaken by the rise of economic and political competitors such as Western Europe, Japan, and the Soviet Union. Within Latin America, regional powers (e.g., Brazil and Mexico) began to challenge the hegemony traditionally exercised by the United States. Resulting global and regional realignments constituted the background of the Carter administration's efforts to redefine policy away from spheres of influence toward an alternative vision of politics based on recognition of the interdependence of nations.

A second explanation for the loss of hegemony, stemming from U.S. military involvement and defeat in Vietnam, is a widespread conviction that U.S. military intervention in Third World conflicts is undesirable for both pragmatic and moral reasons. The "Vietnam syndrome," as well as the abuse of executive power revealed in the Watergate scandal, was responsible for congressional efforts to erect safeguards to constitutional democracy, including commitments to strengthen the role of Congress in order to make the president more accountable for his actions (e.g., the War Powers Act and the establishment of congressional oversight committees); to obtain access to information necessary for accountability and public debate; and to protect civil liberties, including the right to public dissent and opposition.

These changes were accompanied by an increased awareness of North-South relations, of conditions of poverty in Third World countries, and of the problems entailed in sending troops or in supporting undemocratic regimes in these countries. There was an erosion of consensus regarding the use of military force, a recognition of the need to pursue more limited ends at proportionate costs, and a heightened concern for human rights. There was little change, however, in the assumption that U.S. security interests justified and necessitated the maintenance of a war apparatus in times of peace. And underlying the debate was the doctrine of containment and the necessity for the United States to use its influence to prevent leftist revolutionary movements from coming to power. With respect to Latin America, there continued to be a presumption of U.S. dominance and a consensus that further "communist regimes" in the hemisphere should not be tolerated.

A third explanation for the loss of U.S. hegemony, the one adhered to by the Reagan administration, is that the loss was not an objective reality; instead, it was only a perceived erosion, which, along with the Vietnam syndrome, resulted from a loss of confidence and will in the United States. The key to restoring U.S. hegemony lay in convincing the U.S. public and Congress to allow the incoming administration to pursue a more aggressive foreign policy. The Central American crisis was seen not as a problem but, in the words of former Secretary of State Haig, as an opportunity to reassert hegemony and to counter the perception of the United States as a superpower in decline.

It is here, in overcoming the Vietnam syndrome, that the Reagan administration can claim its greatest success. Cynthia Arnson ("The Reagan Administration, Congress, and Central America: The Search for Consensus") argues that while Congress has indeed placed a variety of restrictions on the administration's Central American policy (most notably by directing attention to human rights and tying aid to political reforms), its role in shaping foreign policy has been weakened. Moreover, as noted above, there has been a growing consensus between the executive and legislative branches over the nature of the Central American conflict, if not always over the means to resolve it. Congress and the president seem to agree that Duarte is the only viable alternative for El Salvador and that he has curbed human rights abuses and achieved some degree of social reform. Accompanying this assessment has been a hostile attitude toward both the Salvadoran guerrillas and the Sandinista government in Nicaragua. Congressional defenders of what Michael Conroy and Manuel Pastor describe as the Nicaraguan experiment have become rare.

The new consensus on policy results in part from the increased congressional willingness to view Central American conflicts from the administration's East-West perspective. As Kenneth E. Sharpe ("U.S. Policy Toward Central America: The Post-Vietnam Formula Under Siege") argues, poverty and repression have been de-emphasized as antecedents of revolution, while the role of Soviet aid and the participation of Cuban troops have attained paramount importance. Indeed, the old postwar consensus, which stressed "containment" of revolutionary/communist movements, has given way to the new Reagan doctrine of "rollback." In Nicaragua, as well as in Angola and Afghanistan, the Reagan administration, and increasingly Congress, have supported rebel movements aimed at deposing established leftist governments.

The government's success in strengthening control over the debate on Central America has come at high costs. Sharpe notes that in pursuing its policies the Reagan administration has run roughshod over the safeguards to constitutional democracy established in the wake of Vietnam and Watergate: it has circumvented Congress to launch covert operations against Nicaragua, bypassed congressionally mandated restrictions on increasing military aid to El Salvador, and used military maneuvers in Honduras in order to avoid seeking congressional approval to permanently station U.S. troops in that country.

But the major costs of U.S. policy have been borne by the Central Americans themselves, as is particularly evident in the strategy of "low intensity war." Through this strategy the United States is seeking to reassert its hegemony in Central America without incurring the domestic political costs and geopolitical risks of invasion by its own troops. As Deborah Barry, Raúl Vergara and José Rodolfo Castro explain ("Low Intensity Warfare: The Counterinsurgency Strategy for Central America"), this strategy includes psychological, political, sociological, and economic as well as military warfare, and it targets the civilian support bases of the FMLN in El Salvador and of the Sandinistas in Nicaragua. For the United States this approach, by supposedly lessening the need for direct military intervention, reduces domestic dissent about current policy. Yet the very nature of the low intensity approach, involving a long-term struggle on multiple fronts, will require a prolonged commitment and continuing investment by the United States, which could become a justification for direct military intervention in the future.

The level of intensity is clearly a function of one's vantage point. The low intensity strategy has been accompanied by an increase in military aid to the contras and to the Salvadoran military and an intensification of the air war against civilian areas in El Salvador. In Nicaragua, the contra war has killed thousands of citizens and has strangled the country's economy. In El Salvador, the bombing and strafing of villages, followed by the wholesale destruction of homes, crops and animals, has added to the toll of 60,000 killed and over a million destitute and homeless. The increased militarization of the region has brought countries not directly involved into the conflict. Honduras has become a major base for contra operations against Nicaragua as well as for U.S. maneuvers, and in Costa Rica the civil guard, the only military force in this traditionally neutral country, has tripled in size.

Nevertheless, as Barry, Vergara, and Castro point out, the U.S. strategy in Nicaragua and El Salvador has had only limited success, partly because the Sandinista army and the FMLN have been able to change their structure and shift their operations in response to this strategy. Furthermore, the contras and the Salvadoran army have failed to secure substantial support bases among the populations in the two countries. In Nicaragua, the Sandinista army, initially a guerrilla force, has been reorganized into a regular army, which is complemented by the incorporation of the population into defense units.

In El Salvador the military situation has been characterized as one of "dynamic equilibrium," despite the substantial reaccommodation of strategy and tactics on both sides. As described by Ricardo Stein ("Civil War, Reform, and Reaction in El Salvador"), neither the armed forces nor the guerrillas are capable of militarily weakening the other to the point of imposing negotiating conditions; both recognize that the war will be prolonged. And because both perceive the possibility of an eventual military victory, the process of dialogue and negotiation is difficult. The increased proficiency

of the armed forces and its logistical advantages have been countered by
the dispersion of the FMLN, as well as by "dual power"—the FMLN's
ability to control political and administrative processes within particular
areas in the countryside. While military attacks on its mass base may
represent a setback for the FMLN, the massive displacement of the population
also creates problems for the government and the military.

Ironically, as seen in Gabriel Aguilera Peralta's analysis, the counterinsurgency strategy has been most successful where the United States has
been least involved—in the "hidden war" against the guerrilla forces and
their support bases in Guatemala. Facing the possibility of defeat by the
guerrillas in 1981, the Guatemalan armed forces adopted a multi-faceted
program designed to accomplish two major purposes: to eliminate the
peasant support base of the guerrilla forces by restructuring the countryside
under military control; and to split middle sector support from the guerrillas
by creating political openings within the military regime and ultimately
turning formal power over to an elected civilian government. Zones of
security were established by creating model villages and civil patrols
subordinated to an overarching structure of *coordinadores institucionales*, thus
setting up a form of military dual control in the countryside. The election
of a civilian government that would restore legitimacy culminated in 1985
with the presidential victory of Christian Democrat Vinicio Cerezo.

In the implementation of the military program, up to 75,000 people were
killed, 4,000 villages destroyed, and an estimated 1,000,000 civilians displaced. Nevertheless, the success of the armed forces has not been complete.
The guerrillas, though considerably weakened, have demonstrated their
staying capacity and have not been defeated. Elements on the right still
adamantly resist reform, which frustrates the military's efforts to coopt or
neutralize sectors desiring change as well as reformist policies of the Cerezo
government. Finally, in the context of the present economic crisis, funds to
implement the military's ambitious plans for transforming the countryside
are insufficient, which means that its ability to control and coopt those
groups whose villages have been destroyed and whose lives are disrupted
is limited. As these are the sectors traditionally integrated into revolutionary
processes, the resurgence of revolution in Guatemala cannot be precluded.

In the meantime, one effect of the pursuit of military solutions in Central
America has been the massive dislocation of populations. Between 1 and
2 million Central Americans—Salvadorans, Guatemalans and Nicaraguans—
have left their homes since 1979; many have been displaced within their
own countries, others have crossed international borders. According to some
estimates, there are more than 1 million Central Americans in the United
States, the majority having arrived since 1979. Although the U.S. State
Department routinely denies requests by Salvadorans and Guatemalans for
asylum, claiming that all but a handful come to the United States for
economic reasons, human rights and refugee organizations contend that
they are political refugees, fleeing war and persecution in their own countries.

As argued by Patricia Weiss Fagen ("Central American Refugees and U.S. Policy"), U.S. foreign policy establishes the parameters of U.S. policy toward refugees. Despite the politically neutral legal definition of a refugee as one having a well-founded fear of persecution due to race, religion, nationality, membership in a particular social group, or political opinion, U.S. policy toward refugees adheres largely to political and ideological criteria. There are refugee programs for Vietnamese, East Europeans, Iranians, and Afghans, but none for Salvadorans and Guatemalans. Salvadorans and Guatemalans within the United States who apply for asylum are much less likely to receive it than applicants from Poland, Afghanistan, and Ethiopia. Although the Supreme Court decision of February 1987 may ameliorate this situation, the 1986 Immigration Act has worsened the plight of Central Americans in the United States, many of whom arrived after the 1982 cutoff date for amnesty.

Central America:
External Pressures and Regional Dynamics

Apart from the obvious high costs of the Reagan administration policy, has the United States been able to reassert its hegemony over Central America? The administration can claim success in denying victory to the insurgents in El Salvador and in helping to bring about elections in El Salvador, Honduras, and Guatemala. The guerrilla movements have settled in for a protracted conflict, suggesting, in the words of one of the conference participants, that "the revolutionary moment in Central America has passed." From the administration's perspective, this turn of events is certainly favorable.

It is, however, the qualified nature of these successes that is the key to understanding the limits to hegemony over the region in the recent past. Despite the investment of significant political capital, military support, and economic aid, the administration has been unable to impose its 1980 project of "hyperhegemony," embracing the defeat of both the Sandinistas and the FMLN. Even the elections in Guatemala and El Salvador were hardly unqualified U.S. successes: it is unlikely that these electoral processes would have taken place when and as they did had it not been for the strength of the revolutionary movements in those countries. Furthermore, the elections were not part of the administration's original strategy but, at least in part, a result of pressures from Congress and the region.

Demonstration Elections:
The Unanticipated Effects of U.S. Policy

The fact that these elections often yielded unintended outcomes under-scores the limits of U.S. hegemony. As Terry Karl points out ("Exporting Democracy: The Unanticipated Effects of U.S. Electoral Policy in El Salvador"), the electoral process has an internal dynamic which promotes compromises and opens political space for previously repressed groups. Differentiating the Salvadoran elections from the "demonstration elections" in Vietnam and the Dominican Republic, she argues that the Salvadoran process involved some degree of real contestation for power and that it therefore produced unexpected consequences. In the 1982 constituent assembly elections, for example, far-right parties gained control of the new assembly, threatening to scuttle social reforms deemed essential to the administration's strategy; the U.S. State Department was forced into manipulation designed to prevent ARENA leader Roberto D'Aubuisson from being elected acting president. In 1984 the State Department's preferred candidate, Christian Democrat José Napoleón Duarte, won the presidency, but only after the U.S. government had intervened economically. The newly elected Duarte government was confronted by new contradictions: it was dependent upon the United States, which looked for military solutions and was escalating the war, whereas it had been elected on the basis of promises of reform, negotiations, and peace.

Blocked in its reform efforts by the assembly, still controlled by the right, the Duarte government sought to stem its loss of support through a dialogue with the opposition forces, resulting in the La Palma talks. The subsequent assembly elections of 1985 resulted in a Christian Democratic victory, which ironically revealed the limits of the government's power by exposing its inability effectively to enact reforms. Ricardo Stein describes the dilemma of the Duarte government: pressured by the United States and by the Salvadoran military to give priority to the war effort, Duarte enacted a series of unpopular economic measures which have alienated his support base and left him increasingly isolated. Taking advantage of the new political spaces opened through the election process, increasingly large sectors of the population have mobilized in opposition to the Duarte government and to continuation of the war.

The Nicaraguan Experiment

The Reagan administration has failed in its efforts to defeat the Sandinistas in Nicaragua, but at home it has been more successful in imposing its perspective on the nature of the Sandinista government. As Conroy and Pastor argue, that perspective fails to take into account the variations among socialist and quasi-socialist governments or the uniqueness of the Nicaraguan experiment. Nicaragua differs markedly from most socialist countries, including Cuba, in its response to issues such as state vs. private ownership and the market vs. central planning. Nicaragua operates as a mixed economy, combining private and state ownership; maintains economic relations with Western countries while expanding relations with Eastern European and Latin American countries; and continues to operate as a market economy with limited planning. Nicaragua's electoral procedures constitute another departure from the experience of other socialist countries; and the presidential and assembly elections of 1984 have been recognized as legitimate by numerous international observer groups, contrary to claims by the U.S. Department of State.

The stability and the future character of the Nicaraguan experiment cannot be determined. Many critics on both left and right contend that its contradictions will not permit its consolidation. Military defense against the contra war, consuming up to 50 percent of the government budget, has necessitated severe cutbacks in social programs. External pressures have also forced the government to impose a state of emergency and could further imperil the uniqueness of Nicaragua's experiment. Nevertheless, its survival in the face of increasing U.S. diplomatic, economic, and military hostility is itself remarkable in view of the past history of U.S. domination in the region.

From "Banana" Republics to "AID" Republics

The Reagan administration policy has not begun to address what many see as the underlying structural causes of unrest and instability in Central America. As pointed out by Xabier Gorostiaga and Peter Marchetti ("The Central American Economy: Conflict and Crisis"), the war has in fact aggravated the economic crisis in the region. Between 1978 and 1985 the levels of real income per capita fell by 33 percent. Economic logic has given way to an imposed military logic: in El Salvador and Nicaragua military budgets account for nearly half of public spending and have undercut spending for social services. The imposition of an East-West interpretation on the conflicts of the region has converted the Central American economies into "subsidized and politicized economies"—or, as expressed by one conference participant, from "banana republics" to "AID republics"—with much of the region dependent upon U.S. aid to subsidize its military buildup and supply funds for debt repayment.

But while peace is a necessary condition for economic recovery, it is not a sufficient one. The roots of the crises can be found in the highly inegalitarian economic base characterizing each of the economies except Costa Rica's, and in their vulnerability as primary commodity exporters in the international economy. The formation of the Central American Common Market and the limited industrialization that accompanied it during the 1960s and 1970s failed to address the problem of structural inequality or to end dependency on trade in primary commodities. But as Edelberto Torres Rivas argues ("The Central American Crisis and the Common Market"), the Common Market did achieve the more narrow goals of limited industrialization and increased intraregional trade, although there were severe problems with the regional and industrial structures which resulted. Some form of regional economic cooperation will be necessary for the economic recovery and future development of the region, and the high degree of interdependence among the Central American countries suggests the possibility of reinstituting regional cooperation on new foundations, but the obstacles at present are formidable.

Gorostiaga and Marchetti see the best hope for change in the awakened consciousness and mobilization of what they call the new historical subject: the traditionally exploited sectors in Central America who are questioning the existing economic structures and have become protagonists in the current regional conflicts. The emergence of a new historical subject committed to changing repressive structures and institutions demonstrates a breakthrough in the collective identity of Central America. Whatever the outcome of the current crisis, these actors will continue to play a role in the evolving history of the region.

The Search for Alternatives

The Reagan administration has also enjoyed some success in narrowing the debate about Central America at the international level, although not to the extent it would like. The Latin American countries' efforts on behalf of a negotiated solution to the ongoing conflicts continue to be at variance with the primary emphasis given to military solutions by Washington. But the differences between the position of the Latin American countries and that of the Reagan administration have narrowed even as support for a Latin American alternative in Central America has broadened to incorporate the four Contadora countries and the Lima support group. The differences in perspective among the Contadora countries, such as Mexico (which defends the principles of self-determination and nonintervention and sees the United States as the driving force in the possible regionalization of the conflict) and Venezuela (which promotes the spread of democracy and sees U.S. involvement as a response to Soviet-Cuban intervention), mean that agreement among these countries is possible only on a limited set of goals. The narrowing of differences between the Contadora countries and the United States also reflects the deteriorating economic situation of countries such as Mexico, which makes them increasingly susceptible to pressures from the Reagan administration.

In his analysis of the Contadora peace process, Adolfo Aguilar Zinser ("Negotiation in Conflict: Central America and Contadora") examines Mexico's shift away from its early support for the Sandinista revolution and for negotiations between the FMLN and the Salvadoran government. Pressured by the United States, and weakened politically by the economic crisis in Latin America, the Contadora countries have concentrated their efforts on averting regional military conflict.

Despite U.S. pressures, Contadora has managed to monopolize the scenario for multilateral discussions; it has been endorsed by the United Nations and has blocked U.S. efforts to bring the conflict to the Organization of American States, where the United States has more leverage. With all its limitations, Contadora constitutes one element in a shift in relations between the United States and Latin America, demonstrating the possibility of forums that exclude the United States. This possibility seems to have been reinforced by the agreement of the five Central American governments to the peace proposal of President Arias of Costa Rica.

Within the Central American countries, the most active proponent of negotiations has been the Catholic church, particularly in El Salvador, where the church has had a central role in mediation efforts between the FDR-FMLN and the Salvadoran government. But as Margaret E. Crahan points out ("A Multitude of Voices: Religion and the Central American Crisis"), the church's mediating role is limited by its institutional weakness and its deep political divisions, in many respects reflecting those within the Central American societies themselves. The differences are most evident in Nicaragua, where some sectors within the church strongly oppose the Sandinistas, while others support the Sandinista government. Crahan concludes that, despite a general predisposition toward peace rather than violence, the absence of a civil-military impetus to peace in the region severely constrains what the church can do to promote peaceful resolution of conflicts in Central America.

Despite the difficulties encountered by Latin American institutions and organizations seeking a negotiated solution in Central America, they respond to a strong desire for peace by the populations within Central America, as is evident in the enthusiastic reception given the Arias plan. They have also had an impact on the debate within the United States. As noted above, the Reagan administration's success in restricting the debate on Central America has not been unqualified. The administration's refugee policy—the apparent hypocrisy of granting asylum to Poles and Afghans while denying it to Salvadorans on death lists—has engendered widespread and often dramatic protest on the part of the Sanctuary movement and other groups. Even before investigations of arms sales to Iran and the diversion of funds to the contras revealed the extent of administration circumvention of the law, public opinion polls showed that the majority of the U.S. population disagreed with important aspects of administration policy. These revelations may be expected to strengthen the small but vocal (and growing) minority among the U.S. public and congress which has consistently resisted U.S. policy in the region.

On balance, contributors to this volume and to conference discussions agree that the Reagan administration has failed in its efforts to reassert U.S. hegemony over Central America. Both the goals and the means of current U.S. policy in Central America have come under question. Certainly for the Central Americans suffering and dying at "low intensity," the need for a thorough-going change in U.S. policy is obvious. We hope that this volume, by analyzing the risks of current policy and the ongoing dynamics of the Central American crisis, will further the debate in this country and contribute to the search for constructive alternatives.

Notes

1. We are indebted to Jeff Frieden and Linda Fuller for their suggestions and comments on earlier drafts of this introduction.

PART ONE

U.S. Policy in Central America: Recasting Hegemony

1

U.S. Policy Toward Central America: The Post-Vietnam Formula Under Siege

Kenneth E. Sharpe

In the long run, even the most energetic and ingenious means of reasserting Congressional prerogative will of themselves prove insufficient to the maintenance of constitutional government. As Tocqueville pointed out, war breeds dictatorship. I for one am fairly well convinced that neither constitutional government nor democratic freedoms can survive indefinitely in a country chronically at war, as America has been for the last three decades. Sooner or later, war will lead to dictatorship.[1]
—Senator J. William Fulbright

The Iran-*contra* affair made public an abuse of executive authority which began in 1981. The deeper issues raised by the trading of arms for hostages and the diversion of profits to the contras, however, harken back to the Vietnam period. The impact of the Vietnam War on our constitutional democracy, culminating in the Watergate scandal and the attempt to impeach Richard Nixon, served as a warning of the dangers of an imperial presidency. This essay evaluates the lessons learned, and the reforms instituted, in the aftermath of Vietnam and suggests what it is necessary to do now.[2]

Different people drew different lessons from the Vietnam-Watergate scandals. Some saw the problem as bad men: the abuse of executive power was blamed on the character of the president and his closest advisors, and the solution was their removal from office. Others, seeing the problem as weak laws, supported legislation to strengthen Congress's constitutional prerogatives: its power to check abuses of executive authority and to legislate foreign and domestic policy. Reforms implementing what we will loosely call the post–Vietnam-Watergate formula were enacted to ensure that presidential abuse of power would be less likely again to endanger constitutional democracy in the United States.

Others, like Senator Fulbright, supported legislative action but argued that enactment of laws was not enough. The problem, they contended, was political, not legal, in that Congress lacked the will to enforce its constitutional authority in foreign policy. An exercise of that will also required a challenge to the direction of foreign policy. As long as a belief in permanent Cold War crisis prevailed, it would be difficult to defend the authority of Congress against usurpation by the president and the national security bureaucracy he managed.

The Reagan administration's conduct of Central American policy provided the first sustained test of the post–Vietnam-Watergate formula. It demonstrated the continued willingness of the executive branch to overreach its authority in foreign policy and suggested the limits of legislative reform that was not backed by a strong congressional will.

The Imperial Presidency, the Abuse of Power, and the Post-Vietnam-Watergate Formula

In no part of the constitution is more wisdom to be found, than in the clause which confides the question of war or peace to the legislature, and not to the executive department. . . . The trust and the temptation would be too great for any one man. . . . War is in fact the true nurse of executive aggrandizement. In war, a physical force is to be created; and it is the executive will, which is to direct it. In war, the public treasures are to be unlocked; and it is the executive hand which is to dispense them. In war, the honours and emoluments of office are to be multiplied; and it is the executive patronage under which they are to be enjoyed. . . . The strongest passions and most dangerous weaknesses of the human breast; ambition, avarice, vanity, the honourable or venial love of fame, are all in conspiracy against the desire and duty of peace.[3]

—James Madison, *Helvidius*

The Constitution gave Congress the right to declare war, but it allowed the executive to repel attacks against the country in the absence of a formal declaration of war. The resulting ambiguity has led to continual dispute over the balance of power in foreign policy-making.

The system of checks and balances in the foreign policy arena has indeed been, in Edwin S. Corwin's words, "an invitation to struggle for the privilege of directing American foreign policy."[4] Through more than two centuries of struggle a pattern has emerged: the executive has enlarged its foreign policy powers at the expense of Congress, and Congress has reacted to reassert its constitutional prerogatives when the dangers to its institutional authority have become clear. The long-term effect of such conflicts, however, has been the gradual enlargement of executive power.

The shift in the balance toward the executive began to take on alarming proportions in the Cold War decades that followed World War II. The executive developed a large independent peacetime national security apparatus whose centerpiece was the National Security Council (NSC), created in 1947. Also critical was the Defense Department, which integrated all the military services, the Joint Chiefs of Staff system, and the Central Intelligence Agency (CIA).

As the security apparatus grew and Cold War tensions mounted, the executive branch became increasingly unaccountable to Congress, the press, and the public in the making of foreign policy. Congress usually acquiesced. The rough consensus over foreign policy goals and the seeming imperatives of national security muted fundamental criticism of the shift of power to the executive. The executive branch increasingly bypassed the treaty-making authority of Congress through the use of often secret executive agreements. The CIA developed into an apparatus that not only gathered intelligence but secretly carried out foreign policy, often using covert operations to overthrow foreign governments and assassinate foreign leaders. The president, the Pentagon, the CIA, the NSC, and even the State Department felt less obliged to give Congress and the public information about foreign policy issues.

President Lyndon B. Johnson's commitment of half a million U.S. troops to Vietnam without a declaration of war demonstrated the extent to which Congress's constitutional prerogative had been undermined. The Gulf of Tonkin Resolution (4 August 1964), which some officials in the Johnson administration regarded as congressional approval to escalate the conflict, turned out to be based on a crisis fabricated to justify an already planned escalation.

In 1969, President Richard M. Nixon, by authorizing the secret bombing of Cambodia, took the executive interpretation of war powers even further than Johnson had. The next year, in the face of clear congressional sentiment to terminate the war in Indochina, he authorized the invasion of Cambodia, claiming authority as commander in chief and invoking the need to protect U.S. troops. A few years later the Watergate revelations showed that executive secrecy and the abuse of power had gone even further, putting, Henry Steele Commager wrote, other fundamental principles at risk:

> The principle of a government of laws and not of men. . . . By countenancing burglary, wiretapping, *agents provocateurs,* the use of the Federal Bureau of Investigations, the Central Intelligency Agency and even the Internal Revenue Service to punish "enemies," . . . Mr. Nixon sought to substitute his own fiat for law.

> The principles of freedom and justice in the Bill of Rights. By attempting to impose, for the first time in our history, prior censorship of the press, by threatening hostile television stations with deprivation of their licenses, . . . Mr. Nixon presented the most dangerous threat to the Bill of Rights in the whole of our history.

> The integrity and survival of democratic government in the United States. . . . By corrupting presidential elections through the solicitation of illegal contributions, by a systematic campaign of mendacity, trickery and character assassination against opponents, . . . Mr. Nixon gravely endangered the integrity of our republican system of government.[5]

The reaction was growing support for impeachment and an attempt to strengthen constitutional democracy. Three related commitments, composing a post-Vietnam formula, were embodied in new laws, procedures, and institutional arrangements, or they simply became part of a new ethos. One commitment was to get access to information about executive activities, a necessary condition for the system of checks and balances to work. The second was to restore congressional legislative authority in foreign policy and to strengthen constitutional checks on potential executive abuses of authority at home and abroad. The third commitment was to limit the possibilities for political repression and violations of civil liberties and civil rights, about which I have written elsewhere.[6] In this paper I focus on the first two commitments.

Access to Information

The secrecy, lying, distortion, and claims of "executive privilege," which reached a high point in the Nixon administration, reminded Congress that information is power. Wise judgments, effective legislation, and presidential accountability are based on access to information.

One legislative response was to demand certain critical information. The War Powers Resolution stipulated that the president inform Congress in writing within forty-eight hours of introducing troops (in the absence of a declaration of war) into areas where hostilities existed or were likely to involve the United States. The reasons for introducing the troops, the legal authority justifying the introduction, and the scope and duration of the commitment had to be specified.

The 1974 Hughes-Ryan amendment (amended in 1980) required that the president report, in "a timely fashion," all CIA covert operations, besides intelligence gathering, to appropriate committees, and legislation in 1976 and 1977 created select intelligence committees in both Senate and House. These acts gave Congress a measure of oversight and control, and mechanisms for public disclosure, under certain circumstances, of classified information given to the committees were put in place.

The freedom of the president to make secret executive agreements was limited by the Case-Zablocki Act of 1972, which required all such agreements to be reported to Congress. In 1974 Congress also ruled that arms sales be so reported. If the president declared a national emergency, Congress required him to inform it of the specific laws under which he proposed to act, to file with Congress all executive agency rules and regulations, and to account for expenditures. In 1974 Congress also strengthened the Freedom of Information Act by providing for judicial review of executive agency decisions to keep all parts of a document classified.

Perhaps more important than specific statutes was the general commitment Congress made to monitor presidential actions more carefully and to use its existing powers as leverage to demand that foreign policy decisions be shared. Also significant were the larger number and the foreign policy expertise of staff members, who provided independent sources of information and allowed concerned members of Congress to make better use of existing mechanisms in their oversight of foreign policy.

Restoring Shared Control

Congress's demand for access to information was based on its desire for increased participation in the making of foreign policy and for greater ability to check executive excesses. Constitutionally, much of the necessary power was already in the hands of Congress: it had the authority to declare war and to advise and consent on treaties and appointments, and it possessed an ultimate check on the executive through its power of the purse. But Congress was concerned about existing mechanisms and precedents that allowed the president to circumvent congressional control. A particular problem in the struggle over foreign policy was the president's ability to create situations that forced congressional acquiescense, thus establishing a precedent limiting Congress's use of its existing powers.

Such presidential activity is illustrated in several examples. In 1846 President James Polk sent U.S. troops into an area contested by Mexico and Texas, and when they were attacked by Mexican soldiers, as might have been foreseen, Polk forced Congress's hand. When Theodore Roosevelt sent the fleet around the world in the face of strong congressional opposition, it was Congress that had to vote the funds to bring it back. During and after World War II, congressional acquiescence fostered a dangerous growth of the president's prerogative as commander in chief.

In the Cold War years this kind of initiative, in which the president presented Congress with a *fait accompli*, became more common. Presidents involved the United States in full-scale war by first committing troops to foreign lands (Truman in Korea, Kennedy and Johnson in Vietnam) and then arguing that they could not be abandoned or that commitments made had to be honored to protect American credibility. Presidents also entered into secret executive agreements that bound the United States to certain foreign policies without congressional debate and authorization. Presidents ordered covert operations, thus establishing policies that Congress could disown only at the risk of seeming to undermine national security. By the late 1960s the executive had, through such maneuverings, developed the ability to create situations obliging Congress to stand by the commitments made without its knowledge or consent. This presidential use of power came to have increasing influence on U.S. foreign policy.

Congress attempted to hold the president accountable by insisting on full consultation and shared decision making before the policy die was cast. Part of its effort was legislative. For example, the War Powers Act aimed to "insure that the collective judgement of both the Congress and the President will apply" to the decision to send U.S. troops into hostilities by insisting that the president consult with Congress "in every possible instance" before troops are introduced.[7] The Senate Foreign Relations Committee described the resolution as "an invitation to the executive to reconsider its excesses, and to the legislature to reconsider its omissions, in the making of foreign policy."[8]

Procedures were also established to allow Congress to use the new access to information to insist on participation or to stop the president. For example, the Senate and House Intelligence Oversight committees could try to dissuade the CIA from continuing covert operations by using their control of authorizations for intelligence activities, or by revealing such operations, or by persuading the House or the Senate to pass legislation specifically forbidding or cutting appropriations for such activities. The Clark amendment in 1975 (annulled in 1985), for example, prohibited assistance for military or paramilitary operations in Angola. Similarly, Congress could block or force the modification of executive agreements by denying funds to implement them.

Perhaps the strongest measure was a provision of the War Powers Resolution concerning the unauthorized use of troops. Although recognizing that a president might have to act without congressional authorization in emergencies, Congress wanted to prevent the executive from using extraordinary circumstances as a ploy to circumvent the legislative branch. Hence the War Powers Resolution stipulated that the president must terminate any unauthorized use of troops within sixty days unless Congress takes affirmative action to approve the deployment. The sixty-day period starts when the required report is submitted to Congress. This provision puts the starting of the clock in the hands of the president.

The formula that emerged after Vietnam and Watergate indicated congressional concern about the process of foreign policy decision making as well as the content of foreign policy. There was an awareness in Congress, and later in the Carter administration, that Third World turmoil was often caused by poverty and repression, and that a North-South perspective was more realistic than an East-West perspective. Critics of the Vietnam policy were wary of sending U.S. troops to fight in Third World countries when the goals were not clearly defined and when the conflict was unpopular at home. Many were opposed to supporting corrupt, repressive regimes and sought instead to condition foreign military and economic aid on a regime's human rights performance.

These new commitments to both process and content allowed Congress to play a more aggressive role in shaping U.S. policy for Central America than it had in Vietnam. The shift was clearly visible in the compromises and policy changes the Carter administration was forced to accept in order to get congressional approval of the Panama Canal treaties and of economic assistance to the new Sandinista regime. A much more serious test came when the Reagan administration took office. Its willingness to aid repressive regimes facing domestic turmoil troubled many members of Congress, and its emphasis on a military strategy in Central America raised the specter of U.S. involvement in "another Vietnam." Moderates in Congress were particularly worried that the commitments being made to El Salvador (and later to Honduras and to the Nicaraguan exile army) would eventually draw in U.S. troops. They did not count on the War Powers Resolution alone to give them a say, for they understood that presidential initiatives could make it difficult to oppose the president if he sent troops to Central America. They wanted to participate from the very beginning in shaping policy.

Central America:
A Test Case for the Post-Vietnam Formula

The post-Vietnam formula, like the Constitution itself, was open to interpretation. Would Congress share in shaping the overall direction of foreign policy, in the takeoffs as well as in the "crash landings"?[9] Would Congress be able to prevent the executive from creating a crisis—an antecedent state of affairs—over which it could not easily exert its constitutional authority? Could Congress expect the executive to be forthright and candid in providing information about what it was doing and why? Would the executive respect congressional statutes and stay within the bounds of the law?

El Salvador

From 1981 until 1984 Congress attempted to participate in shaping El Salvador policy by making military aid conditional on certain requirements. The president had to certify that the Salvadoran government was "making a concerted . . . effort to comply with internationally recognized human rights," was "achieving substantial control over all elements of its armed forces, so as to bring an end . . . to indiscriminate torture and murder," was "making continued progress in . . . land reform," and was "committed to the holding of free elections."[10]

The conditionality requirement was weak; once the president had made his certification to Congress, aid was automatically released. Nevertheless, the requirement served a valid purpose: it made clear the broad opposition in Congress to aid for a repressive, reactionary regime, and it underlined the widespread belief that real reform was the only way to stop revolution. Presidential certification every six months also forced a certain public accountability; the congressional hearings connected with each certification provided for careful scrutiny of administration facts and, through media coverage, stimulated public debate and helped to educate the people.

The administration, however, provided false and misleading information in order to certify that the conditions required for aid existed, despite overwhelming evidence to the contrary. Further, it refused to put serious pressure on the Salvadoran military to end its human rights abuses. To cite but one example, it repeatedly denied the well-substantiated charges (confirmed by its own internal documents) that thousands of civilian noncombatants were being killed by government forces and the death squads organized or aided by top military officials.[11] When Congress renewed the certification requirement in November 1983 Reagan pocket vetoed the bill while Congress was not in session and therefore had no opportunity to override the veto. The congressional response to such efforts to undercut or eliminate certification was weak. A majority would not support the strengthening of existing legislation, and congressional willingness to use the power of the purse to cut aid even when the certification conditions were being violated was limited.

The Reagan administration sought to avoid further scrutiny and opposition by refusing to comply with the War Powers Resolution requirement that the president report to Congress within forty-eight hours after U.S. troops had been introduced "into hostilities or into a situation where imminent involvement in hostilities is clearly indicated by the circumstances." Although such reporting had also been avoided by Ford and Carter—it triggers a sixty-day period after which the president must remove the troops or obtain congressional approval—neither of Reagan's predecessors had presented systematically false information about the actual situation of U.S. troops. The Reagan administration maintained that it was "not putting our people in a situation where there is any imminent danger of hostilities."[12] But in fact U.S. military personnel were stationed in brigade headquarters throughout zones of conflict, were traveling to combat areas, had come under fire on at least eight separate incidents (by early 1985), were flying reconnaissance missions over Salvadoran battlefields, and had participated in naval interdiction activities in the Gulf of Fonseca. Congressional critics pointed to the evidence, but they were unable to generate widespread concern.

Congress's ultimate leverage in the foreign policy process lies in the power of the purse. From 1981 until mid-1984 a majority in Congress often did try to limit military appropriations for El Salvador. The president, however, used a number of mechanisms to vastly increase military assistance outside the regular or supplemental appropriations process. In March 1981, for example, using his defense drawdown authority to tap special funds earmarked for military emergencies, he increased congressionally authorized military aid to El Salvador by $20 million (Congress had appropriated only $5.5 million). Then employing power to reprogram budgetary allocations, he sent another $5 million in military aid and $44.9 million in economic support funds. For fiscal year 1982 Congress appropriated only $27 million, turning down an administration supplemental request for an additional $35 million. In February 1982, however, the White House, claiming that the guerrilla destruction of aircraft at the Ilopango air base had created an emergency, again used its defense drawdown authority to dispatch $55 million, over twice the amount Congress had authorized, to El Salvador.

In each instance the president was obeying the letter but not the spirit of the law. The special funds he drew on for military aid were put aside by Congress for use in emergency situations at presidential discretion. Although no emergency existed, the president so defined events in El Salvador in order to circumvent a congressional debate on supplemental appropriations, a debate he was likely to lose. Similarly, reprogramming— which requires only that the appropriations committees be informed and that they offer no objection—was designed to give the bureaucracy flexibility in reallocating funds among budget categories, not to provide a means of circumventing congressional debate on controversial aid authorizations. Yet the limited scrutiny required for reprogramming provided the White House with just such a mechanism. In 1983, as House leaders became more critical of presidential circumventions, the appropriations committee cut the $60 million requested for reprogramming to $30 million. House leaders warned the president not to continue to use his special drawdown authority to fund unauthorized military aid to El Salvador.

The administration tried another tack. In early 1984 it asked Congress for an emergency supplemental appropriation of $93 million; Congress approved $61.75 million. Secretary of State Schultz claimed that the Salvadorans were "running out of supplies," and other officials added that "without these funds, the El Salvadoran Armed Forces will either go back to the barracks or collapse."[13] In fact, there was no emergency, for $32 million of military aid already in the pipeline could have been diverted if necessary. Much of the supplemental aid was used to expand the army by forming new units.

The 1984 and 1985 elections in El Salvador radically changed the character of congressional-executive relations. The election of José Napoleón Duarte, a recognized reformer, reinforced the administration's definition of the government as centrist and reformist. Many moderates grew reluctant to oppose aid despite evidence that the military, not Duarte, was still the real power in El Salvador and that military corruption and repression were continuing. Congress approved the administration's requests for aid. This aid, and particularly the aggressive air mobile tactics it provided for, enabled the Salvadoran military to limit severely the guerrillas' offensive capabilities. This turn of events reassured Congress that the aid was not making U.S. military intervention more likely. The administration continued to provide misleading and false information about the economic and political situation in El Salvador, the growing isolation of Duarte from his own supporters, and above all the repression by the military. There was some decline in politically targeted death squad killings, but the White House denied the documented killing and forced displacement of civilians in air and ground operations, and Congress made few attempts to scrutinize administration claims publicly.[14]

Honduras

Administration attempts to avoid congressional scrutiny and debate by circumventing the normal appropriations process and by tightly guarding information were even more flagrant in reference to Honduras. During U.S. maneuvers in Honduras, for example, the Defense Department took money from a budgeted fund called Operations and Maintenance (supposed to be used for petty cash, not for major military financing) to train and equip Honduran forces and to build permanent basing facilities. In 1984 the House Committee on Appropriations protested that

> the Comptroller General found that funds appropriated for operation and maintenance of our armed forces were used for military construction projects, security assistance activities, and civic action and humanitarian assistance. The Committee believes such diversion of funding from properly appropriated purposes is unwarranted and directs that the Department of Defense take such steps as necessary to prevent recurrence of such improprieties in the future.[15]

Furthermore, the maneuvers, which began in August 1981, turned out to be nearly continuous and thus had the effect of permanently stationing 700 to 1000 U.S. military personnel in Honduras and placing thousands more on ships off the coast—all without congressional consultation or authorization. As the character of these activities became public, some members of Congress raised their voices in protest.

Although the issue was fought mostly on narrow legal grounds, the larger concern was the circumvention of Congress on foreign policy decisions of major importance. The administration was, in effect, using the maneuvers to put military pressure on the Sandinistas and to turn Honduras into a forward basing area for possible use against Nicaragua (and perhaps El Salvador). In doing so, it was not only militarizing Honduras but was putting U.S. military personnel geographically close to areas of high conflict, such as the Nicaraguan border. Had the administration presented this more aggressive plan to congress for funding in 1982 it would have been brought under close scrutiny, given congressional concern over war powers. (The presence of fifty-five advisors in El Salvador was frequently noted, and that number became an informal limit.) When Congress tried to bring such activities under control in 1984 by requiring prior notification of "the complete U.S. construction plan for the region," the administration countered by supplying as little information as possible.[16] A follow-up report by the General Accounting Office (GAO) showed some compliance with congressional requirements, but it also documented a series of new accounting procedures that allowed further circumvention.[17]

Nicaragua

U.S. policy-making on Nicaragua illustrates graphically how emerging patterns of congressional-executive relations are undermining the intent of the post-Vietnam formula. If the examination of congressional participation in Nicaragua policy begins with 1985 or 1986, it would seem that the administration had at least respected the important procedural commitments of the formula. The White House came to Congress and asked for money to aid Nicaraguan exiles fighting to overthrow the Sandinista regime. In 1985, after long public debate, Congress approved $27 million in nonlethal military and in logistical support and, in 1986, $100 million (70 percent of it military). The story, however, started much earlier. Indeed, if the president had asked Congress in 1981 for funds to create an exile army to pressure or overthrow the Sandinistas, his request would have been flatly refused. What happened in the Nicaraguan sequence of events was precisely the creation of an "antecedent state of affairs" which made it difficult, although not impossible, for Congress to say no by 1985. The manner in which the administration managed to get the funding for the contras demonstrates even more clearly than the methods used for Honduras and El Salvador how secrecy, distortion, and circumvention were used by the executive to avoid accountability, consultation, and debate.

On 23 November 1981 President Reagan signed National Security Decision Directive 17 and a secret finding that was submitted to the House and Senate Intelligence committees informing them that $19.95 million in CIA funds would be used to support 500 contras who would infiltrate Nicaragua to interdict purported arms flows to Salvadoran rebels. By providing this information, the administration was carefully observing the letter of the law. The committees did not protest because the interdiction rationale convinced their members of the need to contain a leftist revolution supported by the Nicaraguans.

Although officials in the administration may have initially supported the program simply to interdict arms, major actors—the exiles the CIA was funding, CIA operatives in the field, and hard-liners in the administration— had a very different purpose: to overthrow the Sandinista regime. This view became even more prevalent as the operation escalated in 1982 and 1983. The so-called soft-liners, mostly in the State Department, did not approve of attempts to overthrow the Nicaraguan government, but they believed that building up the contras would threaten the Sandinistas into bargaining over security issues and ultimately over the internal character of their regime. But the broad purposes of Nicaragua policy were not presented to the congressional committees for scrutiny and debate. It was only in later years, as congressional opposition built, that the administration quietly introduced the pressure logic. The president's public position, until the 1985 congressional debates took place, was that his administration was "not doing anything to overthrow the government of Nicaragua."[18]

An effort to misinform or deceive Congress was always an important element in administration policy. But secret wars are never secret from the people being warred on; similarly, they cannot long be kept secret from Congress and the American public. As early as 4 December 1981 articles began to appear in the American press about covert U.S. activities. Soon information came from Florida about training camps for the contras and then reports from the field about contra operations. As the press revealed the scope and the character of the contra effort, the House Intelligence Committee sought to limit American aid to its original purpose. In December 1982 Rep. Edward Boland (D-MA), chairman of the committee, introduced language (the Boland amendment) into the Continuing Resolution for Fiscal 1983 prohibiting the use of funds "for the purpose of overthrowing the government of Nicaragua."

The administration's response was to *expand* contra operations to include sabotage raids on such targets as oil supplies and port facilities. While acknowledging that the aim of the contras might be to overthrow the Nicaraguan government, the administration insisted that it was keeping within the law because its purpose in giving the aid was arms interdiction, not overthrow. The government's position made the Democratic leadership in the House very angry, and in 1983 the House Intelligence Committee voted to cut off all funds for Nicaragua.

As the Republican-controlled Senate Intelligence Committee refused to go along with a total cutoff, a cap of $24 million was put on contra aid for fiscal year 1984. Still, the administration was able to circumvent congressional spending limits: it charged certain expenses (as for the mining of Nicaragua's harbors) to other accounts; an airfield built in Aguacate, Honduras, as part of a Defense Department exercise was then made available to the contras as a logistics and transportation center; and the Defense Department donated aircraft for transporting supplies to contra bases and transferred ships, planes, and guns to the CIA at little or no charge.

Some members of the House and Senate Intelligence committees were particularly disturbed in 1984 when they discovered that the administration had violated the reporting requirements of the 1980 Intelligence Oversight Act by failing to inform the committees of the decision to mine Nicaraguan harbors. In September 1984 Congress learned that a CIA manual entitled "Psychological Operations in Guerilla Warfare" gave explicit instructions for "neutralizing" Sandinista officials and "creating martyrs" for the contra cause, corroborating reports of contra terror in the press and from human rights organizations. A month later the House Intelligence Committee forced the Senate committee, in conference, to accept the Boland amendment, now carefully worded to forestall admininstration circumvention:

> During the fiscal year 1985, no funds available to the Central Intelligence Agency, the Department of Defense, or any other agency or entity of the United States involved in intelligence activities may be obligated or expended for the purpose or which would have the effect of supporting, directly or indirectly, military or paramilitary operations in Nicaragua by any nation, group, organization, movement or individual.[19]

It was further agreed that aid could be restored only by a majority vote in both houses after February 1985.

Again the administration was able to circumvent the law. The National Security Council helped organize and advise a private aid network to fund the contras. According to some administration officials, the plan was approved both by National Security Advisor Robert C. McFarlane and the president. Marine Lt. Col. Oliver North, a member of the NSC staff, was put in charge. North helped reorganize and coordinate operations of the two main rebel groups, gave tactical advice, assisted the contras in raising millions in private and secret public funds, and arranged for supplies and contributions to reach the contras.

Despite the consternation of contra aid critics and the threat of hearings, nothing was done to stop North—and little could be done to undo his work. In the words of Rep. Michael Barnes (D-MD), the White House stonewalled, refusing, for example, to release requested documents on its management of the private network and its circumvention of the Boland amendment. It was not until the Iran-contra affair broke in November 1986 that Congress and the press began to uncover the full details of the NSC's involvement in circumventing Congress. It became clear that millions of dollars in profits from secret arms sales to Iran were diverted to supply the contras; that the NSC had participated in secretly raising millions for the contras from foreign governments (at least $30 million from Saudi Arabia, for example); and that National Security Advisor Admiral John Poindexter and top officials at the State Department and the CIA were also involved. It was further revealed that the contra operation was the centerpiece of an even larger covert effort labeled "Project Democracy" and authorized by President Reagan in a January 1983 National Security Decision Directive (no. 77).

Between 1984 and 1986, as the NSC was flouting the congressional ban, the CIA was also secretly aiding the Nicaraguan rebels. More than $1.5 million was spent to finance "security," to set up and operate a radio station, and to seek political and financial support in Europe and Venezuela. The CIA also helped carry out the elaborate contra supply operation run by the NSC (dramatically revealed after a plane was shot down in October 1986 and American mercenary Eugene Hasenfus was captured by the Nicaraguans and put on trial) and actively tried to reorganize and strengthen contra activities in Costa Rica.

Although full details did not emerge until late 1986 and early 1987, as early as 1985 enough information was available for Congress to demand that future funding of the covert war be openly debated and legislated through normal channels. This debate was different from that on El Salvador, because Congress viewed rollback much more critically than containment. U.S. efforts to overthrow a foreign government raised both moral issues and fears of dragging U.S. troops into a quagmire.

Once the issue could no longer be handled secretly, administration officials sought to impose their definition of the situation. First, alternatives in line with traditional containment doctrine—the efforts of the Contadora countries and of some congressional moderates—were scuttled. Second, the internal character of the regime was presented as so abhorrent and the security threat as so serious that any opponent could be delegitimized as soft on both security and communism. As a result, ideology often replaced fact in the foreign policy debate. This distortion of information (well documented elsewhere) made rational debate about the means and ends of U.S. policy toward Nicaragua increasingly difficult.

Contra aid again came before Congress in 1985. In April the House narrowly defeated an aid measure, but on 12 June 73 Democrats abandoned the House leadership and joined 175 Republicans in supporting a compromise package that approved humanitarian aid but banned lethal military aid and restricted CIA participation in disbursing the funds. A number of conservative Southern Democrats felt that voting against the aid would make them vulnerable to charges that they were "soft on communism." Alluding to this issue, majority leader Jim Wright (D-TX), who himself opposed the aid, said that "to some degree" the country was going through an experience reminiscent of McCarthyism. "Nobody wants to be portrayed as friendly toward Communism."[20]

Many moderate Democrats and Republicans reversed their votes because they felt ill at ease in turning down the president's request in April without providing an alternative. "A good many of our guys," said Wright, "don't believe in waging war to overthrow the Government of Nicaragua, but they feel some responsibility to those doing the fighting."[21] The administration, which had defined the issue in just this way, was reinforced shortly after the April vote when Nicaraguan President Daniel Ortega flew to Moscow to ask for more aid. Rep. Steward B. McKinney (R-CT), who reversed his vote, explained: "There are those of us here who have to recognize the fact that the contra movement against an oppressive dictatorial society does exist. We cannot walk away from it."[22] Others believed that the contras could provide leverage for a negotiated political settlement, which the president claimed he sought. Rep. Bill Richardson (D-NM), who switched his vote, said: "I think the President of the United States for the first time is saying that he is for negotiations and meaning it."[23]

When the crucial vote for $100 million in contra aid came up in the House in March 1986 (it was defeated 222–210) and in June (it passed 221–209), the hook of commitment had already taken hold. Although the majority of Democrats (about 183) opposed any aid, the thirty or so crucial swing votes accepted administration arguments that the contras could not be abandoned and that they were a useful tool in pressing for negotiations.

In both June 1985 and June 1986, the arguments that swayed middle-of-the-roaders would not have made sense if a huge contra force had not already been recruited and if other alternatives had not been undermined or defined out of existence. Administration policies had created the very antecedent state of affairs that the post-Vietnam formula had sought to avoid by insisting that important foreign policy decisions be shared, from the beginning, by Congress and the president. This situation had been created by the very circumvention, secrecy, and deception the post-Vietnam formula had sought to check.

The Post-Vietnam-Watergate Formula Reconsidered

Why did the post-Vietnam legislation not reestablish constitutional balance and check executive abuses of authority? Some analysts argue that the legislation was not well enough designed. The War Powers Resolution could have been strengthened by drawing up a list of binding circumstances under which the president could deploy troops and by setting tougher requirements for prior consultation with and reporting to Congress. The power of intelligence oversight committees could have been strengthened, for example, by requiring the approval, not simply the reporting, of covert operations. Specific proposals have been made to alter the Espionage Act and the Freedom of Information Act to protect more adequately the rights of citizens to hold elected officials accountable.

Some observers of the Vietnam-Watergate period, however, warn of the limits and the dangers of seeing the problem as simply one of laws. As Arthur Schlesinger noted in 1973, "The effective means of controlling the Presidency lay less in law than in politics. For the American President rules by influence; and the withdrawal of consent, by Congress, by the press, by public opinion, could bring any President down."[24]

This conclusion is apt today. When Congress, the press, and the public were willing to exercise political power, the post-Vietnam formula often worked: it helped Congress get access to information needed to participate in the making of foreign policy, and it ultimately helped cut off the private funding network in the aftermath of the Iran-contra revelations. Yet more often than not Congress was unwilling to exercise its potential power. It did not demand to participate in ways that would have limited the president's ability to create an antecedent state of affairs or to break and circumvent the law.

Access to Information

The post-Vietnam formula did not deter the Reagan administration from attempts to limit public access to information. The administration initially misled Congress into supporting the formation of the contra army by arguing that it was setting up an "arms interdiction" scheme. The CIA failed to report the mining of Nicaraguan harbors to the congressional oversight committees. The administration failed to comply with the reporting requirements of the War Powers Resolution in sending U.S. advisors to El Salvador and, to some extent, in handling the Honduras problem. The administration failed to report the secret arms shipments to Iran in 1985 and 1986 to the congressional oversight committees. The executive's rejection of the consulting and reporting requirements of the War Powers Act was evident in respect to Grenada and Lebanon, for the president did not report that troops were being introduced into areas of hostility and thus he avoided starting the sixty-day time clock for automatic withdrawal.

Despite such executive malfeasance, the institutional mechanisms set up by the post-Vietnam formula, combined with a commitment by Congress and the press, provided a framework to check administration attempts to lie, dissemble, and hide information from the Congress and the public. The requirement that the intelligence committees be informed of covert operations proved to be significant. Although information on the covert war was made public by the press almost immediately after it began, these committees provided an institutional locus for information gathering and accountability. Their recognition that the scope was expanding beyond arms interdiction, and later that serious actions had not been reported as the law demanded, led the House committee first to put restrictions on aid, then to support restrictive legislation on the floor of the House, and finally to urge a cutoff of funds. It is important to note, however, that the public outcry, and initial opposition in Congress to the covert war, were stimulated by press coverage; the intelligence committees did not initially assume leadership.

In addition to the mandated legislative mechanisms, the post-Vietnam mistrust of the executive and the desire to get independent information led members of Congress to use existing institutional means of oversight and to establish new methods to generate and check information. The same commitment led a number of reporters to embark on investigative studies which were in turn used by members of Congress.

Restoring Constitutional Checks and Balances
in Foreign Policy

The post-Vietnam legal framework allowed and often encouraged access to information, but Congress needed to use it to insist on full consultation and participation and to react forcefully to presidential efforts to break or evade the law. Congressional efforts to make the formula work were important in forcing a reluctant president to allow Congress to participate in the making of policy toward El Salvador from 1981 to 1984. Congress ruled out the sending of U.S. troops to quell a leftist revolution. It used its power of the purse to restrict funding, to demand public accountability, and to get information through the certification hearings. Administration willingness to take some action against the death squads and to support the election of a civilian government headed by Duarte were a response to congressional pressure. Finally, pressure from the media, the public, and Congress forced an end to White House support for the private funding network after the Iran-contra revelations of late 1986.

Congress, however, was unwilling to confront forcefully the actions of the executive which broke the letter of the law, violated its spirit, or circumvented the constitutional prerogatives of the legislative branch. When the president failed to comply with the reporting and consulting requirements of the War Powers Act, Congress expressed concern but did nothing. When the president met the formal requirements for certifying aid to El Salvador but distorted actual conditions there, Congress did not block aid. Although it cut the president's aid requests, until 1983 the president was able to circumvent Congress's powers of the purse by using emergency powers and his reprogramming authority.

In Honduras, the administration initially forestalled congressional opposition by violating the reporting requirements of the War Powers Act, misusing funds for building unauthorized bases and training Honduran troops, and maneuvering to station U.S. troops in Honduras or place them in ships offshore. What happened in Honduras was exactly what the post-Vietnam formula was intended to prevent: the creation of an antecedent state of affairs which committed the United States to a foreign policy without the participation of Congress. But even when Congress discovered the fait accompli, it did little more than issue a mild reproach, warn against repetition of such a course, and restrict the use of funds. It did not order the bases dismantled, nor did it seriously interfere with the maneuvering to build infrastructure in Honduras or permanently to station U.S. troops there.

The most serious violation of the spirit of the War Powers Act was executive action in Nicaragua. Not only did the contra effort pose an immediate danger of creating an antecedent state of affairs that could draw in U.S. troops; it also established a dangerous precedent for the conduct of foreign policy. Using covert action to thwart the oversight function of the congressional intelligence committees meant that crucial foreign policies were initiated and conducted in a highly secret, unaccountable way. The administration misrepresented the mission of the contras as arms interdiction. It failed to meet reporting requirements on the mining and the terror manual, for example. After the Boland amendment was passed the White House violated the law by continuing to fund the contras. When funds were cut off, it circumvented Congress's power of the purse by helping to organize a private funding network and managing it for more than two years.

An important foreign policy commitment was established with minimum scrutiny and public debate. Congress by and large acquiesced, failing to act even when it learned that private funding was circumventing its ruling and that high-ranking members of the NSC were helping to coordinate the effort. The few members who protested were unable to get enough support to launch a public investigation or to force a halt to such executive actions. At each point the actions were incremental, and as the executive gradually increased its commitment to the contras, Congress found it more and more difficult to share control of policy-making.

Conclusion

The failure of the post-Vietnam formula to check executive abuse of authority did not arise simply from the character of the legislation. Senator Fulbright's 1972 observation is just as true today: "It is not a lack of power which has prevented the Congress from ending the war in Indochina, but a lack of will."[25] Why has Congress not been more vociferous and more forceful in using institutional mechanisms and its authority to prevent executive disregard for the commitments of the post-Vietnam formula? A number of explanations are given: the fragmentation of the foreign policy process within Congress; the president's ability to shape and present information; the difficulty of rallying congressional opposition to small encroachments on its authority.

Although all these explanations contain an element of truth, there is also a more fundamental problem. On the one hand, Congress faces a hard-to-control national security apparatus dedicated to maintaining U.S. hegemony and largely unchallenged by post-Vietnam reforms. The powerful intelligence and security agencies established after World War II embodied norms of secrecy, speed, unity, and efficiency which were antithetical to constitutional democracy. On the other hand, there is no "anti-imperial" political coalition strong enough to force Congress to check the executive and to effectuate legislation against the security bureaucracy.

A coalition to reform the security apparatus in a substantive manner must challenge the foreign policy that justifies the existence of the apparatus itself. "The Imperial Presidency," Schlesinger argues,

was essentially the creation of foreign policy. A combination of doctrines and emotions—belief in permanent and universal crisis, fear of communism, faith in the duty and the right of the United States to intervene swiftly in every part of the world—had brought about the unprecedented centralization of decisions over war and peace in the Presidency.[26]

Although the post-Vietnam commitment did include a reluctance to commit troops and allow some tolerance for leftist regimes, moderates and conservatives still shared the same underlying strategic vision: revolutionary regimes of the left were antithetical to U.S. global interests. The United States still had the right and the responsibility to maintain its hegemony and to minimize the chances of leftist outbreaks and takeovers. The difference between moderates and conservatives lay in means, not ends. Moderates, seeing the causes of revolution in local repression and poverty, argued for human rights and economic development—a position similar to that held by the old Alliance for Progress. Conservatives, discerning the causes of revolution in Soviet-backed intervention and subversion, argued for primarily military responses to Third World revolutions. And no one argued for substantial change in the national security apparatus that planned and administered so large a part of foreign policy.[27]

When the Reagan administration came into office it inherited the existing security bureaucracy, and it brought back the conservative version of the strategic vision. It emphasized not simply containment but rollback of leftist governments ("The Reagan Doctrine"). In this context the new right and the Reagan administration could draw on a continuing fear of communism, and on concern about declining U.S. power and hegemony, to define debate once again in terms of Cold War assumptions.

Such assumptions made it difficult for many of the middle-of-the-road swing voters in Congress to resist the president's persistent demands for a proxy army strategy against Nicaragua. Especially after he had created an antecedent state of affairs, they found themselves trapped between their opposition to communism and their opposition to U.S. troop commitments, between "no more Cubas" and "no more Vietnams." Accepting the end of undermining the Sandinistas, and seeing no alternatives to the contras, members of Congress were open to persuasion.

If Cold War assumptions make it difficult to challenge the executive on specific issues, they make it extremely hard even to put the restructuring of the national security bureaucracy on the political agenda, let alone to challenge its organization and vision against a well-organized and entrenched right. As long as such assumptions guide policy, Schlesinger argues, there will be a demand "for concentration of authority, secrecy, speed and discretion in the Presidency," and Fulbright's 1969 warning will take on greater urgency:

Whatever lip service might be paid to traditional forms, our Government would soon become what it is already a long way toward becoming, an elective dictatorship, more or less complete over foreign policy and over those vast and expanding areas of our domestic life which in one way or another are related to or dependent upon the military establishment. If, in short, America is to become an empire, there is very little chance that it can avoid becoming a virtual dictatorship as well.[28]

Notes

1. J. William Fulbright, *The Crippled Giant: American Foreign Policy and Its Domestic Consequences* (New York: Vintage Books, 1972), p. 241.

2. In preparing this paper I have benefited from the research assistance of Eva Bertram and the critical comments of Charles Beitz, Douglas Bennett, Morris Blachman, Sherle Schwenninger, and Richard Valelly.

3. James Madison, *Writings*, VI (Hund ed., 1906), p. 174. Cited in Christoper H. Pyle and Richard M. Pious, *The President, Congress and the Constitution* (New York: Free Press, 1984), p. 287.

4. Edward S. Corwin, *The President: Office and Powers* (New York, 1940), p. 200.

5. Henry Steele Commager, *The Defeat of America: Presidential Power and the National Character* (New York: Simon and Shuster, 1974), pp. 155–156.

6. Morris Blachman and Kenneth E. Sharpe, "De-Democratizing Foreign Policy: Dismantling the Post-Vietnam Formula," *Third World Quarterly* (October 1986).

7. The War Powers Resolution, Public Law 93-148, 93d Cong., J.J. Res. 542, 7 November 1973; repr. in Pat M. Holt, *The War Powers Resolution, The Intervention* (Washington: American Enterprise Institute, 1978), pp. 43–48.

8. 91st Cong., 1st sess., S. Rept. 91-129, p. 30, cited in Holt, *War Powers Resolution*, p. 4.

9. Senator Vandenberg had advised President Truman: "Let us in on the takeoffs if you want us in on the crash landings." Cited in James Sundquist, *The Decline and Resurgence of Congress* (Washington: Brookings Institutions, 1981), p. 300.

10. International Security and Development Cooperation Act of 1981, Sec. 728(b).

11. See Jim Leach et al., *U.S. Policy in Central America: Against the Law?* (Washington: Arms Control and Foreign Policy Caucus, 11 September 1984), pp. 9–13; Central America Crisis Monitoring Team, *In Contempt of Congress: The Reagan Record of Deceit and Illegality on Central America* (Washington: Institute for Policy Studies, 1985), pp. 32–37; and Raymond Bonner, *Weakness and Deceit: U.S. Policy and El Salvador* (New York: New York Times Books, 1984).

12. Langhorne Motley, before the House Subcommittee on Western Hemisphere Affairs, 2 May 1984 (cited in *In Contempt of Congress*, p. 39).

13. Jim Leach et al., *U.S. Aid to El Salvador: An Evaluation of the Past, a Proposal for the Future* (Washington: Arms Control and Foreign Policy Caucus, 1985), p. 4.

14. See, for example, Kenneth E. Sharpe, "El Salvador Revisited," *World Policy Journal* (Summer 1986): 473–494.

15. 98th Cong., 2d Sess., H.R. Rep. no. 1086, pp. 40–41 (1984).

16. Leach et al., *U.S. Policy in Central America*, pp. 31–32.

17. Comptroller General of the United States, Rep. B-213137, "DOD Use of Operations and Maintenance Appropriations in Honduras," submitted to Rep. Bill Alexander, 30 January 1986.

18. Doyle McManus and Robert Toth, "The Contras: How U.S. Got Entangled," *Los Angeles Times*, 4 March 1985.

19. Jonathan Fuerbringer, "U.S. Aide's Ties to Contras Challenged," *New York Times*, 5 September 1985.

20. Steven V. Roberts, "House Reverses Earlier Ban on Aid to Nicaragua Rebels; Passes $27 Million Package," *New York Times*, 13 June 1985.

21. Steven V. Roberts, "House Gets Compromise on Rebel Aid," *New York Times*, 9 May 1985.

22. Steven V. Roberts, "A Consensus on Rebel Aid," *New York Times*, 14 June 1985.

23. Ibid.

24. Schlesinger, *The Imperial Presidency* (Boston: Houghton Mifflin Co., 1973), pp. 409–410.

25. Fulbright, *Crippled Giant*, p. 194.

26. Schlesinger, *Imperial Presidency*, p. 208.

27. For a detailed discussion see Morris J. Blachman, William LeoGrande, and Kenneth E. Sharpe, *Confronting Revolution: Security through Diplomacy in Central America* (New York: Pantheon Books, 1986), chaps. 12, 13.

28. Schlesinger, *Imperial Presidency*, pp. 298–299. For the Fulbright remarks see *Congressional Record*, 19 June 1969, S6831.

2

The Reagan Administration, Congress, and Central America: The Search for Consensus

Cynthia Arnson

The congressional debate that began in 1979 over U.S. policy in Central America has been one of the most bitter and divisive since the Vietnam War. This is not only because regional instability and the ideological zeal of the Reagan administration revived fears that U.S. military forces may be used in the area, but also because stated U.S. goals in the region and the policies designed to achieve them have appeared inconsistent, contradictory, dangerous, or unattainable.

The Parameters of the Debate

Ideology

Before exploring the roots of the tentative congressional consensus regarding El Salvador and Nicaragua which existed in early 1986, it is important to explain what the debate was and was not about. It occurred within the context of two ideological legacies which were sometimes reinforcing and sometimes contradictory. One legacy was centuries old; for nearly 200 years U.S. policy in the Western Hemisphere had presumed U.S. dominance, even if the expulsion of foreign influences spelled maintenance of a repressive status quo.[1] With the advent of the Cold War, and particularly after the Cuban revolution, broad consensus emerged over the desirability of preventing additional communist governments from coming to power in the hemisphere.[2] U.S. objections had both internal and external dimensions: externally, such governments provided opportunities for the Soviet Union to extend its power; internally, the closed political and economic systems the governments imposed were antithetical to Western values, based on individual rights and free enterprise.

For Central America, this heritage meant there would be little or no debate over the legitimacy or the primacy of U.S. security interests in the region, as defined by successive administrations. Rather, the debate would focus on the best means of protecting those interests. In the case of El Salvador, there would be little discussion of the desirability of preventing a guerrilla victory; instead, the debate would center on the best policies to achieve that end. In Nicaragua, the ideological inheritance of previous decades meant that attempts to influence the internal and external behavior of the Sandinistas could evolve into discussions of whether or not to accept the existence of the Sandinista government itself.

A competing legacy was left by the Vietnam War. The post-Vietnam timing of the Nicaraguan revolution and of the Salvadoran insurgency held out the possibility that U.S. policy in Central America would not be defined by the reflexive anticommunist interventionism of the postwar period. The Vietnam War had signified, among other things, the breakdown of the Cold War consensus over the use of U.S. military force to protect U.S. interests. The Vietnam debacle injected the consideration of limited ends and proportionate means into foreign policy discussions. The U.S. failure in Vietnam also aroused guilt among certain sectors of the public, as well as doubt concerning the purposes of American power.

The Vietnam experience had profound implications for the Western Hemisphere. After decades of tolerating or installing regimes in Latin America which coupled pro-U.S. stability with suppression of their own populations, policymakers in this country began to question the nature of the regimes receiving U.S. support. Internal repression was viewed as fostering a new kind of instability, leading to the very upheavals the United States sought to avoid.[3] In Congress, landmark hearings on human rights in Chile and South Korea (1974), and in El Salvador, Guatemala, and Nicaragua (1976 and 1977), set the stage for an official U.S. distancing from these regimes and, in some instances, for cutoffs of military aid.[4] President Carter sought to harness this momentum and transform it into a major theme of his presidency; Latin America, because of its low strategic importance, was a focus of these efforts. The new spotlight on human rights suggested that the dictatorships in Nicaragua and El Salvador would be met with condemnation, even as their foundations crumbled and revolutionary movements gained in strength.

The debates over Central America are best understood, then, by reference to two historical poles: a centuries-old inheritance of presuming regional hegemony, which intensified with the forging of an anticommunist Cold War consensus; and a post-Vietnam formulation wary of U.S. military intervention to stifle the forces of change, and positing that Third World instability often arose from delayed reforms and domestic repression.[5]

Institutions

Institutional factors also influenced congressional responses to Central America. The Vietnam War and the Watergate scandal set the stage for a congressional attack on the "imperial presidency," in essence an attempt to recoup powers explicitly granted to Congress by the Constitution (to declare war and approve budgets, for example) but subsequently usurped by the executive or given away through congressional deference.[6] The attempts to regain congressional authority culminated in passage of the War Powers Resolution, formation of the intelligence committees, and attacks on the congressional seniority system by a generation of first-term, reform-minded representatives. Such changes signaled both a new attitude in Congress (the desire for greater initiative and closer oversight of foreign affairs) and a new capacity to assert itself in the foreign policy area (through greater democratization within Congress and the establishment of formal mechanisms of control over the executive). The most concrete manifestations of this "resurgence"[7] were directed at U.S. policy in the Third World. For example, Congress cut off covert operations in Angola in 1975 and the Church Committee launched an investigation of the Central Intelligence Agency (CIA) destabilization of the Allende government in Chile.

As the debate over Central America soon demonstrated, however, the congressional role in foreign policy was limited, not only by the residue of an attitude that ceded overall conduct of foreign affairs to the executive branch, but also by presidential prerogatives giving superior resources—information, expertise, flexibility, and propaganda—to the executive.[8] While Congress debated how much military aid to send to El Salvador, for example, the president made use of special discretionary funds to bypass the legislative body. (Between FY/1980 and FY/1983, some 60 percent of all U.S. military aid to El Salvador was sent without the approval of the full Congress.) And when Congress expressed reservations about the number of U.S. military advisors in El Salvador, the Pentagon merely sent them to train the Salvadoran army in Honduras. At times the skirting of congressional prerogatives or the failure to keep Congress informed became the focal point of congressional attacks on the administration. (Recall, for example, Senate Intelligence Committee Chair Barry Goldwater's angry letter to CIA Director William Casey after the mining of Nicaraguan harbors: "I am pissed off," Goldwater wrote. "This is no way to run a railroad.")[9] More often, however, administration determination to pursue its goals in Central America produced exasperation and defeatism on Capitol Hill, a reaction apparently not unintended by administration strategists.

The impact of Congress was also limited by its inability to present and make operational a coherent alternative to the administration's Central American policy. This inability has two principal foundations: (1) the nature of congressional "handles" on foreign policy; and (2) features of the electoral system, including reserves of anticommunism among the U.S. public.

In the first instance, formal power in Congress is based on its ability to pass laws and appropriate money. But the principal mechanisms available to Congress to influence foreign policy—withholding, granting, or conditioning funds—are at best blunt instruments for forcing subtle policy changes. Similarly, laws governing administration behavior can restrain and guide executive action, but they cannot force a new policy direction without the administration's willingness to comply in more than a formalistic fashion. The discussion below of the El Salvador "certification requirement" illustrates the limits of such congressionally mandated procedural solutions.

Second, presenting an alternative—that is, denying resources to the president and promoting an alternative vision—means taking a risk that the future will indeed produce the intended results. In El Salvador, for example, a call for "power sharing" between the government and the guerrillas rested on the assumption that the Salvadoran guerrillas would not come to dominate their non-Marxist allies. Given the Nicaraguan experience, members of Congress saw this proposition as dubious. Similarly, in Nicaragua, calling for a modus vivendi between the United States and the Sandinistas relied on the assumption that they would not seek military alliances in the socialist world, attempt to subvert their neighbors, or repress their internal opponents. With strong anticommunist attitudes existing within the electorate and with administration determination to blame Congress for any policy failures resulting from unwillingness to provide funds, lack of guarantees about the future in Central America produces strong disincentives against the development and support of an alternative foreign policy.[10]

In 1984 and 1985 the Reagan administration clearly played on these reserves of anticommunism in order to gain congressional backing for its policies in El Salvador and Nicaragua. By threatening opponents with being "soft on communism"—at times campaigning openly on this theme in swing districts or engaging in overt red-baiting—the administration and its supporters in Congress were able to heighten the domestic political costs of opposing the president.

The reverse of the negative consensus against communism in Central America was a positive consensus on what was desirable there, based on the American political values of democracy, electoral government, and individual liberty. These values were often taken as absolutes and therefore deemed good for all countries; this observation may help explain why U.S. interventions in Latin America have been justified as uplifting native peoples, even though the results of U.S. policy have sometimes been the opposite. This historical fact, however, does not diminish the extent to which elected representatives in the United States—themselves products of the electoral system—exhibit a deeply held faith in these principles. This belief, as well as agreement on what is undesirable in Central America, is important in understanding the inherent bias in favor of governments perceived as manifesting or striving toward Western democratic forms (Costa Rica, Honduras, El Salvador, and Guatemala) and against those that are not (Nicaragua).

Finally, one particular aspect of party politics influenced the outcome of key congressional debates on Central America: neither of the administration's two major victories—securing full funding for the new Duarte government in El Salvador in May 1984 and aid for contra rebels in June 1985—would have been possible without ideological splits within the Democratic party, closely paralleling regional divisions. In 1984 Majority Leader Jim Wright led a block of southern Democrats in support of Reagan's aid package to El Salvador, which passed the House by a narrow four-vote margin. This same block (excluding Wright) formed the core of the group that changed its votes to support nonlethal aid to the contras between April and June 1985. The split between northern and southern Democrats is principally ideological, particularly on issues related to defense:[11] whereas most conservative districts in the United States are held by Republicans, in the South the post-Reconstruction dislike for the Republican party has meant that many conservatives there still belong to the Democratic party.[12] The split is also linked to the South's geographical proximity to Central America, which raises the specter of an influx of unwanted refugees. The South has also had a special relationship with Central America, deeply rooted in U.S. history.[13]

The following discussion summarizes the evolution of debate over policies toward El Salvador and Nicaragua in order to illuminate the congressional role in foreign policy and to understand how the executive branch came to prevail, despite the ideological and institutional changes that resulted from the Vietnam War. Particular attention is given to the factors that contributed to policy discord, and to the developments that led to congressional support for or acquiescence in administration policy. The debates over El Salvador and Nicaragua followed a similar pattern: at first Congress opposed administration policy but later came to support it. The importance of explaining the turnaround points, or "switches," makes them a major focus of the subsequent discussion. As the debate on Central America demonstrates, the Reagan administration eventually succeeded in gaining majority support for its policies, even though congressional action resulted in policies that were by their nature compromises.

El Salvador

The Reagan administration came into office with the stated intention of "drawing the line" against communism in El Salvador. Yet the extremism of its rhetoric, together with the sordid reality on the ground, provoked a congressional backlash that denied both material resources and political legitimacy to the administration for three combative years.

Throughout the five-year battle over aid to El Salvador, Congress never questioned the appropriateness of the administration's central goal of preventing the Farabundo Martí National Liberation Front (FMLN) guerrillas and their civilian allies from seizing power.[14] Rather, the debate centered on the best means to that end—whether the solution should be political and negotiated or military—and on the appropriate framework for policy discussion. Whereas the administration emphasized the East-West struggle and the dangers of communist penetration, Congress focused on the human rights violations of the Salvadoran military and on the need for political, social, and economic change. Over time the congressional debate, sustained in large part by an active human rights and church lobby,[15] forced the administration to emphasize political reforms (i.e., elections), to support the political center against the right wing, and to move against the most egregious excesses of the death squads in order to guarantee a steady flow of aid to the Salvadoran army. Although it is difficult to find a direct cause-and-effect relationship between congressional protest and administration action, it is undeniable that congressional debate established the general tone of policy, dictating certain outcomes (the need for a political component in administration strategy) while precluding others (the election of right-wing politician Roberto D'Aubuisson as president of El Salvador).[16]

The early policy clashes between the Reagan administration and Congress resulted from the administration's characterization of the conflict and its actions to resolve it. Secretary of State Haig's references to Soviet "hit lists" and "going to the source," and an administration white paper on communist interference in El Salvador,[17] dismayed congressional liberals and moderates. They viewed government-sponsored violence, reflected in the murders of four U.S. churchwomen and two U.S. land reform advisors, along with reports of widespread human rights violations, as the key to understanding the Salvadoran upheaval. Moreover, the Reagan administration's prescriptions—increasing the number of military advisors and tripling military aid—brought back the specter of Vietnam: once again the United States seemed to be backing a corrupt, murderous regime without recognizing that the determination not "to lose El Salvador" would draw the United States into an increasingly greater military commitment.

These concerns, expressed by both Democrats and Republicans in the House and Senate, led in 1981 to the adoption of a certification requirement which specified the conditions that the government of El Salvador had to meet in order to qualify for continued military aid.[18] Certification reflected the basic congressional dilemma regarding El Salvador: Congress accepted the administration's ultimate goal but rejected its means.[19] The certification stopped short of undercutting U.S. support for the Salvadoran junta; instead, Congress was attempting to direct the administration toward a sounder policy based on human rights, economic reform, and political negotiations. Although the president was given ultimate authority to decide whether the conditions were being met (indeed, certification passed the House Foreign Affairs Committee only after a provision giving Congress veto power was dropped), the legislation was a defeat for the administration; it was passed by a Republican-controlled Senate on an issue the administration had made a top political priority in its first year in office.

For the next two years certification became the focal point of congressional debate on El Salvador. Aid levels were reduced, if not slashed, as Congress remained skeptical that progress in El Salvador was as commendable as the administration claimed. But the certification revealed the limits of congressional ability to influence foreign policy through procedural solutions. The Reagan administration complied with the letter of the law by issuing certifications based on its own reading of Salvadoran events, despite vigorous challenges by human rights groups, religious leaders, policy analysts, and former U.S. government officials. At times the administration, in presentations to Congress, made statements that its own cables showed insupportable.[20] Yet Congress remained unwilling to terminate military aid to El Salvador for fear that such a step would lead to a victory by the Salvadoran guerrillas. Both the Reagan administration and the Salvadoran army understood the limits of congressional opposition, an insight that gave them the upper hand in dealing with legislatively imposed aid conditions.

After the first certification debates in 1982, when it became apparent that the administration would comply with the letter but not the spirit of the law, certification hearings became lackluster, biannual rituals. The debate over El Salvador continued to be fueled, however, by political developments in that country, which provided Congress with ongoing reason to maintain its oversight of administration policy.

Elections for the Constituent Assembly in March 1982, for example, gave control of that body to the right wing. Partly in anticipation of a congressional backlash, the Reagan administration sent an emissary to San Salvador to prevent the Assembly from naming Roberto D'Aubuisson, widely associated with death squad activities, as provisional president of the country.[21] Later in 1982, when the Assembly tried to dismantle aspects of the 1980 agrarian reform, the Senate Foreign Relations Committee voted to freeze aid at the preceding year's level. Such actions illustrated that Congress was responding to its own reading of events in El Salvador as well as to administration policy, which was at times a response to the perceived sensitivities of legislators who controlled the disbursements of funds.

The reductions in aid and the conditions placed on the dispensing of aid were Congress's way of expressing doubts about administration policy and events in El Salvador. For its part, the administration complained that congressional aid cuts were contributing to a Salvadoran military stalemate in the war against the guerrillas. To break the impasse without changing the thrust of its policy, the White House shifted tactics in early 1983 and put President Reagan in the forefront of a high-profile effort to gain support for El Salvador funding, specifically for $110 million in additional military aid.[22] In March the president for the first time devoted an entire speech to El Salvador;[23] in April, addressing a joint session of Congress, he emphasized the importance of Central America to overall U.S. foreign policy goals.[24] But the strategy had only mixed results. Key administration supporters in the Senate publicly began to express opposition to military aid, given continuing political violence and government ineffectiveness in El Salvador.[25] Committees and subcommittees in both houses slashed administration aid proposals by up to half.[26] By the end of 1983 the proposed military aid level was less than it had been the year before; moreover, Congress imposed a condition tying 30 percent of the funds to a trial and verdict in the case of the murdered U.S. churchwomen.[27]

In response, an embattled administration moved to appoint a bipartisan commission, headed by Henry Kissinger, to build a consensus on Central America policy which had eluded President Reagan from the beginning of his administration. As evidence of the confusion and infighting within administration ranks and of frustration over congressional activism on El Salvador, President Reagan pocket vetoed an extension of the certification law in late 1983; at nearly the same time the administration sent Vice President Bush to El Salvador to warn that congressional support for aid was in jeopardy as long as death squad violence continued at high levels.[28] The two moves signified administration contempt for congressional meddling in El Salvador policy yet constituted an admission that some kind of partnership with the Congress was essential if the administration was to have the means to implement its strategy.

The Turnaround in 1984

The Kissinger Commission's January 1984 recommendations for higher levels of military aid to El Salvador, coupled with the imposition of strong human rights conditions, underscored the tensions between the Reagan administration and its critics without resolving them.[29] Equally inconclusive were the March 1984 elections in El Salvador, which mandated a runoff between Christian Democrat José Napoleón Duarte and ARENA party candidate Roberto D'Aubuisson. Both the House and Senate balked at the prospect of providing new aid to a government that would potentially be led by a rightist widely reputed to have close ties to the death squads. As if seeing the handwriting on the wall, the Reagan administration provided limited CIA funding to Duarte's campaign, a fact leaked by those opposing Duarte's candidacy.[30]

The triumph of Duarte in the 6 May 1984 presidential runoff election was the event that changed the administration's fortunes in Washington. The key to Duarte's success in confounding the administration's critics in Congress was threefold: (1) his election signified to legislators that democracy was taking root in El Salvador in a peaceful, evolutionary manner; (2) Duarte, a political moderate, announced his plans to improve human rights, carry out reforms, and investigate cases of right-wing violence, all objectives sought by congressional opponents of U.S. El Salvador policy; and (3) as a result, the political costs associated with voting against Duarte were unacceptably high.

On 10 May 1984, the House gave President Reagan the most outstanding Central America victory of his first term by approving, 212-208, a Republican-sponsored aid package for El Salvador; it granted almost all that the administration had requested, with no meaningful conditions attached. Liberal Democrats, making a distinction between Duarte's actual and symbolic power, argued that strong conditions on aid would strengthen Duarte's hand against the intransigent right and the army, thus enhancing the Salvadoran president's ability to carry out his program. But the liberals were ultimately undercut by Duarte himself. In a letter and through personal phone calls to individual members of Congress, Duarte pleaded:

> The people of El Salvador have defied all threats and freely voted in over-whelming numbers for the candidates of their choice. . . .

> In order to avoid the disaster that has befallen our neighboring country, which has seen its legitimate aspirations for democracy frustrated by a Marxist-Leninist takeover, we need adequate economic and military assistance from the American government. . . .
>
> Please help the people of El Salvador and contribute simultaneously to the security and stability of our hemisphere.[31]

House Majority Leader Jim Wright (D-TX) delivered the critical Democrats in the administration's favor, on a vote that was otherwise divided along partisan lines. In an emotional speech during the floor debate following his visit to El Salvador as a member of the official U.S. observer delegation, Wright argued that "—we need steady, emphatic commitment to freedom in El Salvador—not a tenuous, tentative, hesitant, or begruding commitment."[32]

In the 10 May vote, splits between northern and southern Democrats became decisive for the first time on a major Central America vote. In addition to Wright, all four Democrats on the U.S. observer team were Southerners (Montgomery-MS, Boner-TN, Roemer-LA, and Pickle-TX), and all four voted with Wright. Of the fifty-six Democrats who voted with the Republicans, all but seven were from the South. Wright's break with the Democratic leadership was partly offset by support for the Democratic position from the new chair of the House Foreign Affairs Committee (Fascell, D-FL), who maintained the loyalty of an important group of Southerners.[33] In the end, however, the foreign aid bill passed, as Republicans who normally opposed foreign aid voted for the bill in order to hand President Reagan a major foreign policy victory.

After a series of triumphant visits by Duarte to Washington throughout the summer of 1984, Congress approved record amounts of additional military aid to his government. Congressional debate over El Salvador evaporated as legislators agreed to "give Duarte a chance," and as they perceived that no alternative to supporting him and his reformist program was politically viable.

The congressional consensus on El Salvador achieved in mid-1984 has proven remarkably stable. It has survived major challenges to Duarte's leadership within El Salvador and allegations of administration deception in Washington. A February 1985 report to the congressional Arms Control and Foreign Policy Caucus claimed systematic distortions and misrepresentations in administration statements to Congress about policy goals and aid levels to El Salvador. Yet a mere six months after Duarte's inauguration, the document created barely a ripple.[34]

Nicaragua

Congressional opposition to administration policy in Nicaragua prior to 1985 stemmed from a basic rejection of both the administration's goals (gradually perceived as the overthrow of the Sandinista government) and its instruments (sponsorship of a covert proxy war). Initially Congress went along with a covert military operation for what it viewed as the legitimate purpose of intercepting arms going from Nicaragua to rebels in El Salvador. When contra rebels themselves declared their intention to overthrow the Managua government, and skirmishes along the Nicaraguan-Honduran border threatened to escalate into a broader conflict, congressional skepticism turned into alarm, and House Democrats led an effort, successful in late 1984, to terminate funding for the covert war.

Congressional opponents of administration policy thus initially made a fundamental distinction between El Salvador and Nicaragua: it was one thing to support a government engaged in a counterinsurgency war against leftist guerrillas (a policy consistent with postwar containment); it was another to attempt to unseat a left-wing government once it was in power (a new Reagan strategy of "rolling back" Soviet gains in the Third World). In both cases Congress considered the costs associated with the means necessary to achieve U.S. goals. Yet the conflict over Nicaragua was necessarily more intense and bitter, because the legislative branch came to question not only the wisdom of U.S. means but the very objectives they were designed to achieve.[35]

Efforts to limit the covert war began almost as soon as congressional oversight committees were notified of it in 1981. Edward Boland (D-MA), chair of the House Intelligence Committee, at first backed a 1981 Reagan administration proposal to channel $19 million through the CIA to Nicaraguan exiles based in Honduras. Although supportive of the plan, Boland expressed concern in a December 1981 letter to CIA Director William Casey about the number and tactics of the rebels, the U.S. ability to control them, and the possibility of military clashes between Nicaragua and Honduras.[36] In mid-1982 several Democrats on the House Intelligence Committee considered eliminating funding for the covert war during consideration of the upcoming year's intelligence authorization. Boland countered with his own proposal to prohibit use of CIA funds "for the purpose of overthrowing the government of Nicaragua or provoking a military exchange between Nicaragua and Honduras." That provision became public when House Democrats, led by Representative Harkin (D-IA), attempted during a December 1982 floor debate to prohibit U.S. funding for military operations "in or against Nicaragua."[37] Boland's Intelligence Committee proposal, offered as a substitute for Harkin's, was adopted 411-0 with administration support. It thus became the first public law governing the secret war.[38]

Beginning in March 1982 and continuing into early 1983, numerous reports in newspapers, news magazines, and television broadcasts documented the U.S. role in backing paramilitary operations against Nicaragua, the mushrooming of the contra force, their abusive tactics, and their central goal: overthrow of the Sandinistas.[39] The press also reported the readiness of Honduran General Gustavo Alvarez to lend his territory, and his forces if necessary, to the contras' effort. As a result the administration's contention that the only purpose of the covert operation was arms interdiction became all but unsustainable.

In 1982 Boland had staked his prestige on giving the administration the benefit of the doubt about the covert war; he had lent his name to an amendment prohibiting U.S. actions to overthrow the Sandinistas. Yet increasingly frustrated by the administration's perceived failure to comply with the law and genuinely alarmed about the rapid expansion of the contras' ranks and about their real purpose, Boland along with Clement Zablocki (D-WI), chair of the House Foreign Affairs Committee, introduced a bill to terminate funding for the covert war.[40] Boland expressed his fears over the potential outcome of the covert war to the House on 28 July, saying that, although the 1982 Boland amendment "specifically forbade the effort to overthrow the Nicaraguan government or to provoke a military exchange between Nicaragua and Honduras, . . . that is where we are headed."[41] The same day the House voted to end support for the covert war and to provide overt funding only for the limited purpose of intercepting arms going from Nicaragua to El Salvador. House Republicans, calling the cutoff "a policy of surrender,"[42] privately expressed rage to administration officials over leaks before the debate that the United States intended to conduct massive military maneuvers in Honduras and off the Nicaraguan coast. Eighteen Republicans joined all but fifty Democrats in passing the Boland-Zablocki bill by the comfortable margin of 228–195.

In the Senate, however, Democrats lacked the votes to end the covert war, and few senators even rose to denounce it. When the Senate Intelligence Committee approved ongoing funds for the secret war, the House was forced to compromise its no-aid position. The FY/1984 Defense Appropriations bill provided $24 million for the covert operation, but the compromise included a silver lining for the Democrats by prohibiting the use of CIA contingency funds to augment the $24 million. The administration would thus have to gain both House and Senate backing to spend more than the approved amount. The House maintained a veto.[43]

In March 1984 the administration renewed its request for $21 million in supplemental funds for the contras. Despite initial procedural and jurisdictional skirmishes, the Senate Appropriations and Intelligence committees approved the requests and the Senate voted to uphold the funding, defeating a series of amendments to end the covert war. Yet pressure from Senate Republicans persuaded President Reagan to issue an assurance that "the United States does not seek to destabilize or overthrow the government of Nicaragua; nor to impose or compel any particular form of government there."[44]

However, two days later, on 6 April 1984, the *Wall Street Journal* reported that the CIA had participated in the mining of Nicaraguan harbors. The ensuing controversy centered on alleged administration violation of the law and mismanagement of the covert war:[45] the CIA's role in the mining appeared to escalate direct U.S. military involvement in an act of war against the Sandinistas, threatening not only Nicaraguan commerce but the shipping of U.S. allies as well. When Senate Intelligence Committee Chair Barry Goldwater angrily chastised CIA Director Casey, however, his objections seemed to be based less on the substance of the action than on the senator's conviction that the administration had failed to inform his committee.[46] Like Nicaraguan President Daniel Ortega's trip to Moscow a year later, the CIA role was an embarrassment to legislators who had publicly defended their position on the basis of an assessment that later proved to be inaccurate.

In April both the House and the Senate approved nonbinding "sense of the Congress" resolutions condemning the mining; the House voted the next month to defeat the administration's $21 million supplemental funding request; ultimately, the Senate accepted the House position.

The mining of Nicaragua's harbors weakened Senate support for the covert war, setting the stage for a cutoff of funding in October 1984. In June, during consideration of the FY/1984 Defense Authorization bill, four Democratic members of the Senate Intelligence Committee who had previously supported the administration voted to cut off funds for the war. Four months later a proposal by Senator Inouye (D-HI) to fund a phaseout of the covert operation lost by a vote of 57–42. The shifting votes in the Republican-dominated Senate showed that administration bungling, mismanagement, and perceived illegality had begun to reap a harvest of distrust, even among past supporters.

House Democrats opposed to the covert war thus had the upper hand in House-Senate conferences deciding the fate of the contras. During the conference on the FY/1985 Continuing Resolution (a spending bill passed at the end of the fiscal year), Boland emphasized that by then the House had voted four times to end the secret war. He insisted that the Senate yield to the House position. The administration, by exerting heavy pressure on Senate Republicans to continue the program, left them with no fall-back or compromise position. The deadlock was broken when Senate Republicans gave in to Boland, rather than tie up an entire year's appropriations bill. The resulting legislation cut off congressional support for the contras while allowing the president to make a new request—after 28 February 1985— for no more than $14 million. Revelations in mid-October of a CIA-produced assassination manual for the contras added a new scandal to the president's political woes.[47] Nevertheless, a determined administration pressed on.

The Shift

The congressional decision in the summer of 1985, less than a year later, to resume support of the contras by providing "humanitarian" (non-lethal) aid was based on a number of interrelated factors: widespread dissatisfaction with the domestic and foreign policies of the Sandinistas and changes in the composition of their opposition; divisions within the Democratic party over the legitimacy of using U.S. military force to achieve policy goals;[48] changes in the language adopted by the administration to portray the goals and the instruments of its policy; and congressional procedure. President Ortega's trip to Moscow, just after the House voted in April 1985 to reject President Reagan's $14 million contra aid request, has often been blamed for the House switch. More correctly, although the trip did trigger anger and embarrassment on the part of those opposed to contra aid, it also strengthened diverse tendencies within Congress already leading toward acquiescence with the president's proposals.

Although the president did not submit a formal funding request to Congress until April 1985, the campaign to secure its approval began much earlier. Starting in February, Reagan and Secretary of State Shultz went on a rhetorical rampage, calling the contras "our brothers" and "the moral equivalent of the Founding Fathers," threatening those who denied them aid with pushing Nicaragua into "the endless darkness of communist tyranny,"[49] and admitting that the purpose of U.S. aid was to make the Sandinistas "say 'Uncle' " and to "remove . . . the present structure" of the Nicaraguan government. Such hyperbole reinforced critics' doubts about the administration's ultimate objective, but it also helped the administration by narrowing and defining the terms of the debate. The relevant questions became whether and to what extent Nicaragua represented a threat to its neighbors, how totalitarian the Sandinistas were, and whether administration opponents were willingly or unwittingly doing Moscow's work in the hemisphere. To hammer home its position, the administration and conservative domestic groups flooded congressional offices with lobbying materials. In the month of April 1985 alone, the barrage included

1. "The Soviet-Cuban Connection in Central America and the Caribbean," issued by the State and Defense departments;
2. a State Department resource paper entitled "Groups of the Nicaraguan Democratic Resistance—Who Are They?"
3. "The Sandinista Military Build-up," from the State and Defense departments;
4. the "Nicaragua Fact Book," a production of Citizens for Reagan which highlighted Sandinista relationships with terrorist organizations, human rights abuses, etc.;
5. "Central America: Resistance or Surrender?" a conference on Capitol Hill sponsored by Citizens for America and featuring National Security Advisor Robert McFarlane;
6. an offer from Friends of the Americas to make radio spots available to members of Congress in favor of contra aid;
7. personal letters from Secretary of State Shultz asking members of Congress to help strengthen the bipartisan consensus on Central America;
8. the text of President Reagan's remarks at a private fund-raising event for the contras;
9. "Central America: Freedom or Slavery?" a report distributed by Pat Robertson and the Christian Broadcasting Network;
10. "Misconceptions about U.S. Policy toward Nicaragua," a report issued by the State Department.[50]

Despite vigorous opposition to contra policy, a majority in Congress accepted as accurate administration portrayals of the Sandinista's military buildup, their crackdown on internal opponents, and their support for El Salvadoran rebels. The breakdown of efforts to assure participation of opposition leader Arturo Cruz in Nicaragua's November 1984 elections,[51] and Cruz's subsequent incorporation into the contra ranks, exacerbated congressional doubts about the Sandinistas while contributing, in the eyes of some members, to the legitimacy of the contra movement. Given a virtual consensus in Congress against the Sandinista regime, critics of the administration focused debate on the effectiveness of U.S. policy, the extent to which it undermined regional peace efforts,[52] the threat it posed of deeper or more direct U.S. military involvement in Nicaragua,[53] and the extent to which it contributed to, or was responsible for, repression and militarization in Nicaragua.

If Congress was still unprepared in April 1985 to renew military aid to the contras, a new consensus nurtured by conservative, mostly Southern Democrats, had begun to emerge. In a speech to the Coalition for a Democratic Majority, for example, Senator Nunn (D-GA) proposed moving ". . . the military option to the back burner while keeping it on the stove and honoring our commitment to the democratic forces in Nicaragua." Nunn's suggested policy had two central elements: (1) "resuming an adequate amount of humanitarian aid both now and for the future"; and (2) moving "diplomatic and economic options . . . to the front burner." He specifically recommended immediate consideration of an economic embargo "enlisting our allies in the region and other allies throughout the world."[54] The proposal captured the essence of what would emerge over the summer as a position capable of securing enough votes to pass Congress: military pressure to force the Sandinistas to the bargaining table and to guarantee the success of diplomatic negotiations, and "nonlethal" aid to the contras to resolve the dilemma between abandoning the resistance and seeking a military overthrow of the Nicaraguan government.[55]

To avoid a costly defeat in the Senate, where opposition to military aid was expressed by Republicans and Democrats alike, President Reagan compromised his proposal along lines suggested by Nunn and others, agreeing to drop the request for military aid and to use funds only for "humanitarian assistance." In a letter to Senate Majority Leader Robert Dole on the day of the vote, Reagan stated, in language remarkably devoid of the rhetoric of previous months:

> I will provide assistance to the democratic resistance only for food, medicine, clothing, and other assistance for their survival and well-being—and not for arms, ammunition, and weapons for war.
> I intend to resume bilateral talks with the Government of Nicaragua and will instruct our representatives in those talks to press for a ceasefire as well as a church-mediated dialogue between the contending Nicaraguan factions.
> . . .
> The U.S. condemns atrocities by either side in the strongest possible terms. . . .[56]

Stripped of military aid funds, the request passed the Senate by seven votes on 23 April 1985.

Reagan's prospects in the House were bleaker, but the debate indicated that the president had made substantial headway in moving conservative and moderate Democrats toward support of some kind of contra aid.[57] In April the House resoundingly defeated the request for military aid,[58] but a day later it passed a bipartisan alternative which provided no aid to the contras but allotted $10 million to assist Nicaraguan refugees and $4 million to implement any treaty worked out by the Contadora group. But the key House vote that month was on an amendment sponsored by Minority Leader Robert Michel which provided $14 million in "humanitarian" aid to the contras; it lost by only two votes. The slim margin signified that, while opponents of the covert operation had won a series of important battles against the president, they were beginning to lose the war.

Opportunities for reviving the issue of contra aid after the April actions came from two sources: House failure to secure final passage of the bill which contained the bipartisan alternative (noted above) and Ortega's trip to Moscow. The two actions, though independent of each other, became procedurally linked when House moderates, angered by the "absence of a policy," capitalized on Ortega's visit to demand another go-around on the contra aid question.

Ortega's trip was seen as an embarrassment because it appeared to confirm what the administration and its supporters had said all along, that the Sandinistas sought Soviet aid and friendship by choice, not necessity, and that congressional action intended to stop the war would not induce Nicaragua to show restraint in its international policies. One of the many arguments used by administration opponents, for example, had been that Nicaragua's growing dependence on Soviet military and economic assistance was in part a result of pressures caused by the war and could be decelerated by a relaxation of those pressures. In the words of Representative Derrick (D-SC), who ultimately switched his vote in June 1985 to support contra funding, "I took it [the trip] as an international slap at the Congress and a slap at those of us who had gone out on a limb to come up with something" other than direct aid to the contras.[59]

To other leading Democrats who switched their votes, however, Ortega's trip was less important than congressional procedure, specifically the House defeat of the April bill containing the bipartisan alternative.[60] Liberal Democrats who wanted to prevent the legislation from going to conference with the Senate joined with a majority of Republicans who voted against it because its passage would be an overwhelming defeat for the president.[61] The resulting policy vacuum provided an opening for a small group of disgruntled moderates and conservatives to enter the fray as leaders in the search for a new alternative in the House. As one of the key architects of this new strategy, Representative David McCurdy (D-OK), remarked,

> I worked for [the bipartisan alternative] . . . even though I felt that it was less than desirable, because I hoped that once we got to conference with the

Senate a reasonable bill might emerge. When that effort failed, a group of Democrats who had supported [the bipartisan alternative] but opposed the Michel amendment got together and drafted new legislation. *It is often said that the Ortega visit to Moscow was the reason that many people in the House changed their minds about aid. That is just not the truth. Our meeting occurred before that trip actually took place, nor would that trip have made a difference* [emphasis added].[62]

What emerged in June 1985 as the majority position of the House on Nicaragua was virtually identical with the Senate compromise crafted in April, which denied military aid to the contras but provided nonlethal, "humanitarian" assistance. As in other instances, rhetorical changes in the administration's stated policy played an important role in shifting House votes in the summer of 1985. On the one hand, Reagan sent a letter to Michel and McCurdy promising to "puruse political, not military solutions in Central America," to explore the possibility of bilateral talks with Nicaragua, and to promote improved human rights practices by the "democratic resistance."[63] On the other hand, administration supporters launched a concerted campaign to paint the issue as a stark choice between communism and freedom. In early June, Reagan went on a fund-raising trip through Southern and border states where he intensified his attack on the Sandinistas, calling President Ortega "the little dictator in green fatigues" and describing congressional failure to approve funds for the contras as "a dark day for freedom."[64] Capitalizing on Southern fears of a flood of refugees from Central America, House Minority Leader Michel warned his colleagues that ". . . down South, the streets are filling up. It is a fact of life."[65]

Other Republicans were even more direct, hoping that a barrage of red-baiting would force moderate and conservative Democrats to run for cover. "I get the impression that our colleagues on the other side of the aisle feel like we should cower in a corner while the communists march on around this world, taking country after country," said Representative Dan Burton (R-IN). ". . . My friends, don't be soft on communism."[66] House Majority Leader Jim Wright, terming the accusations "to some degree" reminiscent of the McCarthy era, said that "nobody wants to be portrayed as friendly toward communism. That has been true for forty years."[67]

Such rhetorical tactics were partly responsible for the 248–184 House vote on 12 June providing $27 million of "humanitarian" aid to contra forces.[68] All but five of the twenty-six Democrats who changed their votes between April and June 1985 were from Southern or border states.[69] As in the Senate, Southern Democrats had sought to moderate the tone and content of administration policy while recognizing the legitimacy of the contras and providing support for their goals, short of the overthrow of the Nicaraguan government. Thus, overcoming opposition to the covert war in the House resulted not only from the specific factors discussed above, but also from a shift in Congress toward acceptance of the means, if still not the goals, of the Reagan policy.

Prospects for the Future

The agreement between Congress and the executive, however tentative, has different roots in El Salvador and Nicaragua. The consensus on El Salvador policy, achieved with the 1984 election of President Duarte, was an affirmative one, rooted in the conviction that Duarte represented the best hope for democratization and peaceful reform in his country. These beliefs were reinforced by Duarte's opening of talks with the guerrillas in October 1984 and by the guerrillas' adoption of tactics that further delegitimized them in the eyes of Washington: the assassination of U.S. Marines and other civilians in June 1985, the kidnapping of civilian mayors, and the kidnapping of Duarte's daughter in September 1985. The consensus is likely to endure in the Congress as long as Duarte and electoral politics survive in El Salvador, despite periodic outbursts of concern over human rights and over the country's deteriorating economic situation. Should aid to El Salvador again become an issue of congressional debate in the short or medium term, it will most likely be due to cuts in foreign aid spending resulting from budgetary constraints.

As for Nicaragua, the word "acquiescence" is perhaps more appropriate than consensus to describe Congress's attitude. Congress went along with the president's policy, not only out of genuine agreement, but also out of reluctance to bear the political costs of opposing him. The 1986 congressional decision to provide military aid to the contras suggested that the policy of aiding the contras to put pressure on the Sandinistas would probably continue provided the president could maintain the semblance of supporting the goal of "democratization" in Nicaragua through political as well as military means, and as long as contra troops, and not American soldiers, did the fighting and dying. At the same time, the forging of a congressional majority presupposes both a reserve of ideological sympathy for fighting communism, particularly in the Western Hemisphere, and domestic political fears of appearing "soft on communism." Nowhere is the tension between the post-Vietnam reluctance to engage U.S. military forces and the long-standing domestic anticommunist consensus better illustrated than in U.S. policy toward Nicaragua.

The administration's success through 1986 in fostering both consensus and acquiescence in Congress is testimony to three things: (1) the president's enduring structural advantage in setting the foreign policy agenda and in mobilizing and manipulating resources to his advantage, as shown in the contra debate; (2) the ability of Congress to deny the president the means to carry out foreign policy until broad consensus on means and ends has been achieved, as seen in the El Salvador debate; and (3) the impact of regional events, uncontrolled and perhaps unforeseen by U.S. policymakers, on policy decisions in Washington, such as Duarte's election and Ortega's trip to Moscow. It follows that the main actors in the Central American drama, within the executive branch, within Congress, and within the region itself, have both more and less power than each would like, and that outcomes depend on the sometimes subtle interplay, sometimes dramatic clash, among these forces.

Ultimately, however, there remains a central irony: the Reagan administration's success through 1986 in forging winning coalitions in Washington, whether through acquiescence or positive consensus, is not the same as carrying out successful policies in the field. As the Central American crisis deepens, fueled by prolonged guerrilla warfare, weakened economies, and the human suffering both promote, new challenges will present themselves to decision-makers in Washington. When they do, Congress will once again have the opportunity to use its resources either to de-escalate tensions, prolong simmering unrest, or accompany the executive branch down the path of increasing U.S. military involvement. The easiest choices in Washington, based on inertia or political expediency, may well be the most disastrous for the Central American region.

Notes

1. See Cole Blasier, *The Hovering Giant: U.S. Responses to Revolutionary Change in Latin America* (Pittsburgh: University of Pittsburgh Press, 1976); Gordon Connell-Smith, *The United States and Latin America* (New York: Wiley and Sons, 1974); Walter LaFeber, *Inevitable Revolutions* (New York: Norton and Co., 1984); Michael Clark, "The Limits of Moralism: U.S. Policy toward Central America in Historical Perspective," unpublished manuscript, January 1986; Abraham Lowenthal, "The United States and Latin America: Ending the Hegemonic Presumption," *Foreign Affairs*, (October 1976).

2. On the establishment of the postwar consensus, and its breakdown after Vietnam, see Daniel Yergin, *A Shattered Peace* (Boston: Houghton Mifflin, 1977); Irving Kristol, "Consensus and Dissent in U.S. Foreign Policy," and Leslie Gelb, "Dissenting on Consensus," in Anthony Lake, ed., *The Vietnam Legacy* (New York: New York University Press, 1976); James L. Sundquist, *The Decline and Resurgence of Congress* (Washington: Brookings Institution, 1981), esp. chap. 5.

3. See Richard Feinberg, *The Intemperate Zone: The Third World Challenge to U.S. Foreign Policy* (New York: Norton and Co., 1983); Sol M. Linowitz, "A Report of the Commission on U.S.–Latin American Relations", in Kalman Silvert, *The Americas in a Changing World* (New York: Quadrangle Books, 1975).

4. See, for example, U.S. Congress, House, Committee on International Relations, Subcommittee on International Organizations, *Human Rights in Nicaragua, Guatemala, and El Salvador: Implications for U.S. Policy*, 94th Cong., 2d sess., June 1976; U.S. Congress, House, Committee on International Relations, Subcommittee on International Organizations, *Religious Persecution in El Salvador*, 95th Cong., 1st sess., July 1977.

5. Political consultant William Schneider has made the distinction between conservative internationalists, picturing the world in predominantly East-West terms, and liberal internationalists, emphasizing economic and humanitarian problems and rejecting a U.S. hegemonic role. See William Schneider, "Conservatism, Not Interventionism: Trends in Foreign Policy Opinion 1974–1982," in Kenneth Oye, Robert Lieber, and Donald Rothchild, eds., *Eagle Defiant: United States Foreign Policy in the 1980's* (Boston: Little, Brown, 1983), 33–64.

6. See Cecil B. Crabb, Jr., and Pat M. Holt, *Invitation to Struggle: Congress, the President, and Foreign Policy* (Washington: Congressional Quarterly Books, 1984);

Thomas M. Franck and Edward Weisband, *Foreign Policy by Congress* (New York: Oxford University Press, 1979); Alton Frye and Jack Sullivan, "Congress and Vietnam: The Fruits of Anguish," in Lake, *Vietnam Legacy*, 194–215; Arthur M. Schlesinger, "Congress and the Making of Foreign Policy," *Foreign Affairs* (Fall 1978); Douglas J. Bennett, "Congress in Foreign Policy: Who Needs It?" *Foreign Affairs* (Fall 1978).

7. This phrase is used by Sundquist, (*Decline and Resurgence*), among others, to describe Congress's new foreign policy activism.

8. On these points see Lee Hamilton and Michael H. Van Deusen, "Making the Separation of Powers Work," *Foreign Affairs* (Fall 1978); Gelb, "Dissenting on Consensus"; John Rourke, *Congress and the Presidency in U.S. Foreign Policymaking: A Study of Interaction and Influence, 1945–1982* (Boulder, CO: Westview Press, 1982), esp. chaps. 4, 8; Lake, *Vietnam Legacy*, 97; Crabb and Holt, *Invitation to Struggle*, 37; Schlesinger, "Congress and Foreign Policy," 104–112.

9. The complete text of the 8 April 1984 letter is printed in *Congressional Quarterly*, 14 April 1984, p. 833. On 11 April 1984, the letter was printed in the *New York Times*, with expletives deleted.

10. Consider, for example, the following exchange between Secretary of State George Shultz and Rep. David Obey (D-WI), recorded in House, Subcommittee on Appropriations, Hearings, *Foreign Assistance and Related Programs*, 98th Congress, 2d sess., 1984, p. 129:

Shultz: [The people of El Salvador] vote over the opposition of the people that Mr. Obey wants to have brought into the government, people who with armed forces tried to prevent people from voting.
Obey: No.
Shultz: You called for negotiations for power sharing.
Obey: I didn't, I called for negotiation for—
Shultz: By force.
Obey: Quote me accurately. Even the Secretary of State has an obligation to do that.
Shultz: I quoted you accurately.
Obey: No, you didn't. I said we needed negotiations across the board.
Shultz: For power sharing.
Obey: I didn't say you needed to bring in anybody.

11. See "Nicaragua: A New Democratic Family Feud," *Congressional Quarterly*, April 27, 1985, p. 809.

12. For this observation I am indebted to Professor Lars Schoultz of the University of North Carolina.

13. Southerners led a mid-nineteenth century expansionist drive aimed at "re-generating" the nonwhite peoples of Mexico and Central America. Southern support for filibuster expeditions (including that of William Walker into Nicaragua), designed to annex neighboring republics, grew out of a desire to redress the U.S. sectional balance in favor of slave states. See Robert May, *The Southern Dream of a Caribbean Empire* (Baton Rouge: Louisiana State University Press, 1973), esp. chaps. 1, 2, 4, 5.

14. Administration critic Gerry Studds (D-MA), remarked that "you and I and every Member of this Congress . . . would agree with the proposition that a major goal of the U.S. foreign policy in the region ought to be to avoid the coming to power of governments of the extreme left throughout Central America, and the differences which rational men and women have is the means most likely to achieve

that goal" (U.S. Congress, House, Committee on Foreign Affairs, Subcommittee on Western Hemisphere Affairs, *The Role of the U.S. Southern Command in Central America*, 98th Cong., 2d sess., August 1984), p. 25.

15. Religious groups, particularly the Catholic church and Protestant denominations, led public opinion in opposition to U.S. support for authoritarian regimes. Persecution of the church and of the poor was the taproot of this activism, which swelled dramatically after the 1980 murders of Archbishop Romero and four U.S. churchwomen in El Salvador.

16. After both the 1982 and 1984 elections in El Salvador, the United States worked through diplomatic and covert means to prevent D'Aubuisson from assuming the presidency. See notes 21 and 30, below.

17. See Cynthia Arnson, *El Salvador: A Revolution Confronts the United States* (Washington: Institute for Policy Studies 1982), pp. 70–72.

18. The International Security and Development Cooperation Act in 1981 (Public Law 97-113) required the president to certify, among other things, that ". . . the government of El Salvador 1) is making a concerted and significant effort to comply with internationally recognized human rights; 2) is achieving substantial control over all elements of its own armed forces, so as to bring to an end the indiscriminate torture and murder of Salvadoran citizens by these forces; 3) is making continued progress in implementing essential economic and political reforms, including the land reform. . . ."

19. For a full account of the tortuous committee process in adopting the certification, see *Congressional Quarterly Almanac 1981*, pp. 167–185.

20. See, for example, Cynthia Arnson and Aryeh Neier, *Report on Human Rights in El Salvador, Second Supplement* (New York: Americas Watch, January 1983), pp. 67–71; Raymond Bonner, *El Salvador: Weakness and Deceit* (New York: New York Times Books, 1984), esp. chaps. 11–14; Holly Burkhalter and Aryeh Neier, *Managing the Facts: How the Administration Deals with Reports of Human Rights Abuses in El Salvador* (New York: Americas Watch, 1985).

21. Cynthia Arnson, "The Salvadoran Military and Regime Transformation," in Wolf Grabendorff, ed., *Political Change in Central America: Internal and External Dimensions* (Boulder, CO: Westview Press, 1984), p. 112.

22. The request, made on 10 March 1983, represented a fivefold increase over the amount of military aid, $26 million, provided in the preceding year's Continuing Resolution.

23. In his speech on 10 March President Reagan warned that pro-U.S. regimes throughout the region were in danger of being toppled and hinted that the administration would send more military advisors to El Salvador if Congress denied the funds.

24. In concluding his speech to Congress on 27 April 1983, Reagan declared: "The national security of all the Americas is at stake in Central America. If we cannot defend ourselves there, we cannot expect to prevail elsewhere. Our credibility would collapse, our alliances would crumble, and the safety of our homeland would be put in jeopardy."

25. Two of the key supporters were Daniel Inouye (D-HI) and Nancy Kassenbaum (R-KN). In a speech on the Senate floor on 14 March 1983, Inouye, ranking Democrat on the Senate Appropriations Subcommittee on Foreign Operations, likened U.S. policy in El Salvador to the policy that had led the United States into Vietnam. He called for negotiations between the Salvadoran government and its opposition before sending any more U.S. aid. Sen. Kassenbaum, a member of the Senate Foreign Relations Committee, offered a proposal to limit military aid for El Salvador to $50

million (less than half the president's request), cap the number of military advisors, and condition future aid on negotiations.

26. *Washington Post,* 25 March, 20 April 1983; *New York Times,* 27 April, 11 May 1983; *Wall Street Journal,* 11 May 1983.

27. The amendment, offered by Sen. Arlen Specter (R-PA), was attached to the FY/1984 Continuing Resolution appropriations bill.

28. In his toast at a dinner hosted by Salvadoran President Alvaro Magaña on 11 December 1983, Vice-President Bush said that " . . . it is not just the President, it is not just the Congress. If these death squad murders continue, you will lose the support of the American people."

29. The administration provoked yet another bitter quarrel with Congress in early 1984 by declaring a dire emergency in El Salvador and attaching a request for $93 million in supplemental aid to a bill for African famine relief and domestic poverty programs. This time, however, the aid debate was overshadowed by the controversy accompanying a request for $21 million to aid the contras in Nicaragua and by the political furor aroused by the CIA mining of Nicaraguan harbors.

30. In a 29 July 1982 letter to the *New York Times,* CIA Director William Casey admitted having provided invisible ink to stamp voters' wrists in an effort to prevent fraud during the March 1982 elections. Casey also said the CIA provided the Salvadoran government with "information and capabilities" to block arms shipments to the guerrillas from Nicaragua and Cuba.

On 8 May 1984, Sen. Jesse Helms (R-NC) charged that the CIA and the State Department rigged the election in Duarte's favor. The CIA admitted to the House and Senate Intelligence committees that it did provide funds to Duarte. See *Washington Post,* 10 April and 13 May 1984.

31. *Congressional Record,* 10 May 1984, p. H3741.

32. Ibid., p. H3740.

33. Of the twenty-six Democrats who switched their votes in favor of contra aid in June 1985, seven voted with Wright in May 1984 and thirteen voted with Fascell. Of the Republicans who switched in June, six voted with Wright (and the Republican leadership) and one with Fascell. After the vote some liberals complained that Fascell's principal goal—his desire to pass a foreign aid bill in his first year as chair of the House Foreign Affairs Committee—made his support for the Democratic position less than enthusiastic. The logic behind that position was that Republicans opposed to foreign aid would be more inclined to vote for the bill if it included generous aid to an anticommunist U.S. ally.

34. Sen. Mark Hatfield (R-OR), Rep. George Miller (D-CA), and Rep. Jim Leach, (R-IA), *U.S. Aid to El Salvador: An Evaluation of the Past, a Proposal for the Future,* Report to the Arms Control and Foreign Policy Caucus, February 1985.

35. An important underpinning of the controversy over contra aid was the congressional debate during the Carter administration over providing economic aid to Nicaragua. In 1980 the Carter administration gained congressional approval for $75 million in aid for the private sector in Nicaragua by arguing that the government exhibited pluralist tendencies and that not to get involved was to abandon the field to the Soviets and Cubans.

The resignation of moderates in the Sandinista coalition in protest over the direction of Sandinista policy brought a sense of betrayal to members of Congress who, having fought for the aid, developed a stake in the course of the Nicaraguan government.

36. See U.S. Congress, House, Permanent Select Committee on Intelligence, *Report,* Amendment to the Intelligence Authorization Act for Fiscal Year 1983, 98th Cong., 1st sess., 13 May 1983, p. 8.

37. The debate took place during consideration of the Department of Defense appropriations bill for FY/1983, on 8 December 1982.

38. *Congressional Record*, 8 December 1982; Susan Benda, "Covert War: Legislative History," in *Central America 1985: Basic Information and Legislative History* (Washington: Coalition for a New Foreign and Military Policy and Commission on U.S.-Central American Relations, 1985); *Congressional Quarterly*, 20 April 1985, pp. 710–711.

39. See, for example, "U.S. Approves Covert Plan in Nicaragua" and "Motley Groups in Exile Seek to Topple Nicaraguan Revolution," *Washington Post*, 10 March 1982; "A Secret War for Nicaragua," *Newsweek*, 8 November 1982; "Nicaragua: Hill Concern on U.S. Objectives Persists," *Washington Post*, 1 January 1983; "Nicaragua's Elusive War," *Time*, 4 April 1983.

40. A report by the House Intelligence Committee stated the rationale for efforts to end the covert war: ". . . Attempted restraints on the range of activities supported by the U.S. . . . proved ineffective" in limiting the operation to arms interdiction. In addition, the report said, U.S. policy was counterproductive (U.S. Congress, House, Permanent Select Committee on Intelligence, *Report*, 98th Cong., 1st sess., 13 May 1983): "The United States has allied itself with insurgents who carry the taint of the last Nicaraguan dictator, Somoza. It has, in effect, allowed the spotlight of international opprobrium to shift from Sandinista attempts to subvert a neighboring government to a U.S. attempt to subvert that of Nicaragua. *If ever there was a formula for U.S. policy failure in Central America, it would involve two elements: 1) acts that could be characterized as U.S. interventionism in Nicaragua; and 2) an alliance with the followers of Somoza. Both characterizations can now be made*" [emphasis added].

41. *Congressional Record*, 28 July 1983, p. H5848.

42. *Congressional Quarterly*, 30 July 1983, p. 1537.

43. Benda, "Covert War."

44. Letter to Senate Majority Leader Howard H. Baker, Jr., 4 April 1984, quoted in *Wall Street Journal*, 6 April 1984.

45. See U.S. Congress, Senate, Select Committee on Intelligence, *Report, January 1, 1983 to December 31, 1984*, 98th Cong., 2d sess., 1985, pp. 4–15.

46. According to Boland, the House Intelligence Committee had been briefed in March 1984, after having inadvertently learned of the mining in January. See *Wall Street Journal*, 6 April 1984, *New York Times*, 16 April 1984.

47. The manual, *Psychological Operations in Guerrilla Warfare*, advocated the use of "selective violence" to "neutralize" Sandinista officials; the hiring of professional criminals; the creation of "martyrs" through violent, staged demonstrations; and blackmail.

48. *Congressional Quarterly*, 15 June 1985, p. 1140.

49. President Reagan's radio address, 16 February 1985; President Reagan's speech to the Twelfth Annual Conservative Political Action Conference, 1 March 1985; Secretary of State George Shultz's speech to the Commonwealth Club of San Francisco, 21 February 1985.

50. The administration and its supporters sought to offset a strong grass-roots effort led by churches in opposition to the president's request. For practically the first time in the Central America debate, the volume of materials from conservative groups outweighed the volume of those reaching congressional offices from groups opposed to administration policy.

51. Most members of Congress familiar with the negotiations between Cruz and the Nicaraguan government blamed Sandinista Commander Bayardo Arce for refusing a request by the Nicaraguan opposition to postpone the November 1984 elections.

Arce turned down the request during a meeting with Cruz in Rio de Janeiro in early October 1984.

52. Colombian President Belisario Betancur, a leader of the Contadora regional peace effort, called President Reagan's plan "preparation for war" (see *New York Times*, 16 April 1985).

53. A classified annex to the president's request stated that "direct application of U.S. military force . . . must realistically be recognized as an eventual option, given our stakes in the region, if other policy alternatives fail" (*New York Times*, 17 April 1985).

54. Speech to the Coalition for a Democratic Majority (*Congressional Record*, 23 April 1985, pp. S4594–95).

55. Architects of the strategy promoted it as based on the model of El Salvador, in which both Congress and the administration compromised to forge a successful policy (see Bernard Aronson, "Another Choice in Nicaragua," *New Republic*, 27 May 1985, pp. 21–23).

56. *Congressional Record*, 23 April 1985, pp. S4622–23.

57. Though opposing the president's request, Rep. Bill Richardson (D-NM), for example, stated that ". . . there are members of the Contras that used to be Sandinistas that are disappointed and they are out and I think their concerns are legitimate, like Mr. Robelo and the Chamorros and Cruz and Calero . . . there are businessmen, there are students, there are Nicaraguans who have opted to stay in Nicaragua in the opposition rather than become Contras. And I would hope the gentlemen would join me . . . to support these dissident forces within Nicaragua. . . ." And Representative David McCurdy (D-OK) asked: "If we oppose the Sandinistas, why do we buy Nicaraguan beef and bananas? . . . Why do they still enjoy most-favored-nation status? If the regime is illegitimate, and its overthrow a goal of U.S. policy, why do we continue diplomatic relations? If we are serious about meeting the Marxist challenge in Central America, it is time to begin shaping a long-term, affirmative policy. . . ." *Congressional Record*, 23 April 1985, pp. H2341, H2378).

58. The vote was 248–180.

59. *Washington Post*, 14 June 1985.

60. The bill was defeated on final passage by an overwhelming 303–123 majority.

61. Only seventeen Republicans voted for final passage; 161 voted against the bill.

62. "Towards a New Policy for Nicaragua," a conversation with Sen. Sam Nunn and Rep. Dave McCurdy, Coalition for a Democratic Majority, 3 June 1985.

63. The president's identical letters to Michel and McCurdy were circulated to the full house as "Dear Colleague" letters, 11 June 1985. In a tip of the hat to Democratic liberals and moderates, President Reagan insisted that ". . . our policy for Nicaragua is the same as for El Salvador and all of Central America: to support the democratic center against the extremes of both the right and the left."

64. *Washington Post*, 6 June 1985; *New York Times*, 8 June 1985.

65. *New York Times*, 8 June 1985.

66. *Congressional Record*, 12 June 1985, pp. H4162, H4191.

67. *New York Times*, 13 June 1985.

68. One of the reasons the Democrats lost the 1984 election, said Rep. Dan Daniel (D-VA), "was the perception that the Democrats were soft on defense. If we fail now to oppose the spread of communism in this hemisphere and we are once more perceived to be soft on defense, then we could be shut out completely in the next election" (*Congressional Record*, 12 June 1985, p. H4148).

69. Under heavy administration pressure to vote the party line on a key foreign policy issue, seven Republicans also shifted position. The thirty-three representatives who voted "no" on contra aid in April 1985 and voted "yes" in June 1985 are: *Democrats:* Andrews (TX), Aspin (WI), Bustamante (TX), Coleman (TX), Cooper (TN), Derrick (SC), Fascell (FL), Gordon (TN), Hefner (NC), Jones (TN), Jones (OK), Kanjorski (PA), Long (LA), MacKay (FL), McCurdy (OK), Mazzoli (KY), Mollohan (WV), Murtha (PA), Price (IL), Richardson (NM), Robinson (AR), Spratt (SC), Stallings (ID), Watkins (OK), Whitley (NC), Whitten (MS); *Republicans:* Fish (NY), Gradison (OH), Horton (NY), McKernan (ME), McKinney (CT), Snowe (ME), Zschau (CA).

3

Central American Refugees and U.S. Policy

Patricia Weiss Fagen

Since 1980, one to two million Salvadorans, Guatemalans, and Nicaraguans have fled their homes. An estimated 500,000 to 800,000 have crossed international borders, the remainder being displaced within their own countries. As the combined population of the three countries is under 25 million, 5 to 10 percent of their total population—25 percent in El Salvador alone—is either displaced or in exile. Yet only approximately 125,000 Central Americans have been formally recognized as refugees by the United Nations High Commissioner for Refugees (UNHCR) and by host governments.

Nearly all Central Americans who receive protection or assistance from the UNHCR are still in Central America or in Mexico. By conservative estimates, some 400,000 have arrived in the United States since 1980.[1] (The total Central American population in the United States is believed to be perhaps twice this number.) According to the figures of the Immigration and Naturalization Service (INS), only about 1,500 Salvadorans, Guatemalans, and Nicaraguans were granted political asylum in 1984 and considerably fewer in 1985.[2]

The legal and humanitarian support networks that assist Central Americans, as well as large sections of the public and the press, consider the majority of Salvadorans, Guatemalans, and Nicaraguans in the United States to be "refugees" who have fled their countries because of repression, war, and violence. The INS and the Department of State, however, view all but a minute number of them as undocumented entrants who, as in the past, have come here for economic reasons. Government officials advocate the expediting of procedures for handling asylum claims, detention for undocumented asylum seekers, and fewer avenues of legal appeal. Along with some members of Congress, they have also raised fears that hundreds of thousands of Central American "feet people" may add to the already swollen numbers of people illegally crossing the border unless Congress supports administration policies.

59

The formal debate over the appropriate status for Central Americans encompasses three sets of questions: 1) Are the Central Americans essentially economic or political migrants? 2) Can those who claim primarily political motivation establish that they meet refugee criteria as defined by international and national law? 3) Does the continuing violence in the region justify allowing Central Americans unable to establish refugee credentials to remain in the country until the danger at home has passed?

Behind the formal debate two fundamental issues have affected U.S. responses to Central American and other refugees. The first is the deep involvement of the United States government in the Central American region. The second issue, going beyond the Central American question, is the basic lack of preparation for and the general unwillingness in this country to cope with a large-scale influx of first asylum arrivals (i.e., those who come here directly without being processed through other countries). Between World War II and 1980, millions of refugees were admitted to the United States by executive decision with congressional concurrence. Only in the 1980s, however, have large numbers of people desiring to be refugees come directly to the United States.

The United States signed the United Nations Protocol Relating to the Status of Refugees in 1968, and in 1980 Congress passed the Refugee Act, which defines refugees in almost the same terms as the protocol. These documents prohibit the enforced return (*refoulement*) of persons who are physically present in the country or on the border if they can establish that they meet the refugee definition. The protocol defines a refugee as anyone who

> is outside any country of such person's nationality or, in the case of a person having no nationality, is outside any country in which such person last habitually resided, and who is unable or unwilling to avail himself or herself of the protection of that country because of persecution or a well-founded fear of persecution on account of race, religion, nationality, membership in a particular social group, or political opinion.

The Refugee Act, though establishing the statutory right to apply for political asylum and confirming this country's commitment to non-refoulement, primarily elaborates the procedures for refugee admissions rather than for political asylum. In other words, the act establishes the criteria by which individuals and groups still outside the country may be admitted to (resettled in) the United States as refugees, but it develops no new mechanisms for those coming directly to this country seeking refugee status through the asylum process. (Persons granted political asylum in the United States have essentially the same status as refugees admitted from overseas.) As shown later, the Central Americans have found this country relatively unreceptive to their asylum pleas, not only on political grounds, but also because they are among the large number of first asylum arrivals.

The following discussion, describing the impact of U.S. refugee and asylum policies on Central Americans, both here and in other countries in the region, centers on three questions: 1) Given that the Refugee Act removes ideological and geographical limitations from refugee admissions criteria, why have virtually no Central American refugees been admitted to the United States? 2) What disadvantages are faced by Central Americans seeking political asylum compared with other nationalities? What options for protection other than asylum are appropriate and feasible? 3) What factors influence U.S. policies toward Central American refugees in Central American countries and Mexico, and how have these policies affected the treatment they receive there?

Refugee Admissions Selection Procedures

The first question concerns the number of Central Americans accepted as refugees by the United States. Although the ceiling for Latin American refugees in 1985 and 1986 was 3,000, the total number admitted was well under 200 in each of the two years. That level has remained low not because there is a lack of persons who meet the refugee definition and would like to come to the United States, but because until 1987 the formal refugee program applied only to Cubans.

Having passed the 1980 Refugee Act and ratified the United Nations protocol, the United States is obliged to refrain from forcibly returning persons to any nation where they have established that they have a well-founded fear of persecution. Neither national nor international law, however, requires the United States to admit persons simply because they meet the refugee definition. The Refugee Act specifies that persons admitted as refugees should be "of special humanitarian concern to the United States." They must fit within regional quotas and national programs established annually by the executive and Congress and must fall within designated priority categories.

In order of priority, these groups are defined as 1) persons of "compelling" concern or interest, including refugees in immediate danger who have no alternative to resettlement here and former or present political prisoners and dissidents; 2) former U.S. government employees; 3) refugees with U.S. citizens or residents in their immediate families; 4) those with education or employment links in the United States or associated with U.S. based agencies; 5) persons more distantly related to U.S. citizens and residents; and 6) individuals who do not have explicit ties to this country but are "otherwise of national interest." Some national groups are "processed" in all six categories (e.g., eastern Europeans), but most are not. The largest number of refugees come from Southeast Asia and are selected from priorities 1–5. Iranians and Afghans (the only Middle Eastern nationalities for which there are refugee programs) are processed in priorities 1–4. Would-be refugee applicants who are not from nations "of humanitarian concern" may be processed only in the first two priority categories, and each case must be cleared with the State Department.

The overall ceiling for refugee admissions in FY/1987 is 70,000, the same as for the past two years, but the 1987 regional breakdown has been modified.

	1986	1987
Southeast Asia (persons from Vietnam, Laos and Cambodia in first asylum countries)	40,000	32,000
Orderly Departure Program, Vietnam	8,500	8,500
Eastern Europe (excluding Yugoslavia)	9,500	10,000
The Middle East and southern Asia (primarily Afghanistan and Iran)	6,000	8,000
Africa (primarily Ethiopia; small numbers from southern African countries)	3,000	3,500
Latin America (Cubans only in 1986)	3,000	4,000
Reserve for unanticipated refugee admission needs		4,000

The United States has honored the applications of non-Cubans only when they fall into priority categories 1 and 2, as noted above. Since suspension of the Migration Agreement between the United States and Cuba in mid-1985, this stricture applies to Cubans as well.[3]

In recent years U.S. authorities have reviewed the applications of a handful of Argentines, Chileans, and Nicaraguans, refusing nearly all. In FY/1985 the only non-Cuban applicants to be approved were three Nicaraguans; in FY/1986 there were no non-Cuban refugee admissions from South or Central America and only 173 Cubans—69 former political prisoners and their families. New guidelines for FY/1987 mandate the resettlement of one thousand non-Cubans who qualify within the first four priority categories and who lack other alternatives for settlement. As of mid-1987, U.S. Embassy personnel have located few qualified applicants, but undoubtedly FY/1987 will see the first substantial number of Central American refugees in the United States. These are expected to be mainly Nicaraguans.[4]

Patterns of refugee admission indicate that geographic and ideological critéria, supposedly eliminated by the 1980 Refugee Act, continue to be observed in quotas, in ceilings and special programs presented by the executive to Congress, and in the actual numbers of admissions.

Central Americans Seeking Refugee Status Through the Asylum Process

Procedures for applying for political asylum have been established without reference to nationality or ideology. Asylum claims are heard by immigration examiners and immigration judges across the country. What, if any, are the differences between the treatment of Central Americans and that of asylum applicants of other nationalities? What special disadvantages do Central Americans face? Are options for protection other than political asylum feasible in the present context?

Asylum Determinations: A Comparative View

Asylum procedures were established initially to process the small but continuing stream of east Europeans who came to the United States on political grounds. The policies and rules governing the procedures were amended and clarified during the 1970s; in the late 1970s, lawyers and church groups successfully challenged some aspects of INS treatment of Haitians then arriving on the Florida beaches.

During the 1980s public interest groups and lawyers, building on decades of case law relating to political asylum and deportation, have continued to challenge INS practices with regard to other groups as well. Political concerns and bilateral relations, as well as legal factors, have created difficulties for asylum seekers from Haiti and Central America and, in a different sense, for those from many other countries (e.g., Iran, Afghanistan, Sri Lanka). But the issues have been fought over principally in courts of law, and cases have been won primarily on grounds of legal procedure rather than substance. Only recently have members of Congress and other elected officials begun to address asylum controversies from the political point of view.

Today many of those from the Western Hemisphere seeking asylum represent groups that formerly migrated for primarily economic reasons but now also want to escape political repression and civil strife. Unlike Poles, Ethiopians, and Afghans, who also apply for political asylum in the United States, Central Americans have little or no chance of being admitted as refugees.

The approval rate for Haitian, Salvadoran, and Guatemalan asylum applicants is considerably lower than for other major groups.[5] In 1984 only 3 percent of the Salvadorans and 1 percent of the Guatemalans who applied were granted asylum. (Note that the data on asylum grants and denials come from the INS, which processes asylum claims only from people who voluntarily make themselves known to the service. Claims from those who apply for asylum after having been apprehended—the majority of Central Americans today—are heard by immigration judges, who release no figures but who are believed to reject more claims than INS examiners.) The INS asylum approval rate for Poles, Ethiopians,[6] Afghans, and Iranians is markedly lower than the rate for the same nationalities who apply for refugee status overseas, but it is significantly higher than the rate for Central Americans or Haitians.

Because only a fraction of the Salvadorans and Guatemalans who claim political asylum have been accepted, critics contend that the 1980 Refugee Act has not been upheld. In response, U.S. officials argue that few Central Americans meet the standard of proof required for bona fide political claimants.

Central Americans and the Asylum Process

Central Americans, when compared with other groups seeking asylum, face certain disadvantages resulting from their large number, illegal entry, requests for asylum when in detention, and U.S. foreign policy.

Large Numbers. Because the overwhelming majority of Salvadorans in the United States are undocumented, estimates of their numbers may be exaggerated. It is widely believed, however, that more than half a million are in this country and that approximately 300,000 of them have arrived since 1980, when civil strife at home intensified. Guatemalans are estimated at between 100,000 and 200,000; Nicaraguans, at between 40,000 and 80,000.[7] Because many Central Americans describe similar circumstances at home, immigration officials tend to treat them as a group rather than as individuals and to view them negatively. Furthermore, the very size of this population makes it difficult to find the legal and other kinds of support they need.

Illegal Entry. Until the early 1980s many Central Americans could come directly to this country with valid nonimmigrant visas, which most of them overstayed after 1980. Their failure to return home led U.S. consulates to restrict such visas. Since 1982 legal entry has been curtailed for those who cannot establish business or professional reasons for coming to the United States. Nevertheless, the migration has continued to grow. Those who otherwise would have come legally (but probably overstayed) instead undertake expensive and dangerous treks across Guatemala and Mexico, depending on unreliable *coyotes*, and enter this country with no immigration review whatsoever.

Most Central Americans remain in the West and the Southwest (though Nicaraguans prefer Florida), and cities like New York and Washington have also attracted large numbers, since new arrivals often seek established communities where they have relatives and friends and can count on a sympathetic reception. They avoid contact with immigration authorities on the realistic assumption that they will be denied political asylum and deported. Precisely because they have entered illegally, failed to identify themselves to the INS, and joined communities of economic migrants, the authorities can argue that their motivation must have been economic rather than political.

Detention. Because Central Americans seldom make themselves known to immigration officers and do not apply for political asylum unless they are apprehended, they are usually placed in detention when found. Their release is subject to their ability to post bail and, depending on age and circumstances, to meet other conditions. If they attempt to apply for asylum while in detention they face serious disadvantages: the difficulty of obtaining legal counsel and the problems encountered by lawyers in maintaining contact with their clients. Most important, immigration authorities give priority to asylum hearings for individuals in detention, a humanitarian gesture of dubious value, for it means that denial of asylum and subsequent deportation can take place in a few weeks, whereas those not in detention may wait years for their cases to be heard.[8] And when asylum cases are appealed, those in detention, discouraged by long waits and uncomfortable conditions, often succumb to pressures to give up the struggle and return home.[9]

Ideology and Foreign Policy. Possibly the most formidable obstacle confronting Salvadorans and Guatemalans seeking asylum in the United States is their political identification; their claims to refugee status may have potentially embarrassing inferences. Ideological and foreign policy considerations are not the only criteria for determining asylum. For example, until late 1986 Nicaraguans were not particularly favored, although the INS district director in Florida sometimes stayed the deportation of those whose applications were rejected. In 1987, however, the Attorney General issued orders requiring favored treatment for Nicaraguan asylum applicants. Clearly ideological considerations do affect Salvadorans and Guatemalans. Officials in the State Department's Bureau of Human Rights and Humanitarian Affairs (BHRHA), which issues appraisals of conditions in Central America, paint an optimistic picture of the situation in El Salvador and Guatemala. They suggest that repression has all but disappeared, and find human rights prospects encouraging. Such reports ignore the virtually unanimous contrary evidence presented by major human rights groups, as well as statements made by the asylum seekers themselves.

The BHRHA is required to prepare advisory letters in all political asylum cases, analyzing the substance of applicants' claims. In practice the bureau's advice is usually given in a form letter, a common version of which notes the generalized violence and asserts the applicant has failed to fully document his or her individualized well-founded fear of persecution. A review of the asylum process drawn up by an INS staff member in 1983 pointed out that Salvadorans, in order to receive favorable advisory letters from the State Department, had to present "classic textbook" cases.[10] That is, they would have to document that they would certainly be persecuted for politically related reasons.

In most districts, INS examining officers automatically follow State Department advice in issuing initial rulings. Although immigration judges tend to be slightly more independent than INS officers, more often than not they also act in accordance with advisory opinions. Lawyers in different parts of the country say they have encountered judges who have heard hundreds of cases and have never approved a single asylum applicant from El Salvador or Guatemala.

In the future, the burden of proof required of Central Americans as well as other groups applying for political asylum may be somewhat eased. In March 1987, the Supreme Court, ruling in the case of the Immigration and Naturalization Service v. Luz Marina Cardona Fonseca, found that the INS no longer could require asylum applicants to show a clear probability of persecution in order to demonstrate that they had a well founded fear of persecution if returned to their countries of origin.

Legalization

With the passage of the 1986 Immigration Reform and Control Act, Central Americans in the United States since January 1982 may apply for legalization. While estimates of how many Central Americans will be affected by the immigration amnesty remain speculative, most scholars and public officials judge that the majority of them arrived after the January 1982 cut-off date. The post-1982 arrivals will find themselves in an increasingly vulnerable situation due to sanctions against employers who hire undocumented aliens, also part of the new Immigration Law.

Extended Voluntary Departure and
Other Forms of Temporary Protection

If Salvadorans and Guatemalans were given fair hearings under U.S. law, their asylum approval rate probably would jump by several percentage points. Nevertheless, the majority would still remain without refugee protection. In particular, most Salvadorans are unable to establish the individualized evidence of persecution required to obtain refugee status, even if they genuinely fear death. For this reason several religious and humanitarian groups, and some members of Congress, advocate that Central Americans who risk being victims of war, violence, and repression in their homelands be granted temporary haven in the United States.

Early efforts in this direction took the form of advocacy of extended voluntary departure (EVD), an executive order exempting a specified group from deportation for a fixed period of time. Beneficiaries of temporary protection from deportation do not have to prove individual persecution under the Refugee Act. EVD has been supported on humanitarian grounds and tied to adverse conditions in the countries of origin. The thirteen national groups that have been granted such protection in the past obtained permission to work here and access to a few other benefits as well. Temporary haven is presently extended to Poles and Afghans, and until 1987 to Ugandans, on the grounds that they face generally dangerous situations in their home countries. Although the executive has usually cited conditions of violence and insecurity, there are no fixed criteria for an EVD grant. Decisions about EVD are entirely discretionary, and congressional consultation is neither required nor sought in making decisions.

The executive branch has been adamant in its refusal to grant EVD to Salvadorans, despite widespread public support for such protection by religious and humanitarian organizations, citizens' groups, and members of Congress. Churches and synagogues and the mayors of cities across the nation, drawing attention to the plight of Salvadorans and Guatemalans, have provided sanctuary for them. That municipal authorities have joined the sanctuary movement is a setback for the federal government, which opposes it.[11] Congress has recently, through the Moakley-DeConcini bill, elevated the issue to the legislative level. The proposed law would suspend deportation of Salvadorans and Nicaraguans[12] until the situation in their home countries has been investigated and other conditions have been met, over a period of about two years.[13]

The administration has publicly opposed this legislation for the same reasons that it opposed EVD. Laura Dietrich, the then deputy assistant secretary of state in the BHRHA, speaking to the House Subcommittee on Immigration, Refugees, and International Law in November 1985, commented in a typical statement:

The argument is then made that all Salvadorans, even those who do not qualify for asylum, should not be deported to El Salvador. . . . As you know, the Administration does not concur with this view even if it were only a temporary suspension. All suspensions of deportation decisions require a balancing of judgments about several factors, including foreign policy, humanitarian, and immigration policy implications.

The administration advances other arguments against temporary protection for Salvadoran nationals as proposed by Moakley-DeConcini: 1) Salvadorans seek safe haven more because of their desire to work in the United States than because of their apprehension of danger at home; 2) there will be a magnet effect, that is, granting them legal status here will entice thousands more to come, regardless of events in El Salvador; and 3) alternative safe havens supposedly exist elsewhere, either in El Salvador (in areas where fighting is allegedly less) or in other countries in the region. The administration defends its policy by claiming to support refugee protection and assistance programs in Central American countries and Mexico which supposedly make flight to the United States unnecessary.[14]

The State Department briefly changed its position regarding safe haven for Salvadorans upon repeated pleas for leniency and generosity from Salvador's President José Napoleón Duarte. Duarte emphasized that the country could little afford to lose the millions of dollars in remittances that Salvadorans in the United States provided to their families at home, and he also noted that the sudden return of exiles might also add to political instability in El Salvador. Ultimately State Department sympathy for Duarte yielded to Justice Department intransigence and the Administration decided to maintain its opposition to extended voluntary departure for the Salvadorans.

In summary, Salvadoran and Guatemalan applicants for political asylum do face special disadvantages, ranging from the size of their respective populations in the United States to the same ideological and foreign policy considerations that prevent their admission as refugees. Options for protection other than political asylum at this writing (August 1987) hang in the balance, but congressional action to provide a temporary stay of deportation pending improved conditions in the refugees' home countries seems to be moving forward.

U.S. Policies Toward Central American Refugees in Central America and Mexico

What are the factors influencing U.S. policies toward Central American refugees in Central American countries and Mexico? How have these policies affected the treatment the refugees receive in those countries?

The role of foreign policy considerations is even more evident in the U.S. approach to the problems of Central American refugees in the region. Although the United States does provide assistance to refugee programs in

Central America, it is far from adequate to meet the need or to justify refusal to let refugees come to the United States.

Besides Central Americans displaced within their own countries, concentrations of Central American refugees exist from Panama through Mexico. Outside Mexico, the majority of refugees live in designated camps or settlements operated by the UNHCR. A significant minority live in urban areas and receive assistance. A few, mainly Salvadorans in Nicaragua, have been economically integrated into the host countries and no longer require assistance, although they are still under UNHCR protection. Guatemalans do not have formal refugee status in Mexico, but more than 40,000 are assisted by the UNHCR in camps operated by the Mexican National Refugee Commission. Other Guatemalans, Salvadorans, and Nicaraguans in Mexico rarely achieve asylum status or receive assistance even if they are acknowledged by the UNHCR to be refugees.[15]

At least twice as many as those with refugee status lack that status in the countries throughout the region, even if they have fled the same perilous circumstances. For example, the vast majority of Salvadorans in Mexico, and the majority of both Salvadorans and Guatemalans in Belize, are outside UNHCR programs. The thousands of supporters and relatives of the *contras* established on both Nicaraguan borders do not qualify as refugees, although many do receive assistance through political and military channels outside of the UNHCR. Most important, the more than a million displaced persons in El Salvador, Guatemala, and Nicaragua who have not crossed international borders have no access to refugee protection, although they may receive some form of assistance.

The refugee and nonrefugee concentrations are important elements in the mix of U.S. policy concerns in the region. Refugee camps and settlements in the countries of first asylum are deemed essential to stem the flow of Central Americans into this country. Moreover, the U.S. government perceives refugee movements potentially to have serious destabilizing consequences if they are not channeled and controlled and if the refugees' basic needs are unmet.

The U.S. government provides the lion's share of international support for refugee programs in the region. Most of the aid is channeled through the UNHCR, providing approximately one-third of its Latin American assistance. In FY/1985 the United States contributed a total of $107,250,000 to the UNHCR, of which $12 million was allocated for programs in Latin America, most of it by far going to Central America. In FY/1986 total UNHCR budget requests dropped to $86 million, but the share for Latin America rose to $12,500,000. U.S. funding for relief activities that benefit persons lacking refugee status goes principally to the International Committee for the Red Cross (ICRC), which received $3 million in FY/1985 and $3,200,000 in FY/1986 for programs mainly of assistance to displaced persons. Other funds destined for Central America go to the Intergovernmental Committee for Migration (ICM) and some voluntary agencies contracted to handle special projects.[16]

The Agency for International Development (AID) also manages refugee-related programs, providing nearly all the governmental budget for care of displaced persons in El Salvador.[17] AID also disbursed the $7,500,000 allocated by Congress at the end of 1984 for developmental aid and humanitarian assistance in the Honduran Mosquitia. These funds, allocated to the Honduran-Nicaraguan border population, could not be used to assist refugees in the UNHCR settlements. In Costa Rica, AID has channeled the major portion of its developmental funds to the northern border region, again providing indirect assistance to the largely Nicaraguan border population that lacks refugee status.

As noted above, assistance to and protection of refugees in the countries of the region have bolstered arguments by U.S. authorities against Central American asylum seekers in the United States. In public addresses and in yearly reports to Congress on refugees, administration spokespersons have emphasized the regional "tradition" of granting safe haven to refugees:

> Refugees fleeing armed conflicts in El Salvador, Nicaragua, and Guatemala constitute the great majority of refugees in need of protection and assistance in Central American countries. . . . The UNHCR, the ICRC, ICM and many private voluntary agencies are involved in providing assistance to Central American refugees. The United States and other donor countries have been working together with these international organizations in order to ensure that refugees are protected and, where possible, are enabled to return to their homes. Countries in the region, particularly Honduras, Mexico and Costa Rica, have been particularly generous in the provision of asylum to those forced to flee their homelands. Resettlement outside the region has been necessary in relatively few cases.[18]

The contention here is that U.S. government support allows the countries in the region to absorb fleeing refugees and thus presumably absolves the United States from any obligation to admit refugees. This line of reasoning, however, raises problems that go beyond the clear inadequacy of the available support.

First, the argument is built on the dubious premise that there is a regional tradition of asylum. In reality, while there is a tradition throughout Latin America of granting asylum to individuals who have fallen out of political favor in their own countries, there is no tradition of granting safe haven to mass exodus flows.[19] Second, though U.S. influence and support, combined with the presence of the UNHCR and international voluntary agencies, have ensured that the countries in the region do not turn away Central Americans who have crossed into their territories, these factors have not prevented the recurrence of severe protection problems, particularly of Salvadorans in Honduras, Guatemalans in Mexico, and Miskitos in Honduras.

The treatment of refugees in the region varies according to their country of origin and domestic factors in the host countries. Among the countries that receive refugees, Costa Rica, Nicaragua, and Panama have ratified the United Nations Protocol Relating to the Status of Refugees, thereby committing their governments to the nonrefoulement of first asylum entrants, but Honduras and Mexico have not. In Mexico, domestic support ultimately weighed in favor of accepting responsibility for Guatemala's largely indigenous refugees (and Mexico's foreign policy orientation still makes unlikely a concerted effort to deport Salvadorans). In Honduras, however, where public support for refugee admissions is not significant, there is strident hostility to the continuing presence of Salvadoran refugees. (The Hondurans and Salvadorans were technically at war until 1980.) U.S. officials were largely responsible for convincing the Honduran government to admit Salvadoran refugees, but the United States has regularly defended serious assaults against the refugees by the Honduran military. Both U.S. and Honduran officials describe the Salvadoran refugees (close to 90 percent of whom are women and children) as guerrillas or guerrilla sympathizers. Citizens of both Honduras and Costa Rica display considerable ambivalence about the use of their territory by Nicaraguan contras, an attitude reinforced by negative feelings toward the refugees.

The influence of U.S. ideological preferences and its national security agenda has been clearest in Honduras. Honduras is the major refugee-receiving country in the region, as well as the geographic nexus for U.S. policies in Nicaragua and El Salvador. The refugee concentrations of Salvadorans and Nicaraguans on or near the borders of both countries have precipitated acrimonious debates among refugee agencies and governmental actors.

Perhaps the best illustration of conflicting political and humanitarian agendas vis-à-vis a refugee group was the controversy that brewed over several years concerning the proposed relocation of some 10,000 Salvadorans located in camps near the Salvadoran-Honduran border. U.S. officials strongly favored moving them to another location in Honduras. The UNHCR concurred with the desirability of moving the refugees away from the potentially conflictive border, but insisted that the move be consistent with refugee protection and improved capacity for self sufficiency. The refugee agencies working in the refugee camps, and the refugees themselves, argued strongly against moving the refugees, and the latter reportedly organized to resist a move. The Honduran government, for its part, set out to implement the projected move, only to face intense domestic hostility in every proposed location.

Unable to find a location that met UNHCR criteria, Honduran officials reversed their decision to move the border camps. But both Hondurans and U.S. embassy officials maintained their hostility toward the border refugee population. This hostility culminated in August 1985 when a Honduran military contingent entered the Colomoncagua refugee camp supposedly in search of guerrillas; in the ensuing violence three refugees were killed, several wounded, and ten taken prisoner. None were shown to have any connection with the guerrillas.

The U.S. embassy not only supported the Honduran action but went on to criticize the UNHCR and voluntary agencies for attempting to protect the refugees from physical attack. U.S. officials were—and have been—especially critical of voluntary agency personnel (many of whom are U.S. citizens), referring to them as "dupes" of the Salvadoran guerrillas.[20] Before and after the attack on the camp, U.S. and Honduran officials have made statements alleging that the refugees were providing arms and material to Salvadoran guerrillas and giving them safe haven in the camps. At no point, however, have any such allegations been substantiated publicly. The Salvadoran camps, meanwhile, have remained under tight military surveillance to prevent any unauthorized entries or exits.[21]

In contrast, observers of the situation in Honduras as well as in Costa Rica have commented on the lenient attitude toward the young male Nicaraguan refugees in those countries who used to divide their time between the refugee camps and the contra encampments. In the camps and settlements for Nicaraguans under UNHCR supervision, the population of young men used to fluctuate widely, depending on how many were engaged in combat at any time. The UNHCR and voluntary agency staff members have tried, with varying success, to prevent large quantities of food and supplies meant for refugees from being filtered out of the camps, but the population in the camps has remained (unofficially) free to enter and exit at will. U.S. officials have not accused Nicaraguans of treating their refugee status improperly by periodically leaving to serve as combatants.

In both Costa Rica and Honduras, many large areas near the Nicaraguan border have been denationalized, occupied by contra forces, and inhabited by their families and associates. Although these people are by no means refugees, they do receive U.S. assistance and may receive much more, depending on the continuance and distribution of contra aid. Costa Ricans and Hondurans living in these border areas are mostly poor, and the Nicaraguan presence has benefited few of them. Although the governments of the two countries have accepted Nicaraguans—both refugees and non-refugees—in their territories, local hostilities have been growing.

The situation of Central American refugees in Mexico and Central America indicates that existing programs are woefully inadequate to meet their needs and can hardly justify the refusal to accept refugees into the United States. And again there is substantial evidence that U.S. foreign policy and ideology have led to differential treatment of Central Americans in their own region, just as they have dictated treatment of Central Americans in the United States.

*   *   *

The task of finding solutions that are both realistic and humane for the hundreds of thousands of politically motivated Central Americans who have fled their countries of origin is a complicated one for all parties. For the host governments in Mexico and Central America, the presence of large groups of refugees who have connections with or sympathies for different sides in ongoing armed struggles is a destabilizing factor. These governments must weight the refugees' urgent human needs against their own short-

and long-term national interests. They must establish a refugee policy in the face of the often conflicting priorities and demands of the U.S. government, the voluntary agencies, the UNHCR, and their own political well-being. The refugees have constituted a serious drain on national resources. Perhaps even more troubling is the perception that the refugees—miserable as they are—are living better than many citizens, who also live in misery.

As for the refugees, some in all three groups have decided to return voluntarily to their homes, although to date repatriation has not been extensive except in the case of the Miskito Indian population. Clearly pressures to repatriate refugees will continue to grow, despite the inadequacy of conditions in the home countries for a large-scale refugee return. Given the participation of the United States in Central American affairs, any large-scale refugee movements from El Salvador, Guatemala, and Nicaragua are obviously of concern to foreign policy officials. Debates about these refugees invariably raise questions about U.S. involvement in Central America. The presence of Central Americans in the United States has had a particularly strong political impact. It has raised criticism of U.S. foreign and domestic policies in regions and among groups that might otherwise have been indifferent to or unaware of this country's role in Central America.

Apart from foreign policy issues, the Central Americans have made manifest the shortcomings of the United States as a country of first asylum. U.S. institutions are designed to serve the needs of refugees whom the government has itself chosen to admit. Besides the Central Americans, other groups, differing widely in ideology and in relationships to the United States, are also seeking asylum in growing numbers, among them Haitians, Iranians, Afghans, Ethiopians, Chinese, and eastern Europeans. Most of them, like Central Americans, leave their own countries for a mixture of economic and political reasons that cannot be disentangled. This country's institutions have been found lacking, in both humanitarian and political terms, in their capacity to handle groups that arrive, uninvited, in search of refuge. What is needed is not only a fair policy for dealing with Central Americans, but recognition by the government that the United States will continue to receive a large and ideologically varied population of exiles and refugees, and willingness to accept their right to remain.

Notes

1. Although somewhat arbitrary, the 1980 date is used to mark the beginning of what is considered the politically motivated flight from Central America.

2. Political asylum was approved in 1985 for 499 Nicaraguans and 71 Salvadorans, according to figures in the State Department *World Refugee Survey*, Report submitted to Congress as part of the Consultations on FY/1986 Refugee Admissions. Another 53 approvals were for all others, except Cubans, presumably most of them Guatemalans and Haitians. Although not specified, these figures refer only to INS asylum grants and omit approvals by immigration judges.

3. The Latin American refugee allocation rose in FY/1985 from 1,000 to 3,000 and to 4,000 in FY/1987 in order to accommodate Cuban political prisoners and

ex-prisoners. Refugee processing for these groups had ceased in previous years because the Reagan administration decided to "punish" the Cuban government for its refusal to accept the return of Mariel entrants who were in federal custody. The special program for former and current political prisoners stemmed from the 14 December 1984 Migration Agreement between the United States and Cuba which obligated the Cuban government to take 2,746 Marielitos and the United States to resume processing refugees from Cuba. The Cuban program in 1985 was to include both people from Cuba and some who wished to enter the United States from other countries. Only 28 Cubans had entered the United States, however, when Cuban authorities suspended the Migration Agreement in mid-1985 to protest the establishment of Radio Martí. Since then, as before, Cuban refugees are being processed from overseas in the first two priority categories. In 1986, thanks largely to the intervention of prominent individuals such as Jacques Cousteau, Catholic agencies were able to process small numbers of former political prisoners. The State Department expects a much large influx of former political prisoners in 1987, although it is highly unlikely that Cuban refugees will come close to reaching 4,000, the number of refugees allocated for Latin America.

4. In 1984 the United States (and other countries), responding to a request from the UNHCR, accepted about 100 persons from El Salvador as refugees. They were among those persons eligible for an amnesty declared by the Salvadoran government, which could not guarantee their safety if they remained in El Salvador. For this reason the UNHCR undertook to resettle them elsewhere.

5. Groups from other countries with poor human rights records, such as Tamils and Ghanians, fare about as badly as do the Central Americans, although in the past they have not migrated to the United States in large numbers. They constitute only a tiny portion of the asylum pool.

6. Poles and those Ethiopians who arrived before July 1980 have extended voluntary departure status, exempting them from deportation.

7. These estimates appear in a study prepared by the Urban Institute for the office of the assistant secretary for planning and evaluation, *The Impact of Central American Migrants on Social Security Programs,* 16 December 1985, chapter four.

8. Both the INS and immigration judges have expedited their procedures substantially in most places, thereby reducing the waiting period for asylum applicants.

9. At present Central Americans are not treated differently from other nationalities in these respects. In response to persistent criticism in the early 1980s that the INS was discriminating against Haitians and Central Americans, particularly in its detention policies, the service responded by subjecting all nationalities to the same rigid policies. Nevertheless, Central Americans do represent a disproportionate number of the people held in detention, because so many of them enter the country illegally.

10. *Asylum Adjudications: An Evolving Concept of Responsibility for the Immigration and Naturalization Service,* 1982, p. 59.

11. Undoubtedly, many of the local officials who support sanctuary not only feel sympathy for the Central Americans but also see an advantage in saving local budgets and personnel from the thankless and difficult task of helping the federal government search for status offenders. The INS might also profit if Salvadorans were to be granted EVD or another form of safe haven. Unofficially, some INS officials seem to recognize this possibility and thus to distance themselves, at least verbally, from State Department policies. If such a policy were implemented, INS officials and immigration judges would have fewer asylum applicants who were seeking safety from violence. Moreover, the INS would not have to build or contract for costly new detention centers; the strains on the border patrol would be eased; fewer lawsuits

would be filed; the sanctuary movement would no longer confront the INS on behalf of Salvadorans; and immigration officers could more easily ascertain how many Salvadorans are in the United States.

12. The bill makes no provision for Guatemalans because of the formal, though not fully effective, return to democracy in that country.

13. The arguments of those opposed to the administration's position have been elaborated during congressional debates on EVD and the Moakley-DeConcini bill and in connection with the sanctuary movement. See Ignatius Bau, *This Ground Is Holy: Church Sanctuary and Central American Refugees* (Ramsey, NJ: Paulist Press, 1985); Gary McEoin, ed., *Sanctuary: A Resource Guide for Understanding and Participation in the Central American Refugee Struggle* (New York: Harper & Row, 1985).

14. These arguments, which have appeared in numerous statements and newspaper articles, were elucidated in government testimony in hearings of the House Judiciary Subcommittee on Immigration, Refugees, and International Law on 7 November 1985 in connection with the Moakley-DeConcini bill. See also Elliott Abrams's statement before the subcommittee of the House Committee on Rules on 20 June 1984; and Alan Simpson, "We Can't Allow All Salvadorans to Stay," *Washington Post*, 10 July 1984.

15. See chapter appendix for an enumeration of refugee and exile groups in Central America and Mexico.

16. Office of the U.S. Coordinator for Refugee Affairs, *Proposed Refugee Allocations for FY/1986*, Report to Congress, September 1985, p. 37.

17. Department of State, *Migration and Refugee Assistance, FY/1985: Request for Appropriations*.

18. Department of State, *World Refugee Survey*, FY/1986, p. 53.

19. See *Declaración de Cartegena sobre los refugiados*, final document prepared under the sponsorship of the Organization of American States and the UNHCR, 19–22 November 1984; see also the annual report of the Inter-American Human Rights Commission, OEA/CIDH *Informe anual de la comisión interamericana de derechos humanos, 1984-1985* pp. 187–190.

20. Voluntary agency officials have also created problems for U.S. policy-makers in El Salvador by refusing to accept funding from USAID or to cooperate with the Salvadoran government's program for displaced persons. It has been difficult for USAID to find private agencies willing to implement its humanitarian programs in El Salvador.

21. Editors' note: In October 1987, some Salvadoran refugees in the Mesa Grande camp in Honduras began to return to their homes in El Salvador.

APPENDIX

TABLE 3.A1
Refugees and Displaced Persons in and from Central America: A Statistical Profile

	Salvadorans	Guatemalans	Hondurans	Nicaraguans	Totals
Internally displaced	500,000[1]**	100,000 to 250,000[2]*	35,000[3]*	250,000[4]*	885,000 1,035,000
In Panama	900[5]	NA	NA	300[5]	1,200
In Costa Rica	6,200[5]	200[5]	NA	22,000[5] 100,000[2]	28,400 106,400
In Nicaragua	7,600[5]	500[5]	NA	----	8,100
In Honduras	24,000[5]	1,000[5]	----	43,000[5]	68,000
In El Salvador	----	NA	NA	400[5]	400
In Guatemala	10,000[5]	----	NA	2,000[5] 20,000[6]	12,000 30,000
In Mexico	120,000[5] 250,000[7]	45,000[5] 150,000[7]	NA	NA	165,000 400,000
In the United States	500,000 to 800,000[8]	100,000 to 200,000[8]	50,000 to 100,000[8]	40,000 to 80,000[8]	690,000 1,180,000

(continued)

TABLE 3.A1
Refugees and Displaced Persons in and from Central America: A Statistical Profile *(continued)*

	Salvadorans	Guatemalans	Hondurans	Nicaraguans	Totals
In Canada	4,600[9]***	485[9]***	NA	NA	5,085
In Australia	600[10]***	NA	NA	NA	600
In Belize	3,000[5]	6,000[5]	NA	NA	9,000
Totals	1,176,900	253,185	85,000	357,700	1,877,785
	1,606,900	608,185	135,000	493,700	2,893,785

Note: All data are for 1987 except * =1986; ** =1985; *** =1984.

Sources:
[1] El Salvador government and voluntary agencies estimates.
[2] Costa Rica government estimates.
[3] Estimates of voluntary agencies in Honduras.
[4] Government Social Security Institute and Evangelical Committee for Development Aid (CEPAD), Managua, Nicaragua.
[5] U.N. High Commissioner for Refugees.
[6] Guatemala government estimates (Comisión Especial para la Atención a Repartiados).
[7] Mexican voluntary agencies.
[8] Urban Institute, U.S. Department of Health and Human Services, *The Impact of Central American Migrants on Social Security Programs*, Washington, D.C., December 1985.
[9] Canada government data.
[10] Australia government data.

4

"Low Intensity Warfare": The Counterinsurgency Strategy for Central America

Deborah Barry, Raúl Vergara, and José Rodolfo Castro

The victory of the Sandinista National Liberation Front in Nicaragua in 1979, coinciding with a new surge of revolutionary organization and struggle in El Salvador and Guatemala, created a dilemma for U.S. policy in a region the United States had traditionally taken for granted. The conflicts in Central America arose during a period when the dominant elite within the United States was reflecting on its future as a world power, and Central America became a cardinal issue in the U.S. debate over foreign policy. After President Reagan came to office in 1981, Central America's conflicts were seen as an opportunity for the United States to reassert its hegemony in the region and to test the new counterinsurgency strategy developed as a result of the Vietnam experience. The conflicts thus became key elements in the emerging Reagan doctrine, a doctrine that might be applied to similar conflicts in other Third World countries.

This study examines the development of the new U.S. strategy, with particular emphasis on the influence of the national security doctrine, the effects of the Vietnam experience on counterinsurgency policy, and the specific postulates of the Reagan doctrine. It then focuses on the implementation of this policy in Central America, particularly in El Salvador and Nicaragua, and its effects on the targeted countries.

Reconceptualizing Conflict

The politico-military defeat in Vietnam—the first such experience in U.S. history—led to a breakdown in the national consensus about policy in the

Translated by Ricardo Anzaldúa Montoya, Center for U.S.-Mexican Studies, University of California, San Diego.

Third World and the evaporation of public confidence in government leadership exacerbated by the Watergate scandal.[1] The Vietnam experience was not the only challenge to U.S. hegemony: between 1974 and 1981 significant social and political changes brought new governments not aligned with the United States to power in thirteen other countries.[2] During the same period U.S. interests in the Middle East were profoundly disrupted by the oil crisis and its obvious economic consequences for the U.S. consumer.

As a result of these crises, U.S. strategists began to recognize that revolutionary conflict in the Third World was a permanent phenomenon and that the United States was ill prepared to confront it. At the same time, as the notion of nuclear parity between the two world powers began to gain general acceptance, the probability of conventional war in Europe decreased. According to many U.S. strategists, small-scale Third World conflicts will be the focus of U.S. involvement for the rest of the century and beyond.[3] This probability in turn requires the United States to restructure its political and military institutions in order to deal more effectively with such crises.[4]

The Reagan Doctrine

During the Carter administration, government officials and military strategists began to redefine national security policy and the underlying premises of that policy, based on a recognition of waning U.S. leadership in the Western world. In reassessing U.S. foreign policy, the Reagan administration asserted that the loss of leadership should have been avoided and could be reversed. A document written during Reagan's first presidential campaign, commonly known in Latin America as the Santa Fe Document, clearly states this new conception:

> America's basic freedoms and economic self-interest require that the United States be and act like a power of the first order. The crisis is metaphysical. America's inability or unwillingness either to protect or project its basic values and beliefs has led to the present nadir of indecision and impotence and has placed the very existence of the Republic in peril. . . . It is time to seize the initiative. An integrated global foreign policy is essential.[5]

Such thinking has penetrated the very pores of U.S. politics, but neoconservatives have established their position most tenaciously in the area of foreign policy. Since the new right views any change in the status quo of any country as a gain for one superpower at the expense of the other, they see world events in the framework of East-West polarization. Theoretically, any country experiencing a conflict that threatens the status quo becomes a vital and high-priority interest of the United States, forcing this country to intervene globally simply to maintain its credibility. In this context, a revolutionary government in Nicaragua (a questionable geopolitical danger at best) becomes a central threat to the "crusade of ideological internationalism."

Although the neoconservative ideology has increasingly characterized U.S. policy in Central America and elsewhere since Reagan first came to office, it was not until 1985 that the so-called Reagan doctrine emerged as a coherent body of political thought designed to guide U.S. actions. The doctrine rests on four basic principles: (1) to promote and support, by overt or covert means, any military and political forces opposing revolutionary governments in Third World countries; (2) to intervene in potentially revolutionary situations so as to control change while preserving the essence of the regime in power; (3) to undertake an antiterrorist campaign; (4) to reserve the threat of direct, massive intervention by U.S. forces for highly vulnerable revolutions, either incipient or already consummated.[6]

The Reagan doctrine is a response to a crisis in the world political and economic system which was consolidated under U.S. leadership during World War II. More specifically, its self-stated purpose is to respond to the Soviet strategy of supporting movements of national liberation and, particularly, to the Brezhnev doctrine of 1968 which states that "once part of the Soviet block, always part." The Reagan doctrine is intended to regain for the United States the global strategic initiative by reversing the gains of Third World liberation movements and by positing such reversals as an historic trend (particularly in Nicaragua, Angola, Cambodia, and Afghanistan).[7]

What came to be known as the Reagan doctrine in 1985 apparently departs from earlier policy in at least two ways. First, a new policy of condemning dictatorships of both right and left replaces an older policy of defending authoritarian right-wing dictatorships as against totalitarian regimes, described in the well-known article by Jeane Kirkpatrick.[8] The shift implied that Washington would be prepared to foster changes in allied governments threatened by internal social discontent and pressured by international opinion, with the aim of preserving political control in those countries. This strategy was dramatically implemented in Washington's support for Corazón Aquino against Ferdinand Marcos in the Philippines and in its lack of support for Jean-Claude Duvalier in Haiti.

Although it is difficult to date this change in presidential doctrine precisely, U.S. policy toward El Salvador reflects the shift and perhaps even served as a test of the new strategy. In 1982 the transitory civilian-military junta was already giving way to an electoral process, beginning with the election of the Constituent Assembly, and preparations were underway for presidential elections, which were scheduled for 1984. One of the administration's earliest public allusions to this policy change was in President Reagan's speech before the British Parliament in June 1982, when he declared "abhorrence of dictatorship in all its forms."[9]

The second departure from earlier policy lay in the administration's proposal to elevate the formerly secret work of the Central Intelligence Agency (CIA) to the level of official public policy, particularly in supporting counterrevolutionary armies in the Third World. The administration gave enormous political importance to, and gained extensive media coverage for, support of the *contras* in Nicaragua, not only to legitimate the counterrevolution but also to turn the contras into protectors of Western freedom.[10]

To a large extent the Reagan doctrine is inward-looking, aimed toward the U.S. population in an effort to overcome the Vietnam syndrome. A certain degree of public support and congressional cooperation is central to carrying out policy, especially a policy of prolonged warfare (see below). By mid-1985 the Reagan doctrine had made considerable inroads, as a hard-won liberal bloc in Congress began to break down. The turnabout was evident in four measures in June and July of that year: (1) the ten-year old legislative prohibition against military aid for Angolan counterrevolutionaries (the 1975 Clark amendment) was repealed; (2) the House of Representatives, in a dramatic reversal, voted "humanitarian" aid for the Nicaraguan contras; (3) for the first time, aid for the Cambodian opposition forces received public congressional sanction; and (4) also for the first time, Congress voted publicly to fund opposition forces in Afghanistan.[11]

The Iran-contra investigations of 1986–87 have begun to reveal the extent to which implementing Reagan's policy defied congressional will and public sentiment. The high concentration of decision-making power and responsibility vested in the hands of the National Security Council and private networks (at the risk of blatant illegality and executive credibility) demonstrates the administration's desire to maintain control over this policy. The first step in the Iran-contra investigation was the president's appointment of the Tower Commission. According to the introduction to the commission's report on its investigation,

> The report pictures a National Security Council led by reckless cowboys, off on their own on a wild ride, taking direct operational control of matters that are the customary province of more sober agencies such as the C.I.A., the State Department and the Defense Department. In this instance, the report says, a kind of parallel government came into being, operating in secret, paying scant heed to laws, deceiving Congress and avoiding oversight of any kind. Poindexter and North, the report adds, "functioned largely outside the orbit of the U.S. government."[12]

The Reagan doctrine has made it very expensive for revolutionary regimes merely to exist. Furthermore, the campaigns of military support and legitimation for counterrevolutionary forces are efforts to make the downfall of revolutionary governments seem the result of internal incompetence. This policy, designed to prevent the use of U.S. military forces in Third World conflicts, increases the likelihood of U.S. intrusion in the domestic politics of the countries affected.

The New U.S. Vision of Counterinsurgency: "Low Intensity Warfare"

The resurgence of conflicts in the Third World has revived the counterinsurgency strategy that evolved in the shadow of Vietnam. The result is a close correspondence between new-right ideologues' proposals for global politics and the accepted military doctrine for confronting low-intensity conflicts.[13]

The concept of "low intensity" is derived from the idea that conflicts which imperial powers confront in the late twentieth century may be arranged on a spectrum of warfare intensity, ranging from high-intensity global nuclear war to incidents of low intensity civil disobedience and armed confrontation between local government forces and liberation movements. Intensity is thus based on military factors such as relative quantities of armaments, firepower, duration, and troop deployment. The term "low intensity warfare" misleadingly suggests that the incident in question is simply a small-scale conventional conflict, obscuring the fact that, for the countries concerned, the intensity is anything but "low."

A central concept of the doctrine of low intensity warfare is the recognition that small wars are political wars, which suggests using the same tactics against liberation movements which the revolutionaries themselves use. As its proponents state, "the enemy is likely to be employing a combination of political, economic, psychological and military measures, so the government will have to do likewise to defeat him."[14] This policy should enable the government forces to have political influence in the same local, national, and international arenas.

Only in the post-Vietnam context is it possible to weigh the effect of that war on U.S. counterinsurgency strategy. One lesson learned from the confrontation in Indochina was that superior military capacity does not guarantee victory over irregular popular forces. Another lesson, this time relearned, was that the issues in dispute cannot be resolved militarily and that this type of struggle is fundamentally political. Political considerations should therefore inform the counterrevolution: the objectives are not achieved by physically eliminating enemies, as in conventional warfare, but rather by so delegitimating, undermining, and isolating them that they lose credibility as a viable political alternative. On a practical level, then, the war must focus strategically on the civilian population, with the intent not of eliminating it but of neutralizing its support for the revolutionary forces or, ideally, winning its support for counterinsurgency.

The realization that social change in Third World countries is necessary, and perhaps inevitable, has increased support for a low intensity warfare doctrine holding that "the initiative rests with those who can influence or exploit the process of change."[15] The challenge then is to formulate reforms as alternatives to those advanced by revolutionary forces and to wrest from those forces their social bases of support. Another obligation is to adopt a less alienating style of repression, to shift from massive repression, which does not distinguish between guerrilla and civilian populations, to selective repression. The latter policy requires a relatively sophisticated security and intelligence apparatus.

Recognition that the key to successful revolutionary wars is a support base at the local level has generated the notion that effective counterinsurgency means total war at the grassroots level, implying the widespread participation of nonmilitary institutions. The need for change in the traditional role of soldiers and in their relationship to the civilian population requires a high level of coordination by all participating institutions. Success depends on the professionalization of the armed forces, the police, and security agencies and on improvement in intelligence capabilities. It requires the organization and training of local security forces in each country and, in areas like Central America, the regional integration of intelligence gathering. A successful intelligence program includes spying from the air to detect troop movements, supply lines, displaced populations, and the like; efficient communication equipment for counterinsurgency forces; and sophisticated instruments for tracing electronic information. Furthermore, the immigration and customs agencies of the countries in the region should be merged so as to control the movements of suspected persons within the area.[16]

To keep the conflict at the low-intensity level desired by the United States, responsibility must be divided between the United States and the affected country, with the former concentrating on logistical help and intelligence training. In Central America, the security systems of countries with ongoing conflicts are subsumed within the U.S. security system. Developing the Central American security apparatus implies changing the role of the Southern Command[17] and coordinating U.S. military bases throughout the region. Also required are the training and equipping of Special Forces and the CIA and expanding their activities in the region.[18] For U.S. forces, a successful intelligence operation requires complete integration into the environment, mastery of the language, and deeply ingrained knowledge of national cultures in the region.

The principal objective of low intensity warfare is attrition or exhaustion of the revolutionary forces, whether guerrilla or governmental. In this instance, however, attrition (an objective in all wars) is achieved by political as well as military means. In the application of this objective in the area of diplomacy in Central America, counterinsurgency forces have focused on neutralizing international support of revolution. Militarily, the counterrevolution aims to force guerrillas into continuous movement and to keep revolutionary armies on perpetual alert. These tactics, combined with policies that block access of international finance and trade, have devastating economic repercussions and can destroy alternative revolutionary economic models.

The goal of physical, psychological, moral, and material attrition is to delegitimate and isolate revolutionary forces from their bases of support. In concert with politico-psychological work among the masses, a war of attrition can eventually weaken the revolutionary power to the point of collapse, a collapse that appears to be self-induced. A revolution's bases of political and military support (here, a rearguard) become a central objective in this model of counterinsurgency.

The Rearguard: The Creation and Mobilization
of Popular Forces

In contrast with conventional war, in which the rearguard consists of logistical support systems within a clearly defined physical space, in unconventional warfare the rearguard is a popular, ideological base of support. Acceptance of an insurgent force as a legitimate alternative depends on its success in generating grass-roots support and particularly on the viability of its political program. The population as yet uncommitted represents a potential rearguard and therefore a political target of the insurgents.

In the relationship between a belligerent force and its base of support, each party influences and defines the other. Human and military resources for the guerrilla struggle are derived from the grass roots; the development and achievements of military forces engender the political consolidation of their bases of support. These bases are not only sources of provisions and reinforcements; they are also active participants in, and ultimately beneficiaries of, the process of change. The broad alliance between combatant units and their supporters breaks down psychological and ideological barriers that separate them, in spite of physical distances between them. This definition broadens the range of possibilities of those who can be considered a part of the rearguard. It may include representatives of diverse social sectors: a sympathizer working in a government agency, an urban labor organizer, a peasant messenger, a sympathetic catechist, a human rights activist, the mother of a combatant or of one of the disappeared, a businessperson, a bureaucrat.

It is useful to distinguish between the rearguards located inside the country and those existing abroad. The former usually comprise the masses who live in zones under insurgent control, their allied political organizations, and humanitarian and labor organizations. External rearguards include sympathetic governments and governmental institutions, solidarity groups, political organizations, and private organizations, each with its own level of commitment and capacity to lend legitimacy to a revolutionary movement or government. For government armies engaged in counterinsurgency wars, the proximate, material rearguard is the state apparatus itself.

Because of the unique connection between rearguard and combat forces, counterinsurgency assigns the highest priority to undermining and converting the enemy's rearguard. Tactics range from psychological warfare (aimed at winning "the six inches between the peasant's ears"[19] (instead of territory) to massive saturation bombing of populated areas in "liberated zones" (intended both to reinforce psychological tactics through terror and to "remove the water from the fish"). The underlying goal is to remove the masses as a support for revolutionary forces and recruit them into the rearguard of "national security."

The Doctrine of National Security
and Third World Military Ideology

Although linked to the general U.S. concept of national security, the doctrine of national security as used here refers to a set of concepts and ideas which inform a deeply rooted ideology within the Latin American armed forces. National security doctrine incorporates elements of Nazi geopolitics as well as the experiences of England and France in resisting the independence of former colonies.[20] It is based on the postulate that all Western democracies, particularly those in the Third World, are under permanent siege by a hostile transnational force, international communism. This confrontation is a battle for supremacy between two allegedly incompatible systems, Western Christianity and atheistic Marxism. Unlike traditional military encounters, the enemy in this conflict is not a foreigner with an unfamiliar flag but a compatriot with "ideas inimical to society," a society invariably defined as democratic regardless of its true character. This enemy, presumed to engage unremittingly in subversive activity against the system and its values, is classified as an internal enemy or a terrorist.[21]

National security doctrine assumes an astute, underhanded enemy who can disguise his or her ideas and infiltrate every aspect of society; included are individuals and organizations that endorse social change and eventually anyone who does not support the repressive policies required by the dictates of the doctrine. Effectively combating this amorphous enemy requires drawing lines of battle in every area of national life where the enemy might operate— the economy, diplomacy, unions, and religious organizations, all potential components of the rearguard.

National security defined as the defense of an ideological frontier becomes the driving force in national life, and the armed forces become its leading proponent. As a result, military forces and methods penetrate regular political processes, transforming them into new forms of counterinsurgency warfare. The military assumes this national project as its own, independent of and aloof from the classes in conflict. By its nature, however, the project is compatible with that of the dominant classes.

Within the Third World, specifically in Latin America, the doctrine of national security has been used to justify the repression of groups agitating for structural change, especially groups based in the urban and rural wage-earning and marginalized sectors. The immediate goal is to prevent progressive groups from achieving political power. Whether repression will be indiscriminate or selective, however, depends on such factors as the ability of the security apparatus to obtain information and maintain control and its capacity to make unified political decisions the moment repression is "needed."

Such a strategy favors the dominant classes because repression of the working masses and their labor organizations permits levels of exploitation which can raise levels of profit and soften or postpone economic crises. Thus so-called national security is invariably associated with the perpetuation of the most exploitative relations of production.

The belief that democratic states, particularly those in the Third World, are vulnerable to subversive agitation may be expressed in the idea of protected or restricted democracies. In this conception the degree of democracy varies from country to country, depending on how acutely the system or group in power feels threatened by the forces that oppose it. As formal democracy is valued universally, however, a regime must somehow adopt or revive it or run the risk of international rebuke. Institutions of formal democracy may even be manipulated as new instruments designed to legitimate counterinsurgency. This unique notion of "democracy-under-counterinsurgency" requires a security apparatus and an authoritative body to define the institutional limits within which democracy will operate, two functions assumed by the armed forces.

Nevertheless, relations between the government and the armed forces in national security regimes are necessarily conflictive, as formal power rests in restricted democratic institutions and real power belongs to the army. Although committed to the same antisubversive ends, the two groups use different and sometimes even contradictory means. The clearest example of this contradiction occurs in disputes over the allocation of resources. Given the precariousness of underdeveloped and dependent economies, a nation's ability to satisfy the demands of the army is limited and must be assessed in terms of the pressing needs and demands of the population.

Counterinsurgency Policy in Central America

The Internalization of National Security Doctrine

The national security doctrine in Central America has aspects that are particular to the region and to each country within it, the most significant of which has been the role of the United States. Earlier revolutionary or socialist movements in the southern cone of South America, such as Unidad Popular and MIR (Revolutionary Left Movement) in Chile, the Montoneros and ERP (People's Revolutionary Army) in Argentina, and the Tupamaros in Uruguay, appeared in societies that were more highly developed politically than those in Central America. These movements confronted modern, professional, ideologically well-prepared armies which had their own military traditions[22] and thus possessed more autonomy relative to the United States. As a result of these and other factors, the violent application of national security doctrine quickly annihilated the revolutionary movements, at least militarily. The U.S. role was largely limited to ideological and political support.

In Central America, however, the United States has taken on the additional task of financing and implementing the doctrine of national security; its assumption of a more comprehensive program has increased the military, political, and economic dependency of countries in the region. Having defined the Sandinista revolution and the insurgent movements in El Salvador and Guatemala as threats to its security, the United States is using local forces to defend its interests. The armies of the region, through their long, complex relationship with the U.S. military, have begun to adopt and, indeed, internalize U.S. conceptions of hemispheric security as their own.

Although national security actions are portrayed as internal, nationalist initiatives, in practically every instance they preserve U.S. hegemony while strengthening economic dependency. Such endeavors seek to establish stable models of nation building which retain bourgeois hegemony in a given country and U.S. hegemony in the region. The resulting imposition of development models, heavily conditioned aid packages, and recessive economic measures adversely affects the most defenseless of the masses. Still, the measures recommended by the United States do not always coincide with the interests of groups in power; they often aggravate conflicts between dominant groups and between those groups and the masses. This tendency has been particularly evident, for example, in the growing opposition of both the labor movement and right-wing groups to austerity measures proposed by President Duarte in El Salvador.

Political war in Central America, transcending the conduct of classical military confrontations, penetrates practically every aspect of social and political life. Although the war has taken a distinct form in each country and has set its own pace and level of development, the decision of the United States to respond with an undifferentiated counterinsurgency strategy has unified the national crises into a single regional conflict.

Low-Intensity Warfare and the Central American Armies

Under U.S. influence and control, Central American armies have had to adapt to the fundamentally political character of the war. The process has not been easy. Honduras, for example, has had to forge a tactical military alliance with the army of El Salvador, with which Honduras was at war in 1969.

El Salvador. The low intensity model of irregular warfare and the national security doctrine have required Central American armies organized to engage in conventional warfare to make adjustments. The coexistence in the armed forces of strongly conservative, pro-oligarchical sectors and professionalist, apolitical, and even progressive elements had allowed nationalist ideals to exist within the army. The recent militarization inspired by low-intensity warfare, however, has changed the picture. As the costs of militarization far exceed the country's economic capacity, the military has become dependent on the United States, not only technically but also economically. This double dependency has undermined nationalist political and military ideals as well as their political applications.

As nationalist sectors inside the Salvadoran armed forces lost support, factions supporting a more antinational, antipopular view of how to deal with the internal conflict consolidated their power. Later, as the war developed and expanded, disputes over political and military direction brought about political shifts within military structures, strengthening groups more in accord with the U.S. notions of how to conduct the war.[23]

After the first major FMLN (Farabundo Martí Front for National Liberation) offensive in January 1981, the Salvadoran army mobilized all its forces and deployed large regular units in an attempt to annihilate its adversary. The army's inability to adapt to changing tactical situations and to control territory away from its bases, however, revealed its inadequacy in the conduct of irregular warfare.[24] The army's failures and the losses it suffered allowed

U.S. advisors to impose their concept of "troops without quarters." The new strategy dictated that units be permanently deployed in the field, with a high degree of mobility and a clear offensive strategy. But these offensive forces lacked roots among the masses in the areas where they fought, which left them dependent on the regular army's logistical structures and limited their mobility and autonomy. They also lacked knowledge of local areas, and their officers were unable to adapt to unfamiliar operational techniques in which the enemy had a significant advantage. Military campaigns were accompanied by massive human rights violations; sometimes entire village populations were massacred.

From mid-1982 to late 1983 the guerrillas gained sufficient territorial control to consolidate their forces and form brigades and battalions. This regularization permitted broader actions, such as taking over the army barracks in El Paraiso, Chalatenango, in December 1983. Military actions like this takeover demonstrated the weakness of security systems recently installed on U.S. advice. While the FMLN was demonstrating its strength, the so-called government of national unity suffered a major political crisis in the crucial period preceding the 1984 presidential elections.[25] By the end of 1983 the FMLN was in control of roughly one-third of El Salvador's national territory. Under these circumstances, the United States was able to persuade Salvadoran military officers to abandon conventional warfare, thus permitting a fundamental deregularization of the Salvadoran army. The number of infantry brigades was doubled, and search-and-destroy units were organized and deployed in various parts of the country. The army also reinforced its helicopter units and activated long-range reconnaissance patrols, antiterrorist battalions, navy piranha battalions, and Immediate Response Battalions. Thus the basic structure of the army gradually became oriented to counterinsurgency warfare under new U.S. military policies.

These changes in military structures and units implied a political shift in the conduct of the military. The reduction in the size of operative units permitted them to become the so-called launching pad of counterinsurgent political warfare. Also, closer contact was established with the civilian population at the community level in an attempt to create better civilian-military relations, a fundamental principle of any guerrilla war. Another objective of the strategy was to force the guerrillas into constant movement in order to wear them down and break up their close relationship with the civilian population in the eastern part of the country. This tactic has been called "an attempt to out-guerrilla the guerrillas."

Thus two parallel processes were being developed in the Salvadoran war: the regularization of the FMLN forces and the deregularization of the government army. The tactical shifts of the latter were partly responsible for the FMLN's decision again to disperse its forces, a decision based in part on an evaluation of the military and political costs of continuing to function in large concentrations. Not only were large units more vulnerable to air fire, but they were losing daily contact with their bases, making it easier for the government army to contend for the support of the masses.

By again dispersing their forces in small detachments, the guerrillas began an inverse process of persecuting the "hunters" through a series of small-scale attacks aimed at continuing erosion of government forces. At the same time the FMLN sought to maintain the unity of command to permit the effective concentration of its forces in attacks at predetermined points.[26]

Another key component of the U.S. security policy for Central America, designed to increase public support for counterrevolution, is reinforcement of the "democratic center." As carried out in El Salvador, the policy implies the creation of a political system that will bring civilians to formal power and will help to consolidate alliances in support of counterrevolutionary plans, while the military concentrates on the war or on the neutralization or prevention of popular mobilization. This war, however, is clearly political, and as such it is not based on military activity alone. Despite the clear-cut division of functions in the counterinsurgency plan between the civilian government of Duarte and the armed forces, the political aspects of the war tend to maintain the real power of the military. The objective of setting up a restricted democracy is to smooth over the harshness of military power, not to eliminate or limit it. Indeed, the opposite occurs: the civilian power that has been instituted "is limited in its scope and has no decision-making power beyond determined limits."[27]

The development and conduct of the plan called United to Reconstruct has clearly revealed the relationship between civilian power and military power. Given the political limitations of the Duarte government, the military has taken on a central role in the direction and promotion of the plan, coordinating with the private sector and seeking the cohesion of all groups involved in the plan as a national unit.

The U.S. strategy also aims to set this process of democratization (in Honduras and Guatemala as well as El Salvador) in opposition to the presumed Sandinista totalitarianism in Nicaragua. The objective is to de-legitimize the experience of national self-determination in Nicaragua and present the situation in Central America as a confrontation between democracy and totalitarianism.

Nicaragua. In contrast with the Salvadoran army, which was forced to transform itself from a conventional organization into a more effective counterinsurgency force, the Nicaraguan army was formed by a reverse process: the transformation of guerrilla forces into a regular army. Later it again had to readjust its organization and doctrine to enable it to confront irregular counterrevolutionary warfare. The early perception that the principal danger was a foreign invasion led by the United States has also influenced its evolution.

The two major tasks in Nicaragua were the incorporation of the masses, the rearguard of the Sandinista revolution, into national defense and the organization of permanent defense bodies, the Sandinista Popular Army and the Ministry of Defense. Political conviction together with severe economic constraints reinforce the strategy of developing small, efficient, professional armed forces with various forms of popular participation.

The transformation of guerrilla and militia forces into a regular national army requires bringing existing forces, which tend toward dispersion and *caudillismo* (domination by a military leader), under a single military command. The factors making this process a difficult one included the resistance of guerrilla mentality to the new demands of discipline, norms, and lifestyles, as well as the lack of material resources to support a regular army.[28] An important aspect of the development of the Sandinista Popular Army has been the voluntary incorporation of large numbers of civilians, through popular militias, into national defense.[29] The concept of popular defense underlying this process requires the formation of close linkages between popular and regular forces.

The transformation of the Nicaraguan army began in 1982, when harassment by small bands of former members of the National Guard (Somocistas) shifted to larger and more systematic counterrevolutionary operations.[30] Beginning in 1982, the active forces of Sandinista military defense were organized around Reserve Infantry Battalions, military units of civilians who served six-month tours of duty. The heterogeneous composition, inadequate experience, and limited combat training of these units, however, placed them at an operational disadvantage with respect to the better-trained and better-equipped Somocista forces, now directly supervised and supplied by the CIA.

The contra forces were able to take the initiative and carried out a well-planned strategy of irregular warfare. By 1983 the counterrevolutionary struggle took the form of large-scale, broadly dispersed irregular operations which exceeded the capabilities of Nicaragua's small regular army and its nonprofessional militias, made up largely of reserve infantry battalions. Nicaragua had to reassess its assumption that the small counterrevolutionary bands were playing only a marginal and complementary role in a larger strategy of invasion by the United States.

This realization dictated the second major change in the Nicaraguan army: the development in mid-1983 of its capacity for offensive irregular warfare and the creation of the Patriotic Military Service, based on obligatory two-year periods of military service. The unavoidable economic and political costs of this policy were seen in the opposition of affected families, reinforced by the propaganda of opposition groups within Nicaragua. Its impact proved less disruptive however, than mobilizing militia fighters, most of whom would have to have been taken away from productive work. In early 1984, 10,000 young recruits were organized into mobile shock battalions known as Irregular Warfare Battalions (BLIs).[31] The initiation of obligatory military service was a qualitative and quantitative leap in strategy which would definitely reverse the course of the war.

The unremitting threat of invasion (made evident by continuous, massive maneuvers in Honduras and continuous deployment of conventional U.S. military units along the coasts of Nicaragua) and growing hostility on the part of the Reagan administration obliged the Sandinistas to maintain the training and equipment needs of their regular army. At the same time the army has developed abilities and technologies to conduct irregular warfare against the contras. The popular forces, meanwhile, have been reinforced through the organization of territorial militias, self-defense committees, and other units which perform a variety of tasks, both offensive and defensive, throughout the country.[32]

Little by little, the contras' task forces and operational command posts were dispersed; by the end of 1984 they had lost the initiative. Despite the escalation of U.S. military aid beginning in 1985 (as well as unknown quantities of aid from other foreign governments and private sources), the contras have failed to develop a significant local rearguard in combat zones, much less political support in the cities. Nor have the contras achieved any significant military objectives.

An important element in the development and transformation of the Sandinista Popular Army is aid from predominantly socialist countries in supplying technical military equipment. This support and its origins have been used by the Reagan administration to characterize Nicaragua as a country under Soviet influence and a military threat to the region.

Numerous military specialists have clearly established the defensive character of the Sandinista Popular Army, however, based on both its structure and equipment and its professional capacity.[33] The most dramatic characteristic of the development of the Nicaraguan army is indeed that its rhythm of growth has corresponded closely to open and direct military threats and concrete aggressions.[34] Nor is the source of supplies accidental. From the moment of their victory, the Sandinistas worked assiduously to construct their national army, searching for appropriate resources in Western countries, including the United States. Commander Tomás Borge led these unsuccessful efforts.[35] Direct pressures exercised by Washington on countries in a position to provide needed supplies affected even the government of François Mitterrand in France. After initiating military assistance in December 1981, the French government suspended it in mid-September 1982. Thus socialist countries became the major military suppliers because of the lack of alternatives.

Beyond the dictates of solidarity and good diplomatic relations, few ideological similarities or political objectives link the Soviet Union and Nicaragua. Recognition of this fact has led prestigious institutions in the United States which engage in military and political analysis to affirm that Soviet influence in Nicaragua is limited and that its military presence is "very small."[36]

Apart from Soviet reasons for maintaining a limited and nondominant relationship with Nicaragua, the Sandinistas have their own logic in desiring to keep Nicaragua independent and autonomous. In the words of one of the Sandinista commanders, "If they ask me if I want the Nicaraguan revolution to be like that of the Soviet Union, I tell them no. Like that of Cuba, I tell them no."[37]

The success of the Sandinista army, in comparison with that of El Salvador, may be attributed to the character of the armed forces, the revolution they are defending, and the enemies they are confronting. The Salvadoran army had to transform itself from a conventional into a counterinsurgency army, capable of operating in small units with high mobility and of conducting political and psychological as well as military warfare. The Sandinista army transformed itself from a guerrilla army into a regular national army prepared for possible U.S. invasion and at the same time capable of fighting an irregular war against the contras.

Perhaps the most significant difference between the two armies is that the Sandinista army has roots in the population, both in its origins and in the popular militia created after the Sandinista victory and subsequently reorganized into territorial units to complement regular army operations. The Sandinistas have thus enjoyed the continued support of a substantial rearguard among the population. In contrast, the Salvadoran army has been unable to obtain popular support; its military operations against the civilian population have given it the character of an antipopular army, despite the reforms attempted by the Christian Democratic government. In fact, the Salvadoran army continues to be regarded as a defender of the dominant class in El Salvador and, increasingly, of U.S. interests.

Significant differences also distinguish the Salvadoran guerrilla forces united in the FMLN from the Nicaraguan contras, particularly the FDN (Nicaraguan Democratic Forces, the major contra force). The Salvadoran guerrillas' base of popular support is evident in the mass organizations that supported them in the 1970s and in the community bases in the liberated and contested zones, which have not been eradicated after nearly three years of bombardment by the Salvadoran armed forces. The relationship between the FMLN and its rearguard is revealed in its political program, which is oriented to meet the needs of the different social sectors that constitute its base of support. This program might be considered as the beginning of an alternative form of government administering production, distribution of goods and services, a judiciary body, and other aspects of communal life. Although the contras receive some support from small farmers in the central mountainous areas of Nicaragua and from the small indigenous populations of the Atlantic Coast region, their leadership has been drawn largely from the Somoza National Guard. Their dependence on U.S. training, organization, and financing, not to mention their obvious lack of a political agenda independent of that of the United States, belies any effort to portray them as a genuine popular force. To date, the contras' only political project has been merely to spread anti-Sandinista propaganda.

Thus, in contrast with El Salvador, where two hostile armies confront each other, in Nicaragua the army confronts a force that is essentially foreign, by virtue of its absolute dependence on the United States as its rearguard.[38] The contras thus resemble an expeditionary force using irregular warfare tactics rather than an insurgent guerrilla force.

Conclusions

Development of the U.S. counterinsurgency strategy for Central America has been a dynamic process. In it an initially simplistic vision of rapid military victory has been transformed into a more sophisticated strategy incorporating political, psychological, economic, and diplomatic, as well as military, elements. This transformation has resulted partly from pressures within the United States but primarily from the realization that a quick, easy military victory over the Salvadoran guerrillas or the Sandinistas was not possible.

The current U.S. policy toward the region, based on the Reagan doctrine, incorporates the ideology of the national security doctrine, which has characterized U.S. foreign policy since the end of World War II, and new counterinsurgency strategies developed in the wake of the Vietnam War. In some respects, this policy is a throwback to the hard-line strategies of the 1950s, but it also includes elements of a more sophisticated policy, embracing the promotion of restricted democracies and limited reform, rather than support for right-wing regimes as an alternative to revolutionary change. The most original component of the Reagan doctrine is the notion that revolutions are reversible, not only in Latin America, where the United States has traditionally exercised hegemony, but also in the rest of the world. Central America has thus become a spearhead of the Reagan doctrine— a model that may be emulated in the rest of the world.

The strategy of low intensity war implies an indefinite prolongation of conflicts that have already taken a high toll in Central America; thousands have been killed and hundreds of thousands displaced; the region has been militarized, and its economy has been pushed to the brink.[39] Nevertheless, a U.S. victory over the guerrilla forces in El Salvador and the Sandinistas in Nicaragua remains elusive. Although the failure of U.S. counterinsurgency strategy to date may be attributed to many causes, the existence and the nature of the popular bases of support for both the Sandinistas and the FMLN, and the virtual absence of such a rearguard supporting the Salvadoran army and the contras, are undoubtedly important factors. A related factor is the inability of the Salvadoran army to develop a political program to meet the needs of its population. And the contras lack even an agenda distinct from that of the United States.

In the meantime the strategy of low intensity war is generating contra-dictions for the Reagan administration. On the one hand, low intensity warfare strategy requires the prolongation of conflict in order to achieve its objective of wearing down the enemy. Recent investigations have revealed that the present application of policy in the Central American region has been overly secretive, highly centralized, defiant of Congress, improperly directed, and illegally conducted.[40] On the other hand, as the Reagan administration draws to a close, the pressure to resolve the conflict mounts. The dilemma will thus be whether to abandon the strategy and negotiate, or to escalate the war through the last available means: direct U.S. inter-vention.

Notes

1. The debate that has arisen regarding the Reagan doctrine has gone beyond the determination of the correct premises for U.S. policy into the elaboration of

policy positions. For a sense of the complexity emerging from this debate, see Irving Kristol, "The War of Ideology," *National Interest* 1 (Fall 1985): 16–25; Christopher Layne, "The Real Conservative Agenda," *Foreign Policy* (Spring 1986); Alan Wolfe, "Crackpot Moralism, Neo-Realism, and U.S. Foreign Policy," *World Policy Journal* (Spring 1986): 251–275; and Stephen Rosenfeld, "The Guns of July," *Foreign Affairs* (Spring 1986): 698–714.

2. The thirteen countries are Mozambique, Zimbabwe, Angola, Grenada, Nicaragua, Iran, Afghanistan, Laos, Cambodia, Guinea-Bissau, São Tomé, Cape Verde, and Ethiopia.

3. Robert Kupperman and William J. Taylor, Jr., eds. *Strategic Requirements for the Army to the Year 2000* (Cambridge, MA: Center for Strategic Studies, 1983), chaps. 10, 11.

4. This thesis is the subject of innumerable reports, documents, and other studies, including Robert Kupperman Associates, "Low-Intensity Conflict" (study prepared for the U.S. Army Training and Doctrine Command, 1983); Richard H. Shultz et al., "Low Intensity Conflict," in Heritage Foundation, *Mandate for Leadership II: Continuing the Conservative Revolution* (Washington, 1984); and Kupperman and Taylor, eds., *Strategic Requirements*, chaps. 10, 11, 14.

5. Committee of Santa Fe, "A New Inter-American Policy for the Eighties" (Santa Fe, NM: Council for Inter-American Security, 1980).

6. Fred Halliday, "Beyond Irangate: The Reagan Doctrine and the Third World" (London: Transnational Institute, 1986).

7. Eduardo Lucio Molino y Vedia, "Los Conflictos de Baja Intensidad y el Mito de la reversibilidad de la historia," *Panorama* (Mexico City), 9 (May–June 1986): 15.

8. Jeane Kirkpatrick, "Dictators and Double Standards," *Commentary* (November 1979).

9. Reagan said that "any system is inherently unstable that has no peaceful means to legitimize its leaders. In such cases, the very repressiveness of the state ultimately drives people to resist it, if necessary by force. While we must be cautious about forcing the pace of change, we must not hesitate to declare our ultimate objectives and to take actions to move toward them" (Don McLeod, "A Doctrine at work," *Insight*, 10 March 1986, p. 3).

10. One demonstration of the privileged role of the Nicaraguan contras in the media is evidenced in a recent study of the coverage of Latin America in the major U.S. press (*Wall Street Journal, Washington Post, New York Times, Miami Herald, Los Angeles Times,* and *Christian Science Monitor*). The study shows that in 1985 Nicaragua monopolized 20 percent of all articles covering Latin America; Mexico, with 11 percent, was in second place. "Of course, the major concentration of information on Nicaragua occurs in the months prior to votes by the U.S. Congress on aid to the contras, thus becoming almost 30 percent of the total news on Latin America in the month of June," (see "Cómo nos ven?" *FLACSO* [Santiago, Chile; December 1986–March 1987], pp. 20–21).

11. Rosenfeld, "Guns of July," pp. 698–714.

12. *Tower Commission Report*, introduction by R. W. Apple, Jr. (New York: Bantam/ Times Books, February 1987), p. xv.

13. We are not attempting to attribute the outcomes of internal struggles over policy formation and its implementation in conflict areas in the Third World solely to the increased influence of the new right over the Reagan administration. Certainly, the arguments for resorting to low intensity warfare in Central America involved political influences antagonistic to new-right thinking (see reactions and debates over the naming of the Kissinger Commission). From our perspective, however, new-right thinking has been conducive to the implementation of low intensity war by providing

the ideological rationale, as well as by openly supporting this doctrine in such publications as *Mandate for Leadership II* (Heritage Foundation, 1985), among several others.

14. Frank Kitson, *Low Intensity Operations: Subversion, Insurgency, Peace-Keeping* (Harrisburg, England, 1971).

15. Major General Donald R. Morelli and Major Michael P. Ferguson, "Low-Intensity Conflict: An Operational Perspective?" *Military Review*, November 1984: p. 4.

The increased debate on counterinsurgency strategy in the U.S. armed services, particularly in the army but also in the air force, is evident in the dramatic growth in the number of articles dealing with it in military journals, such as *Military Review* and the *Air University Review*, as well as in definitive works like Summers, *On Strategy: A Critical Analysis of the Vietnam War* (Novato, CA: Presidio Press, 1982), and Krepenvitch's *The Army and Vietnam* (Baltimore: Johns Hopkins University Press, 1986).

As suggested in current military literature, the forces stationed at the U.S. Southern Command in Panama throughout the 1980s have played an important role in urging that the lessons learned in Vietnam be applied to the Central American crisis (see: *Analytical Review of Low-intensity Conflict*, prepared by the Joint Low-intensity Conflict Project, United States Army Training and Doctrine Command, Fort Monroe, Virginia, August 1986).

16. See "Memorandum of the Department of State to National Security Advisor Robert McFarlane on Financing for Political Training in Central America" (Washington, June 1985), pp. 4–8; Joanne Omang, "The Winds of War Blow through Washington," *Washington Post Weekly Edition*, 28 July 1986, p. 2; and Ricardo Wheelock Román, "Preparaciones de la intervención," *Barricada*, 8 July 1986.

17. Raúl Leis, *Commando Sur, poder hostil* (Panama City: CEASPA, 1985); "SWORD [Southern Command's Small Wars Operations Research Directorate] Puts Cutting Edge on US South Commission," *Southern Command News*, July 1986, pp. 25–71.

18. Alfonso Chardy, "Debate Grows in Washington on Management of *Contra* War," *New York Times*, 3 July 1986, describes the future role of the CIA in Nicaragua as "operational control, battle strategy and tactics, and communications, logistics, intelligence and combat advice." See also Richard Halloran, "C.I.A. Is Reported Set to Channel Aid to *Contras*," *New York Times*, 17 March 1986; Omang, "The Winds of War."

19. John Waghelstein, "Low-Intensity Conflicts in the Post-Vietnam Era" (lecture delivered at American Enterprise Institute, Washington, 16 January 1985).

20. Alvaro Briones, *Economía y política del fascismo dependiente* (Mexico City, 1978), p. 308.

21. Jorge V. Tapia, *El terrorismo del Estado: la doctrina de Seguridad Nacional en el Cono Sur* (Mexico City, 1980), p. 118.

22. Brian Loveman and Thomas M. Davies, Jr., ed., *The Politics of Antipolitics: The Military in Latin America* (Lincoln, NE: University of Nebraska Press, 1978), p. 14.

23. Two parallel processes were generated within the armed forces: (1) the displacement and destruction of the "institutionalized" sectors (marginalization of the forces of Col. Adolfo Arnaldo Majano and of the military youth in the Permanent Council of the Armed Forces [COPEFA] who had been responsible for the 1979 coup; and (2) reinforcement of the U.S. perspective in the upper echelons of the Salvadoran army, resulting in an adjustment of accounts between General García (at that time minister of defense) and Lt. Col. Ochoa in the crisis of January 1982,

which resulted in the displacement of García and abandonment of his traditional perspective on the war. See José Rodolfo Castro Orellana, "La Guerra Contrainsurgente en El Salvador: ¿Militarización de la política o politización de lo militar?" (Sixth Central American Congress of Sociology, Panama City, March 1985), pp. 16–17, and his "El Plan de contrainsurgencia norteamericana para El Salvador," in *Centroamérica: La guerra de Baja-intensidad, Agresión vs. Sobrevivencia, Cuadernos de Pensamiento Propio* (Managua, February 1986), p. 58.

24. See Castro, "El plan de contrainsurgencia norteamericano."

25. During this period the political situation in El Salvador was marked by intense political activity centered on the elections, which were to be the final step toward an elected civilian government. (See article by Terry Karl in this volume [editors' note].) Christian Democrat José Napoleón Duarte was seen as the candidate most likely to win; he was already enjoying enormous support from the United States. The pre-election period was also characterized by high levels of disagreement among the three major parties participating in the elections, including the Christian Democratic party, ARENA (National Republican Alliance), and the PCN (Party of National Conciliation).

26. For a more in-depth treatment of this dynamic relationship between the tactical shifts of both armies, see Castro, "El Plan de Contrainsurgencia," pp. 55–57.

27. Franz Hinkelammer, interview in "La Guerra, la Paz y las Ciencias Sociales en Centroamérica," Universidad de El Salvador, January 1987, p. 25.

28. Commander of the Revolution Humberto Ortega, "El pueblo en armas garantiza la victoria" (speech delivered 7 February 1985, published by Dirección Política, Ejército Popular Sandinista [EPS]).

29. Efforts have been made in both El Salvador and Guatemala to incorporate sectors of the civilian population into civic action patrols as part of the counterinsurgency strategy. The efforts in El Salvador have failed. In Guatemala they have been more successful, but many of the patrols are unarmed or poorly armed and recruitment seems to have been largely coercive. (See article by Gabriel Aguilera Peralta in this volume [editors' note].)

30. Philip Brenner and William LeoGrande, "Congress and the Not-So-Secret War against Nicaragua: A Preliminary Analysis" (Washington, 1985), p. 4.

31. Press conference by Commander Joaquín Cuadra, vice-minister of defense, EPS, 14 October 1985.

32. Interview of Comandante Roberto Calderón, EPS, by Agencia Nueva Nicaragua, September 1985.

33. Lt. Col. (ret.) Edward King, "Report on the Military and Political Situation in Central America," Unitarian Universalist Service Committee, Massachusetts, September 1984. King's assessment was confirmed in conversations with him by one of the authors, Managua, August 1985.

34. Marc Edelman, "Lifelines: Nicaragua and the Socialist Countries," in NACLA, *Report on the Americas*, Vol. XIX, no. 3 (May/June 1985), p. 49.

35. Robert Matthews, "The Limits of Friendship: Nicaragua and the West," in ibid., p. 25.

36. *The Defense Monitor*, Vol. XV, no. 5, 36 (Washington: Center for Defense Information, 1986), p. 30.

37. Commander Bayardo Arce, interview, in Gabriele Invernizzi et al., "Sandinistas" (Managua, 1986), p. 86.

38. According to one UPI report, even U.S. officials shared this assessment. A spokesperson was reported as saying that "in the judgment of the government, the

contra cannot survive as a force of struggle without renewed military aid" (UPI wire story, dateline Washington, published in *La Prensa* [Managua], 15–16 February 1986, p. 1).

39. The number of regular troops in the five Central American countries was estimated at 207,350 in 1985, a figure approaching the size of the armies of Mexico (250,000) and Brazil (277,100), countries whose populations, at 75 million and 130 million respectively, dwarf that of Central America at 25 million. The addition of irregular combatants—the contras in Nicaragua, the FMLN in El Salvador, foreign military personnel—would raise the total still higher (Council on Hemispheric Affairs, "A Special Report," Washington, March 1985). The militarization of the region is further evident in its costs: approximately 50 percent of the government budgets in Nicaragua and El Salvador, 20–30 percent in Guatemala, and a rising proportion in Honduras and Costa Rica.

40. See article by Kenneth Sharpe in this volume (editors' note).

5

Negotiation in Conflict: Central America and Contadora

Adolfo Aguilar Zinser

The search for peace in Central America has been marked by frustrated expectations and lost opportunities as well as important though limited achievements. Essentially a Latin American initiative, it has in certain respects challenged the military orientation of U.S. policy. Given the hegemony traditionally exercised by the United States over the region, as well as other problems, some of them avoidable, efforts to negotiate, particularly those of Contadora, have tended to be limited, reactive, and abstract. Nevertheless, Contadora has devised an avenue for hemispheric cooperation and has obtained broad regional support for an agenda independent of U.S. influence.

The purpose of this article is to analyze the Latin American initiatives for negotiations. It examines the development of such efforts from 1979 to mid-1987, describing their transformation over time from initiatives with a clear political definition to legal and diplomatic initiatives with little political content. It then analyzes the limitations and achievements of the Contadora process. A final section comments on the future prospects for negotiation, taking into account the implications of the Iran-*contra* affair.

The Origins of Negotiation

To understand the parallel between the process of the Central American conflict and the Contadora efforts, it is necessary to review the origins of Contadora, its criteria in proposing a solution to the conflict, and the use of these criteria by different actors with opposite intentions. The issue of a negotiated arrangement in Central America was first raised in 1978 by President Carter in connection with the Sandinista insurrection and the imminent fall of Anastasio Somoza. The moral, political, and practical impossibility of supporting Somoza did not stop the Carter administration

Translated by Maria Irene Alvarez.

from trying to prevent the collapse of his regime and the destruction of the National Guard. Democratic party strategists hoped that negotiations could displace Somoza and at the same time prevent the Sandinistas from coming to power.

When Mexico was invited with other Latin American nations to join an effort to mediate between the Nicaraguan opposition and the dictator under the auspices of the U.S. Department of State, the Mexican Ministry of Foreign Relations categorically declined, claiming that the action would be an intervention in Nicaragua's internal affairs. Carter's negotiating effort and Mexico's intransigence became the first episode in political negotiation in Central America. Subsequently, in June 1979, Washington called upon the foreign ministers of the Organization of American States (OAS) to meet in an effort to avoid total destruction of the National Guard and the triumph of the revolutionary army through a multilateral cease-fire backed by Latin Americans. A negative response came from Mexico's minister of foreign relations, Jorge Castañeda: "What can the OAS do in these conditions? The essential point is what it cannot do. The OAS cannot legally, politically, nor morally intervene in this purely Nicaraguan affair." As he pointed out later, "For us the worst and most serious intervention would consist in trying to impose a solution from outside to a purely internal Nicaraguan problem, to block its natural culmination."[1]

Shifting Roles in the Negotiation Process

The "natural culmination" of the Nicaraguan war on 19 July proved Castañeda right: the Sandinistas took power without ties to any other nation or compromises with the old regime. And Carter's frustrated attempts at mediation discredited the negotiation process as a means for guaranteeing the national security of the United States in the region. Carter's failed effort led to one of the main criticisms leveled at his foreign policy by conservatives and Republicans: "We lost Nicaragua."

Consequently, when Ronald Reagan became president in 1981, the respective positions of the United States and Mexico in relation to negotiations took a diplomatic swing of 180 degrees. Carter in his last months had already established in El Salvador a new military strategy of containment of revolutionary processes in the region. There was already talk of Soviet and Cuban intervention, of arms traffic, and therefore of the need to support the established governments with military aid for national security reasons, on the basis, of course, of social reforms and respect for human rights. Reagan followed Carter's lead but emphasized the containment of Soviet intervention by any means and minimized interest in reforms and human rights. The new Republican administration decided openly to support armies besieged by revolutionaries and to form a political and military alliance in the region so as to strengthen local counterinsurgency.

The Salvadoran revolutionary movement thus found itself directly confronting U.S. strategy and weapons, which were transferred in large numbers to the Salvadoran army. The balance of power in El Salvador was altered in a few months, although not to the point that the revolutionaries lost their impetus or were subjugated by force of arms. In the short run, however, a revolutionary triumph that had seemed conceivable was prevented.

At the same time that U.S. involvement in the Salvadoran civil war was growing, Washington's hostility toward the Sandinistas was also increasing. The establishment of the war machine in El Salvador, the recruitment of neighboring governments against the Nicaraguan revolutionaries, the military and naval maneuvers in the zone, the economic blockade of Nicaragua, and covert and later overt support to the contras all jeopardized the very existence of the Sandinista revolution.

The French-Mexican Communiqué: Inadmissible Negotiation

The position of Mexico respecting negotiation also shifted. Convinced that the Gordian knot of the conflict lay in El Salvador and that the Reagan administration's determined backing of the Salvadoran army appreciably altered the situation in comparison with that in Nicaragua in 1979, Mexico now attempted to force negotiations in an effort to neutralize U.S. intervention. The first initiative was the French-Mexican communiqué of September 1981, which had three political components. First, it granted diplomatic recognition to the Salvadoran opposition forces (FMLN-FDR) with the explicit aim of ensuring their acceptance by the international community as legitimate contenders for power and valid actors in an eventual negotiation with the Salvadoran government and the United States. Second, it proposed a negotiation plan that included genuine democratic elections as preliminary to the peaceful formation of a new government. Third, it implicitly underlined the belief of a European ally of the United States (France) and a friendly neighbor (Mexico) that acceptance of the revolutionaries and their demands as a starting point for the solution of the conflict was not incompatible with strategic U.S. interests.

The Reagan administration strategy, however, calling for the total destruction of the revolutionary forces, could not be reconciled with the concept of their legitimacy. Thus the Mexican-French initiative was not only unacceptable but was interpreted as a serious breach of Mexico's understanding with the United States. Given the Republican party position that revolutions originate in the East-West confrontation, the Mexican solution was seen as supporting, either unintentionally or by design, the interests of the East.

The joint initiative of López Portillo and the Socialist president of France, François Mitterrand, did have the effect of encouraging other European political forces, particularly members of the Socialist International, to continue pushing for a negotiated solution to the Salvadoran conflict and a mutual understanding between the United States and Nicaragua. But these conciliatory efforts were consistently blocked by the United States. The European perspective that the Central American revolutionaries had to participate in any solution deeply irritated Washington, and Reagan's inflexible reaction to the advice of his Western allies demonstrated the diplomatic risks of interfering in the U.S. "backyard."[2]

At the same time, the Latin American countries, including Mexico, understood that the search for a negotiated solution to Central American conflicts was interpreted by Washington as irresponsible support for the guerrillas. The Europeans, for their part, realized that without Latin American leadership in promoting a just solution the European position would be stranded in isolation. Gradually the Socialist International had to abandon its negotiating efforts.

Negotiation: A No-Exit Policy

In February 1982 Mexico made a final effort to mediate a settlement defined in strictly political terms. Before a large gathering in the Revolution Plaza in Managua, President López Portillo specified the three areas where agreement was necessary as El Salvador, Nicaragua, and the relations between the United States and Cuba.[3] In addition to the local participants, the United States and Cuba would be parties to the general agreement. Mexico committed itself to use its influence and prestige in the region to guarantee that the national security interests of the United States would not be damaged by the coming era of revolutionary change in Central America.

The United States paid little attention to the Mexican proposal. Going beyond simple rejection of its ideas, Washington explicitly disapproved of Mexico's becoming a political actor in Central America without regard for the U.S. definition of its strategic interests. At this point the Mexican government became convinced that an essential element in the Reagan administration's concept of national security was reinstitution of U.S. political and military hegemony in Central America.

By the end of 1982 the Latin American countries, particularly those neighboring on the area of conflict, were showing increasing alarm at the prospect of a regional war and of direct U.S. intervention. Neither Mexico nor Venezuela, which had thus far held antagonistic positions on Central America, had the will or the political means to implement its policy on its own. Mexico, just entering upon the most serious economic crisis of its history, felt highly vulnerable to U.S. pressures. In Venezuela, the Christian Democrats had become more closely identified with the stand of the United States; correspondingly, they were almost diametrically opposed to the Mexican position. They had distanced themselves from the Sandinistas (who had had the support of the preceding Venezuelan government of Carlos Andrés Pérez); they were now hostile to the Salvadoran revolutionaries, and were partisan to Christian Democratic reformism in the region. The Christian Democrats' identification with U.S. strategies had been detrimental to their electoral position and their international prestige.

In September 1982, almost a year after issuance of the French-Mexican communiqué, López Portillo and Venezuelan President Luis Herrera Campíns put forward a new negotiating proposal calling upon the governments of the United States, Honduras, and Nicaragua to agree upon a peaceful solution of the border conflicts between the two Central American countries. This proposal marked an important change in the criteria for negotiations. For the first time, they were based on the premise that the main causes of regional conflicts were not internal political forces and that each government had an immediate responsibility to conserve peace among the states. The axis of Latin American diplomacy toward peace in Central America thus shifted from political concern over the revolutionary struggles in El Salvador and Guatemala to diplomatic and legal efforts to influence the conflict among states, a conflict heightened by U.S. hostility toward the Nicaraguan government.

Although the Reagan administration ignored the Mexican-Venezuelan proposal, it was evident that in omitting reference to El Salvador the Mexican government, seeking a safer stand for its Central American policy, had abandoned certain positions opposed by the United States. This first Mexican retreat gave the United States more latitude for its political-military maneuvers in El Salvador. Still, the joint effort by Venezuela and Mexico was unsettling for the Reagan administration in that it enhanced the prospects for a broad Latin American initiative free of direct control by the United States.

Intent on blocking Latin American diplomatic initiatives, the White House undertook its own arrangements. In October 1982 the Department of State organized the Forum for Peace and Democracy, known also as the Enders Forum because of the role played by Under Secretary of State Thomas Enders. Its first and only formal meeting was attended by official representatives of Belize, Panama, Jamaica, Colombia, and the Dominican Republic and by the foreign ministers of Honduras, Costa Rica, and El Salvador. The United States acted officially as observer. Guatemala and Nicaragua were excluded because of allegations that their governments were not democratic. Notwithstanding its ambitious title, the forum had no other purpose than to vote a censure of Nicaragua and Cuba, regarded by the Reagan administration as the major enemies to peace and democracy on the continent. Some of the participant governments, who had expected open support for the development and peace of the region, were displeased by what they saw as a crude diplomatic manipulation to make them accomplices in the Reagan administration's aggressive policy toward Nicaragua.

Contadora: Multilateral Refuge

On 8 and 9 January 1983 the foreign ministers of Mexico (Bernardo Sepúlveda Amor), Colombia (Rodrígo Lloreida Caicedo), Venezuela (José Alberto Zambrano), and Panama (Juan José Amado) met on the Panamanian island of Contadora.[4] The official purpose of the meeting, promoted by Mexico, was to discuss the dangers to regional peace and security posed by the Central American crisis. The common concern of the participants was, and continues to be, the military buildup in the area and the U.S.

objective of finding a military solution to the political and social conflicts in Central America. The document issued by the ministers stated that the root causes of the region's instability lay not in East-West tensions but in the economic and social backwardness of the countries, reaffirmed the validity of the principles of nonintervention and self-determination, and called for dialogue and negotiations.[5] The Contadora group did not officially launch its drive for peace until three months later, in April, when Colombian president Belisario Betancur made a quick trip through Venezuela, Panama, Costa Rica and Mexico. By then, the urgent need for mediation that would lead to negotiations and avert regional war had become clear. The four Contadora countries would work toward that end.[6]

The international situation and the specific circumstances of each country fortuitously combined to facilitate the birth of Contadora. The Mexican government needed to break away from its isolation in Latin America, brought on by the French-Mexican declaration of 1981, and to avoid a bilateral conflict with the United States. To abandon completely its Central America policy in order to ensure Washington's goodwill during its financial crisis would have cost Mexico political trouble at home and the loss of international prestige. Joining its sister countries and removing itself from internal revolutionary struggles to deal with conflicts among states—from the relative security of multilateral diplomatic and legal declarations—was an almost perfect solution for Mexico. The United States, however, instead of accepting this adroit retreat, increased its pressures against Mexico under the Contadora pretext.

For its part, Venezuela also found in Contadora a timely refuge from the uncomfortable closeness to Reagan's position stemming from its support for Christian Democracy, the fundamental element in Washington's efforts to legitimize the Salvadoran government. Joining Mexico in a multilateral initiative, President Herrera Campíns could diffuse much of the internal and external suspicion directed against his government. At the same time the innovator of Colombian policy, President Belisario Betancur, could give his country a tenable foreign policy through Contadora and simultaneously enhance the internal and international standing of his government. Moreover, Colombia's role in the Contadora process gave Betancur valuable arguments and political means for initiating his program of internal pacification and amnesty for the guerrillas who had been fighting in Colombia over the years. Finally, Panama, in search of a diplomatic excuse for not becoming directly involved in its neighbors' wars, joined Contadora to strengthen its negotiating position with the United States so as to avoid difficulties with the Reagan administration in implementing the Panama Canal treaties.

The need to maintain consensus among the four Contadora countries called for adjustments and mutual concessions which further limited the initiative. For example, the Salvadoran civil war could not be discussed because Mexico supported the FMLN-FDR while Venezuela favored the Christian Democrats and José Napoleón Duarte. Nor could the behavior of international actors in the region be openly debated: Mexico attributed the intervention only to the United States; Venezuela blamed it on Cuba and the Soviet Union as well.

In the long run Mexico has had the strongest motivation for keeping Contadora alive. Despite the fact that Mexico has not always taken a position of leadership, the persistence of its government largely explains why Contadora has not been abandoned after numerous disappointments and failures.

Contadora Abstractions

On the basis of over four years of experience, it is possible to identify four practically inviolable norms, some implicit, others explicit, that have characterized the Contadora efforts: (1) as Contadora is an initiative of four Latin American governments subsequently supported by another four in South America, only Latin Americans actively participate in its efforts; (2) Contadora is concerned only with conflicts among states, not with struggles within them; (3) Contadora is not concerned with placing blame and refrains from any judgment on or censure of any Central American state; (4) Contadora is committed only to establish by common accord general principles, international legal norms, and recommendations for peaceful coexistence and cooperation, applicable to all, including third parties.

This "behavior code" allows Contadora to carry out diplomatic pacifying functions rather than attempt real political mediation as it shifts peace deliberations to an abstract level. The Contadora forum, its very existence dependent upon its political ingenuity and legal precision, accepts as valid two premises that are in fact invalid. First, on the basis of international principles of the equality of states, sovereignty, and self-determination, Contadora assumes that the Central American governments are indeed sovereign governments able to negotiate on their own and to commit themselves to fulfill agreements without having outsiders dictate their behavior. Second, Contadora undertakes its tasks with the hope (not the certainty) that the observation of international rules of peaceful coexistence among states will neutralize external pressures and condition the behavior of other countries not in the region. Contadora's hope was that progress in the negotiations—a task considered easier in the absence of the United States—would present a real obstacle to Washington's war plans.

Without the United States being present and free from the East-West framework, Contadora did not have to address the issue of extraregional responsibilities. The diplomatic purity of the initiative was thus maintained, direct confrontation with the Reagan administration was avoided, and Latin American countries could work together to find a solution to a conflict involving sister countries. At the same time, internal power struggles within the Central American countries would not contaminate the negotiating climate Contadora was trying to establish.

The presumption that the Central American states were sovereign entities, capable of negotiating agreements among themselves in terms of their own interests, confined the diplomatic negotiations to the regional governments.

By encouraging these countries to sit at the same negotiating table, Contadora also offered them a genuine opportunity, in face-to-face meetings, to design effective mechanisms of nonaggression and peaceful coexistence. Contadora's first task, certainly not an easy one, was to bring the five governments together. Not only was it necessary to place the states under Contadora's diplomatic jurisdiction; it was also necessary to persuade them that proceeding in this way was more beneficial than seeking a different forum, either on their own initiative or under pressure from Washington.

In Search of Peace on Paper

On 20 April 1983 the Contadora foreign ministers held the initial joint meeting with representatives of Honduras, El Salvador, Nicaragua, Costa Rica, and Guatemala in an effort to set the general rules for negotiations. A few days later, however, an obstacle appeared when Costa Rica, ignoring Contadora, accused Nicaragua before the OAS of a troop incursion into its territory. From that point on, Costa Rica would try repeatedly to obtain international backing against Nicaragua in the OAS,[7] where the United States could easily force adoption of resolutions in its favor and against Nicaragua. Far from facilitating conciliation, such an outcome would have instigated a confrontation among Latin Americans as occurred in the cases of Guatemala in 1954 and Cuba in 1962 and 1964. To prevent the Central American issue from being moved to the OAS became a prime objective of Contadora.

Paradoxically, Contadora was able to use Costa Rica's claim against Nicaragua to validate its procedural criteria and legitimize its mediating role. On 7 May the OAS Council rejected Costa Rica's claim and asked Contadora to intervene. A few days later Contadora's ministers agreed to form a commission to observe and render an opinion on the events taking place on the Costa Rica–Nicaragua border. Although nothing concrete was achieved and tensions between the two countries eventually increased, the commission formally initiated the process, through consultation and coordination, of drafting and discussing proposals that would characterize the subsequent endeavors of Contadora.[8] The commission's goal was to persuade the Central American countries to sign an agreement or a treaty that would commit them to (1) begin a process of disarmament, (2) refrain from aggressive and destabilizing actions against one another, (3) prevent foreign military advisors and the installation of foreign military bases in their countries, (4) refrain from arms traffic in the region, (5) resolve their differences peacefully, and (6) promote national reconciliation, human rights, social development, and democracy.

The first, and thus far the only, summit meeting of the four presidents of the Contadora countries took place in Cancún, Mexico, in July 1983. The resulting Declaration of Cancún formalized the basic concerns of Contadora: (1) control of the arms race; (2) elimination of foreign advisors; (3) creation of demilitarized zones; (4) prohibition of political or military activities in any country intended to destabilize another country; (5) elimination of arms traffic; and (6) prohibition of aggressive or political intervention in the internal affairs of another country. These criteria served as the basis for subsequent Contadora documents, the first of which, the Document of Objectives, was presented to the Central Americans in September 1983. Its twenty-one points, the Contadora nations asserted, had to be embodied in any agreement to strive for peace in the region.[9] In December, before the first anniversary of Contadora, the second document, entitled Norms for the Execution of Commitments Assumed in the Document of Objectives, was issued.[10] The favorable response of the Central American governments to the principles outlined by Contadora fed the illusion that a concrete agreement, or at least a firm basis for such an agreement, could be achieved quickly.

In June 1984 Contadora presented the Central American foreign ministries with a draft of the Act of Peace and Cooperation for Central America, setting 15 July as the deadline for comments and proposals for amendments.[11] By that date, supposedly, all points of the draft would have been widely discussed and would win a general consensus. This hope, however, was illusory, and the concept of progress in negotiations proved to be a mirage. When the nature of the proposed accords became known, the U.S. Department of State protested that their adoption would unfairly favor Nicaragua inasmuch as they did not guarantee that the Sandinistas would really abide by them. Honduras, El Salvador, and Costa Rica, influenced largely by Washington, raised objections to the accords, proposed substantial changes and reforms, and expressed doubts about Contadora's ability to guarantee fulfillment of the agreements and Nicaragua's compliance. In November, after numerous consultations which merely sharpened differences, Nicaragua—until that time the only country to express its willingness to sign the agreement without reservations—declared that it would not sign the Contadora peace act if it was altered in any way.[12]

At that point Contadora's mystique collapsed and a painful period of internal struggle and attrition began. The very existence of Contadora was threatened by several disintegrating tendencies, some arising from its own deteriorating process and others from inherent problems until then obscured by the earlier optimism. Honduras, Costa Rica, and El Salvador, openly encouraged by the U.S. State Department, bombarded Contadora with new proposals that would have required the reinitiation of negotiations. These initiatives targeted Nicaragua, now regarded as the instigator of regional conflict, rather than assigning responsibility to all five countries for peace in the region.

Even while incorporating the suggestions of those impugning the act, Contadora sought to maintain control of its original agenda and to resist the challenge by U.S. allies to its freedom of action. These efforts nearly caused the breakdown of agreement among the four sponsors of negotiation. Venezuela wanted Nicaragua to yield, on the grounds that its intransigence would wreck the efforts toward peace and prevent the signing of the

Contadora Peace Act. On the contrary, Mexico, concerned about its credibility, hoped to keep Contadora from becoming one more instrument of U.S. opposition to the Sandinistas. Panama and Colombia wavered, shifting from one position to another according to circumstances and the harshness of the winds blowing from the north.

The Central American countries identified themselves less and less with the Contadora initiative. Nicaragua feared that the proposed agreement, far from ensuring a halt to U.S. aggression, would seriously limit its own defense and would become an advantage to its opponents. Guided by this concern and ignoring Mexico's advice, the Sandinistas withdrew from the Contadora forum and took the debate to the UN Security Council and General Assembly, where they have found many Third World countries sympathetic to their cause. For its part, Costa Rica repeatedly urged that the OAS invoke the Inter-American Reciprocal Assistance Treaty (Rio Treaty) to assist in its defense of its border in conflicts with Nicaragua, provoked in part by Costa Rica's tolerance of contra activities on its territory. The frequent bypassing of Contadora led the four governments to insist that any discussion of the issue in the United Nations or the OAS be based on the documents and resolutions of Contadora and not on the request of one of the parties in conflict.

After an important Contadora meeting had to be canceled early in 1985 because of another incident between Costa Rica and Nicaragua (the capture of a Nicaraguan army deserter sheltered in the Costa Rican embassy in Managua), the Latin American countries came to recognize the imminent danger of Contadora's demise.[13] In July 1985, to avert that danger, a support group comprising Peru, Argentina, Brazil, and Uruguay was organized in Peru.[14] The cooperation of these South American countries revitalized Contadora and raised new hopes. Latin American support, however, was not enough to neutralize the United States or to pressure the Central American states to sign a peace agreement. The third Contadora anniversary, in January 1986, was marked by promulgation of the Caraballeda declaration, signed by the Contadora and support group countries. It called for conciliation rather than for celebration of efforts toward peace.[15] After more than three years of a fruitless search for peace, it became clear that, so long as the United States rejected the negotiating option, all further efforts would be in vain.

The United States Versus Contadora

Although no country had been willing to address the problem politically, each knew that the most serious obstacle to Contadora was the Reagan administration. From the beginning of 1983, Washington showed its determination to prevent Latin American initiatives from influencing the outcome of the regional conflict, from limiting its own scope of action, and from facilitating a cessation of hostilities which would guarantee the survival of the Sandinista regime.[16] Reagan always looked upon Contadora as a development opposed to U.S. interests, inspired by the anti-American and pro-Sandinista inclinations of some of its participants. Contadora's proposed solutions to Central American problems were looked upon as alien to U.S. concerns for national security.

The Reagan administration manifested its indifference to Contadora at its creation, and soon thereafter, on 28 April 1983, named a special envoy to explore prospects for a political settlement of Central America's problems.[17] In July, one day after he received a letter from the four presidents of the Contadora countries inviting the United States to cooperate in the search for peace in the area, Reagan gave another revealing response in announcing plans for military and naval maneuvers in Central America, Ahuas Taras II (Big Pine II). Immediately thereafter, on 21 July, the White House appointed the Kissinger Commission, a bipartisan body directed to recommend political measures to resolve the Central American problems. The commission's report, presented in January 1984, totally ignored Contadora's point of view, saying only that "the interests of the four Contadora countries are not identical, nor coincidental to those of the United States, and hence the United States cannot use the Contadora process as a substitute for its policies."[18]

In other efforts to bypass or at least to neutralize Contadora, the United States convoked other forums and devised alternative mechanisms and initiatives to build consensus and promote multilateral actions. Unable to reestablish the Enders forum that had met in Costa Rica the preceding year, the Reagan administration tried unsuccessfully to revise the Council of Central American Armies (CONDECA), which had been inactive for fourteen years.[19] It was rivalries among Central Americans for leadership of the council, along with the suspicion that the real intent of the United States was to substitute CONDECA for its own troops in any intervention against Nicaragua, which defeated the attempt.

That the Reagan administration, unmindful of Latin American predilections for a peaceful solution, was committed to military options was confirmed on 25 October 1983. On that date, even as the Contadora nations were meeting in Panama, U.S. troops occupied the tiny island of Grenada. The pretexts for invasion were the political chaos following the fall of Prime Minister Maurice Bishop and the presence of Cuban advisors. At the same time the United States was continuing its military activities in Central America, including the shipment of huge quantities of arms to the area; the installation of military bases and contra camps in Honduras; the mining of Nicaraguan harbors; and the organization, training, and financing of the contras. It was also exerting political-economic pressure on the governments of Honduras and Costa Rica to cooperate in the anti-Sandinista campaigns.

Contadora could not, and did not even try, to halt these actions. Its promotion of a radically different solution raised no real barrier to the military-political strategy of the United States. Contadora's tactic was to run on a track parallel to that of the United States in the hope of reaching its goal of peace before the Reagan administration could achieve its objective of war. The Contadora governments considered it suicidal to cross the path of Reagan, and indeed in most circumstances such an attempt would be extremely imprudent. On occasion, however, Contadora might have been able to present an obstacle to Reagan's plans without incurring grave danger; for example, instead of seeking only a cautious dialogue with the Reagan administration it might have tried to convince Congress and the U.S. public of the legitimacy of its efforts toward a peaceful alternative. Contadora also failed to take advantage of an opportunity to invoke international law when the United States mined Nicaragua's harbors, rejecting a French offer to send minesweepers for removing the mines and to reestablish the right of free navigation in Central American waters.

Contadora: A Peace Without Attributes

In addition to U.S. opposition, the achievements of Contadora have been limited by the diplomatic environment in which it operates and by its deliberate exclusion of certain realities with which it cannot deal. The difficulty is most evident in the contradiction between Contadora's recognition of extraregional provocation as a major factor behind the confrontations among the Central American states, on the one hand, and on the other its assumption that this intervention does not inhibit the sovereign will of the states to negotiate. Contadora deliberations thus assume an abstract character, evident in the absence of political allegations in its documents in favor of or against a particular protagonist and in the concentration on general principles and behavioral norms to which all should subscribe. For example, in condemning the arming of irregular forces to destabilize a country's government from another country's territory, Contadora might be referring either to the contras in Nicaragua or to the guerrillas in El Salvador. References to foreign bases and advisors might mean the U.S. presence in Honduras and El Salvador or the Cuban and Soviet presence in Nicaragua. Contadora's assertion that states should abstain from initiating military and naval maneuvers in foreign countries is simply ignored by Washington, the main perpetrator of such exercises and a nonparticipant in Contadora. The United States believes that there is nothing to keep it from exercising its military superiority in areas neighboring on Nicaragua and El Salvador.

Although all states could agree on the abstract categorizing of the conflicts and the legal and diplomatic prescriptions to resolve them, the possibility for agreement is nonexistent when the commitment to fulfill particular responsibilities, in specific times and circumstances, is dealt with. At this point Contadora's negotiations come to a standstill. The legal nature of the diplomatic proceedings determines that peace is essentially the maintenance of the status quo, a disengagement or at least a cease-fire, without victors or losers. No one wins anything new in the negotiating arena, but everyone has to give up armed struggle or intimidation to achieve the overriding purpose of peace—a peace that holds no one responsible and consequently gives rise to opposite interpretations regarding what each party must do to fulfill the agreements. A peace that entails diplomatic agreements but does not include political negotiations places the parties in conflict at their point of origin.

Nevertheless, the achievement of Contadora—and one of its principal merits—is that it defines an agenda and proposes actions which are not limited to the boundaries imposed by the United States. To the extent that Contadora defines the conflicts to be resolved, the actors participating in them, and the instruments to be used in solving them, its proposals, if they are utopian, visualize a different utopia from that of the United States. And even if they do not impede the application of the Reagan strategy, they do neutralize whatever role the region's own diplomatic negotiations might play on behalf of that strategy.

Contadora: Limitations and Achievements

The dynamics of negotiation on Central America have paralleled, and responded to, the dynamics of confrontation of Reagan administration policy in the region. The highly uneven character of these two processes has been evident in the reactive nature of the Contadora efforts and their confinement to legal and diplomatic initiatives rather than significant political action.

Failure to achieve a peaceful settlement of regional conflicts cannot be attributed solely to the weakness of the instruments of negotiation. The major factors are the historical complexity of the social problems and power struggles within Central America and the aggressiveness and intransigence of the Reagan administration's policy. Nevertheless, negotiation efforts have been more a display of diplomatic skills than a real and effective political effort to block U.S. intervention or to prevent the escalation of war and tensions in the region. Contadora has been unable to meet the political challenges raised by the conflict and has failed to explore all the possible ways of thwarting U.S. actions in Central America.

One example is the failure of the Contadora countries to exercise their economic leverage with the Central American countries. This leverage might seem to be slight, given the difficulties faced by most of the Latin American countries because of the debt crisis. Nevertheless, the four Contadora participants, especially Mexico and Venezuela, have pursued a modest program in the isthmus in the areas of trade, financing, and direct investments. Although limited in volume, economic activity could be specifically targeted to meet the needs of the Central American countries so as to lessen their dependence on U.S. aid; it could also be used to reward fulfillment of peace commitments. Mexico and the other Contadora countries have not taken advantage of these opportunities.

Another area in which Contadora might exercise stronger political leverage is in influencing U.S. public opinion and in lobbying Congress. The Contadora countries have clearly, and perhaps deliberately, not used their frequent opportunities to inform the U.S. media, universities, members of Congress, and business groups of the Contadora initiatives and their compatibility with long-term U.S. interests in the region. Apart from occasional press reports, statements from formal meetings of Contadora, or visits to Washington and New York by Contadora officials, the U.S. public has received little information about the Contadora initiatives.

Supporters of Contadora claim that its primary and undeniable achievements have been to prevent direct armed intervention by the United States in El Salvador and Nicaragua and to keep Central American armies from engaging in a fratricidal struggle. Yet there is no convincing proof that either of these accomplishments is attributable to the efforts of the Contadora group. For example, the first claim would be valid only if the United States had intended to send troops to Central America or if Contadora had presented the only obstacle to such an invasion. In fact, the Reagan administration has followed the versatile strategy of demonstrating U.S. armed power while limiting its use in the so-called low intensity war. In this way the United States has been able to wear down its adversaries, align the governments and armies of the area, neutralize dissenting forces and voices, create a limited consensus in Congress, and legitimate the position of protagonists allied to its cause. In essence, Reagan has succeeded in setting the stage for a political, economic, and military siege against the Sandinistas in Nicaragua and also in keeping the Salvadoran regime viable.

By making the possibility of an invasion credible and at times apparently imminent, the Reagan administration may have achieved more than it would have by an actual armed intervention. The point here is not to eliminate the possibility of a U.S. invasion but to question the claim that Contadora has been able to prevent it. The forces restraining Reagan are to be found, not in external pressures, but in internal U.S. politics: public opinion, the media, and Congress. And, as noted above, despite its appeal to U.S. liberals and Democrats, Contadora has been extremely cautious about projecting itself into the United States; consequently, it has been unable to play a decisive role in political debate in the United States.

Nor has Contadora been responsible for preventing an anti-Sandinista regional war that might embroil Honduras, El Salvador, and/or Guatemala. The fact is that Reagan's Nicaragua policy is not sufficiently mature to have unleashed a generalized war among neighboring countries. The Sandinistas themselves have been careful to avoid actions that might cause such an outbreak. Moreover, the Central American governments have excellent reasons for shunning a fratricidal conflict, despite their differences with the Sandinistas. In any event, the frictions between Nicaragua and its two neighbors, Honduras and Costa Rica, have not only continued but have also increased in intensity.

At the same time it would be incorrect to say that Contadora has served no purpose or to deny that prospects for a negotiated peace have been increased because of its efforts. A major achievement has been to bring all the countries of the region, which had lost the ability even to talk to one another, to the negotiating table. Contadora has legitimized itself as the only multilateral forum for the discussion of regional problems, a forum recognized by the United Nations and international political forces as appropriate for exploring the prospects for a peaceful agreement in Central America. The eminently Latin American nature of Contadora, and its international reputation, have prevented Washington from getting the OAS to act on its behalf or from establishing its own forums to initiate multilateral actions against Nicaragua. Contadora occupies an international space that deprives U.S. diplomacy of alternatives and resources.

In fact, Contadora's prestige and credibility are based less on its actual performance in the Central American peace process than on the support it has gained among Latin American governments as a concrete example of hemispheric cooperation. Contadora and its support group are seen in Latin America as a new arena for collective diplomacy, independent of the United States, where Latin countries can discuss their mutual problems, strengthen their criteria and ideas on inter-America relations, and attempt to neutralize manipulations and pressures from Washington. The initiative of Mexico, Venezuela, Colombia, and Panama, later joined by Argentina, Brazil, Peru, and Uruguay, is seen less as an effective instrument for negotiation in Central America than a conscious effort to revive the spirit of inter-American diplomacy and to offer an alternative to the docile pro–United States stance of the Organization of American States.

Negotiation Prospects

The Iran-contra hearings have revealed to Congress the weakness of the Reagan administration strategies and have diminished the legitimacy of the contras. These revelations may lead to a revision of U.S. policy based on accepting the existence of the Sandinista regime and the abandonment of efforts to overthrow it or change its character.[20]

One possible implication is a return to a more narrowly defined concept of the national interest and of U.S. security in Central America. From the conservative perspective of the Reagan administration, national security can be preserved only by gaining absolute political, ideological, and military dominion throughout the isthmus. Such undisputed power would not only prohibit the transfer of Soviet, Cuban, or East European arms to the area and the expulsion of all foreign advisors from Nicaragua; it would also entail the overthrow of any indigenous political group not tractable to U.S. demands. In other words, for the Reagan White House national security is nothing less than the establishment of hegemony.

The Iran-contra affair and the widespread criticism of covert operations as a legitimate tool of foreign policy have damaged the validity of Reagan's ambitious approach to national security. More than the president's authorization to sell arms to Iran—in disregard of his own public commitments—the diversion of funds thus obtained to buy arms for the contras, circumventing explicit congressional restrictions, has attracted widespread condemnation by members of Congress.

The main obstacles to a real change of policy toward Nicaragua in Washington are the reluctance of most Republicans and many Democrats to accept the Sandinistas as reliable partners in negotiation with Washington and the fear that the United States could not enforce an eventual agreement with the Nicaraguans. Even under a new Democratic administration in 1989, financial support to the contras could be used as a negotiating card to bring the Sandinistas to a substantial political compromise with Washington.

For some U.S. politicians, a possible solution in Central America—saving face and at the same time avoiding the direct use of U.S. troops—is to condition recognition of the authority of the Sandinista regime on Nicaragua's willingness to terminate its dependence on the Soviet Union. In contrast with the Reagan administration approach, the concept of Nicaraguan neutrality is less ambitious and less ideological, contemplating only concrete strategic and geopolitical objectives. According to this concept, the ultimate interest of the United States would be to prevent a Soviet presence in Nicaragua and not to decide what kind of government the country should have. In fact, proponents of the idea claim that they could accept a Marxist regime in Nicaragua.[21]

In such a scenario, what would be the role of Contadora? Even if they were more receptive to the idea of negotiation with Nicaragua, many Republicans and Democrats would be unwilling to accept the nonintervention and self-determination criteria of Contadora. On the contrary, as the Reagan strategies continue to show their futility, many U.S. politicians might try to impose their own agenda on Contadora, suggesting that the group could survive only by explicitly accommodating itself to U.S. positions.

Contadora might also be viewed in Washington as a tool for bringing Latin American pressure to bear on the Sandinistas, forcing them to relinquish control over key areas of power in return for suspension of U.S. military, political, and economic actions against Nicaragua. This kind of role might be acceptable to some Contadora countries, like Venezuela, but it would be highly embarrassing for others, like Mexico; it would also negate the principles of self-determination and nonintervention explicit in the legal framework of the Contadora negotiations.

In the event of a U.S. policy change based on Nicaragua's strict neutrality, Contadora could be called upon to devise the rules for implementation of disarmament, departure of foreign advisors from Nicaragua, and elimination of any Sandinista assistance to rebels in El Salvador, or anywhere else. It is unlikely, however, that the United States would negotiate its own military retreat and the dismantling of the contra forces within the Contadora framework. Nor is it likely that U.S. politicians, whether liberals or conservatives, would accept the jurisdiction of Contadora, or of any other international organization, over removal of the U.S. military apparatus and withdrawal of personnel from Central America. At best, Contadora would be acceptable only if its role was limited to guaranteeing that the Sandinistas would honor their undertakings in any agreement, leaving to the United States the implementation of its own peace commitments. And the United States would almost certainly demand that the sanctions against Sandinista violations of neutrality be enforced by the United States.

It is noteworthy that the most viable version of this Nicaraguan neutrality option has come, not from Contadora or any of its members and supporters in Latin America, but from Costa Rica, which has distinguished itself as one of the most belligerent detractors of Contadora. The so-called Arias peace plan, presented in February 1987, attracted more attention in the U.S. Congress than most of the documents issued by Contadora, largely because it explicitly addressed the political and military questions raised by the conflict and proposed hard political commitments, not simply legal and diplomatic procedures. From the perspective of Costa Rica, Nicaragua is the principal obstacle to peace, and to some extent the plan reflects this view. Yet its specific content is not necessarily unacceptable to the Sandinistas; the Arias plan, surprisingly, is the most attractive proposition of coexistence made thus far to the Sandinistas by any of their neighbors.[22]

In some political circles in the United States, the Arias plan has been perceived as a blueprint for discussion of a new U.S. approach to peace with Nicaragua. This perception has been reinforced by the fact that the Costa Ricans have lobbied their initiative in the United States in a way that Contadora never pushed its program.[23] Although the Contadora group expressed support for the Costa Rican plan, Arias did not want to negotiate it within Contadora; rather, he sought approval in a series of consultations parallel to those sponsored by the Contadora countries. The text of the plan makes explicit references to the Contadora proposals, but the draft specifies that Contadora would become involved only after the document had been formally subscribed to by the respective parties and after a supervisory committee, including Contadora, the support group, and the general secretaries of the UN and the OAS, had been appointed.

Even if the United States enters into direct negotiations with Nicaragua and agrees to a de facto recognition of the Sandinistas, the problem of negotiations in Central America will not be solved. The civil war in El Salvador and instability in Guatemala will create tensions and will supply incentives for U.S. intervention. Washington will remain suspicious of the Sandinistas, perhaps blaming them for all regional disturbances, an attitude that would certainly undermine any agreements between the Sandinistas and the White House. It is predictable that Contadora's comprehensive approach and its Latin American character will continue to have diplomatic importance, perhaps close to the center of discussions. If it maintains its political elusiveness and does not shift from abstraction to concreteness in its proposals, however, it will continue to fall short of expectations.

Notes

1. *El Día* (Mexico City), 22 June 1979.

2. For an analysis of the Central American situation from the viewpoint of European social democracy and an account of Socialist International initiatives in 1981, see Pierre Schori, *El Desafío Europeo en Centro América* (San José: Editorial Universitaria Centroamericana [EDUCA], 1982).

3. *Cuadernos de Política Exterior Mexicana* I,1 (Mexico City: CIDE, 1984): 205–209.

4. See Stella Calloni and Rafael Cribari, *La Guerra Encubierta contra Contadora* (Panama City: Centro de Capacitación Social, 1982), p. 2.

5. After four years of frustrated diplomatic efforts to secure the signing of the Peace Act, as of June 1987 only one of the founding foreign ministers, Bernardo Sepúlveda of Mexico, continued to represent his country in Contadora. Either the others were removed from their positions, or their governments lost in elections or were overthrown. If changes in Contadora's leadership have demonstrated the endurance of the initiative, they have also been symptom and cause of the fragility of political consensus within the group. See Adolfo Aguilar Zinser and Veronica Marina Cortés, *Contadora: Crónica de una Paz Inconclusa* (Mexico City: CIDE, 1987).

6. Between the first meeting of Contadora in January 1983 and the April follow-up, there was strong international endorsement of mediation: in January the Coordinating Bureau of the Non-Aligned Group, meeting in Managua, backed Contadora and declared itself in favor of a negotiated peace; in March, Pope John Paul II visited the area and spoke insistently for the same objective; in the same month President Felipe González of Spain offered to mediate in the conflict, and Nicaragua announced in the United Nations Security Council its willingness to negotiate with Honduras in a direct bilateral summit, with Mexico and Venezuela as witnesses. President Betancourt of Colombia took advantage of the favorable conditions to restate the Contadora initiative more forcefully. See Aguilar Zinser and Cortés, *Contadora*, pp. 3–6.

7. Several factors were responsible for Costa Rica's involvement in a conflict with Nicaragua which could have been avoided: lack of political vision on the part of Costa Rica's president, Luis Alberto Monge; pressures from the United States; and the sympathy of Costa Rica's right wing for the contras.

8. Aguilar Zinser and Cortés, *Contadora*, p. 7.

9. Calloni and Cribari, *La Guerra Encubierta*, pp. 164–166. The twenty-one points were divided into five categories: relations among states, peace and internal stability, national security, refugees and human rights, and cooperation among states for social and economic development.

10. Ibid., p. 235.

11. Aguilar Zinser and Cortés, *Contadora*, pp. 41–43.

12. Ibid., p. 69.

13. Adolfo Aguilar Zinser, "El Caso Urbina Lara," series of five articles in *Uno Más Uno* (Mexico City), 6–10 May 1985.

14. Aguilar Zinser and Cortés, *Contadora*, p. 173.

15. The Caraballeda declaration called for a renewal of negotiations and reiterated the points of earlier documents. It was subsequently endorsed by the Central American foreign ministers.

16. *Excelsior* (Mexico City), 8 September 1985.

17. Aguilar Zinser and Cortés, *Contadora*, p. 196.

18. *Report of the National Bipartisan Commission on Central America* (Washington: Government Printing Office, 1984).

19. Calloni and Cribari, *La Guerra Encubierta*, p. 177.

20. De facto acceptance of the Sandinistas would not necessarily lead to negotiations between the United States and Nicaragua. As exemplified by Cuba in the 1960s, the costs and difficulties of toppling a revolutionary government might convince Washington that the only valid choice is to pull back, accepting the regime as a reality but not recognizing it as a legitimate international actor.

21. The idea of "Finlandizing" Nicaragua has been advanced by some U.S. politicians. According to Zbigniew Brzezinski, national security advisor in the Carter administration, it would achieve two basic goals: (1) strategic security for the United States and its southern neighbors and (2) self-determination for Central America. Nicaragua's neutrality would be specifically protected against violations by previously defined and multilaterally accepted instruments of U.S. coercion, ranging from economic and diplomatic sanctions to the use of military force (remarks by Brzezinski at the conference, "Study Group on U.S. and Mexican Relations," Overseas Development Council, Huaxtepec, Morelos, Mexico, 3 April 1987).

22. The peace plan presented by President Oscar Arias of Costa Rica in February 1987 calls for the demilitarization and democratization of the region under specific rules that initially seemed to be directed exclusively to Nicaragua. With later amendments, however, the plan includes an implicit but clear and unprecedented recognition of the established Sandinista order and of the validity of its constitution. It is also clear that the real purpose of the plan is not to demand far-reaching internal changes in Nicaragua but to explore the demilitarization of the Sandinista regime in exchange for a cease-fire formula that applies to other countries fighting internal wars, calls for dismantling of the armed contra bands, and specifies disarmament requirements for all nations in the region. For the full text, see "Procedimientos para Establecer la Paz Firme y Duradera en Centro America," Presidencia de la República de Costa Rica, 15 February 1987, mimeograph.

23. The U.S. Senate passed a resolution, by 97 to 1, supporting the Arias plan, and the House Foreign Affairs Committee approved a $20 million "peace bonus" to "encourage" the diplomatic efforts of the Costa Rican government.

PART TWO

Central America: External Pressures and Internal Dynamics

6

The Central American Economy: Conflict and Crisis

Xabier Gorostiaga and Peter Marchetti

Central America is passing through an economic crisis of unprecedented proportions. After enjoying the steadiest economic growth in Latin America for nearly three decades (1950–1978), all the countries in the region, regardless of the severity of their military-political convulsions, have entered into a prolonged economic crisis. As noted below, the "miracle" of Central American growth in 1950–1970 was a miracle without a future. Although the growth continued in the 1970s, its basis was more artificial, and in the 1980s it yielded to a crisis that had been brewing during the preceding decades.

The performance of the gross domestic product of each country during the past thirty-five years (see Table 6.1) demonstrates the magnitude of the current economic crisis. These statistics do not show what eight years (1978–1985) of increasing economic misery have meant for Central America's majorities, on whom the burden has fallen most heavily. During this period the levels of real income per capita dropped by 33 percent. Guatemala and Costa Rica regressed to the levels of 1972, Honduras to that of 1970; in the countries most affected by war, Nicaragua fell back to the level of 1965 and El Salvador to that of 1960. The poorer classes have experienced a decline in their standard of living even more precipitous than that shown by the national averages. With the prolongation of the military conflict, the prospect for improvement in the economic situation in the coming decade is dim.

The continuation and the sharpening of the economic crisis have intensified the search for its causes. What is significant is that for the first time in Central America, not only economists and other specialists but also the

This article is based on a broader work published in a special issue of the Spanish edition of *Envío* (Managua: Instituto Centroamericano Histórico, January–February 1986). It was translated by David Ayón, Department of Political Science, University of California, San Diego.

population sectors suffering the most are seeking an answer, and the different groups are coming up with divergent explanations.

Interpretations of the Crisis

Some observers of the Central American crisis, taken in by the rhythm of economic growth between 1950 and 1978, assert that the problem is not the inequality of economic structures, but a lack of internal democracy in the various countries. They argue that what Nicaragua needed was a Raúl Alfonsín, not a Sandinista social transformation; that in El Salvador, Duarte should control the military more effectively; and that the programs for change advanced by the Sandinista Front for National Liberation (FSLN) and the Farabundo Martí Front for National Liberation (FMLN) are not realistic in the backyard of the United States.

This view is mistaken for two reasons. First, it ignores the specificity of the emergence of a new historical subject[1] with a viable program of armed struggle in Central America and not in other Latin American countries suffering the same economic hardships. Second, it presupposes that people rise up when their misery increases, whereas they really rebel when economic growth allows them to lift their heads. Such growth evokes superficial changes in the economy but opens cracks in the social system which, in turn, leads to questioning the validity of existing structures.

The failure to take underlying structural inequalities into account is also harmful because it implies that all was well in the isthmus before the Sandinista revolution began and the FMLN emerged in El Salvador. These observers either ignore the inequality existing in Central American countries or assume it was a minor evil necessary for capitalist development. This philosophy helped to generate the Reagan strategy aimed at eliminating the FSLN, the FMLN-FDR (Democratic Revolutionary Front), and the Guatemalan National Revolutionary Unity (URNG); it also revived faith in the model of dependent capitalism which had seemingly yielded so many benefits during the preceding three decades. In other words, the failure to understand the economic specificity of the isthmus may lead to blaming the crisis on those sectors of the population which have suffered the most from it.[2]

In a different interpretation, some revolutionary militants, the well-to-do classes, and the Reagan administration hold that the principal cause of the economic crisis is the revolutionary wars that are raging in several Central American countries. They seem to believe that when the wars end the economic problem will be resolved. Although this opinion is shared by people across a broad ideological spectrum, we believe that it is illusory and that to propagate it serves only to mislead the poor with false hopes.

The economic crisis began to make itself felt in the 1970s. It was not generated by the armed struggle, as the rightist ideologues maintain; on the contrary, it was the crisis itself which triggered the new wave of armed struggle. The war has indeed deepened the crisis, but it does not follow that the achievement of peace and the restoration of political stability will automatically end the crisis.

In the following analysis we advance three hypotheses on the origins and development of the economic crisis and discuss eight tendencies that will probably affect its direction in the near future.

Three Hypotheses on the Central American Economies

1. Central American Economies in the International Market

Our first hypothesis is that, given the way they are structured and the way they function in the international market, the Central American economies are not viable, regardless of whether their governments are of the left or of the right. Central America's economic recovery therefore requires not only (1) peace, (2) an end to restricted democracies, and (3) the social reforms that the dominant classes refused to make earlier, but also (4) a new form of regional integration and (5) a new mode of insertion by the region as a whole in the international market by way of agro-industrialization and the diversification of exports.[3] The latter two changes should have been initiated in the period 1950–1978, when the extraordinary economic expansion was taking place.

The crisis presently afflicting the Central American economies is not an isolated phenomenon. Rather, it has coincided with fluctuations in the world economy which began to deepen in 1966 with the break from the postwar liberal Keynesian model of growth. In the 1970s, throughout Latin America, rates of profit in productive activities began to decline, speculative movements of capital notwithstanding. As part of the international recession during that decade, all Latin American countries rapidly became debtor nations, due to easy international credit policies.

What makes the crisis in Central America especially intense is not only that it followed three decades of steady growth but, above all, the particular vulnerability of the region's countries resulting from their participation in the international market as exporters of agricultural products. Their economies thus became overly vulnerable to the cycles of the world capitalist economy. The resulting Central American crisis is so severe that even if the changes listed above were initiated, it would be a long time before the majorities would benefit. And the military conflict, stimulated by U.S. aggression in the region, does not allow even the initiation of the enormous project of transformation Central America needs if it is to emerge from the crisis.

The situation in the isthmus in the decades preceding advent of the crisis was exceedingly complex. The twenty years (1950–1970) of stable economic growth and superficial changes did not bring needed structural changes. The growth, far from being self-sustaining, was artificially engendered by external factors; as import-substitution industrialization was not integrated with agriculture and natural resources, no internal market sufficient to generate its own demand was created. Economic growth over a period of nearly thirty years did not result in the accumulation of funds because resources were concentrated in a small proportion of the population. The

TABLE 6.1
Rate of Growth of GDP,[a] 1950-1985 (percentage)

Year	Guatemala	El Salvador	Honduras	Nicaragua	Costa Rica
1950-1960	3.7	4.8	2.8	5.4	6.4
1960-1970	5.2	5.5	5.0	6.5	5.9
1970-1978	6.0	5.4	4.7	3.9	6.3
1978-1983	0.8	-4.6	1.7	-2.0	-0.4
1984	-2.6	-1.5	-0.6	-5.8	3.6
1985[b]	-1.1	1.6	2.6	-2.6	1.6

[a]At constant prices of 1970
[b]Preliminary figures
Source: Comisión Económica para América Latina (CEPAL), Centroamérica: Bases de una política de Reactivación y Desarrollo (Santiago, Chile, May 1985), pp. 3, 22.

beneficiaries of the accumulation of resources indulged in excessive foreign-oriented and artificial consumption, a pattern that did not permit the growth to be transformed into permanent forms of self-sustaining development.

The phenomenon of economic growth without structural development is basically what a recent study by the Economic Commission for Latin America (ECLA) calls "additive development" (desarrollo aditivo): "The considerable transformations of the three postwar decades were characterized essentially by the manner in which they juxtaposed new economic and social strata to the old within a process of change and modernization which did not fundamentally threaten the preexisting economic structure."[4]

An important factor in the economic growth in Central America between 1950 and 1970 was the conservative management of the economy at a time when the terms of trade were favorable. The stability depended on management of four macroeconomic factors: (1) the balance of payments; (2) the balance between supply and demand; (3) the fiscal balance; and (4) the monetary balance. For the most part, from 1950 to 1970 the Central American economies had no debts, no inflation, no fiscal deficits, and no monetary instability. Tables 6.2–6.6, however, show that, from 1970 on, indebtedness, inflation, and budget deficits were beginning to afflict all Central American countries. Monetary instability and devaluations were affecting Costa Rica and Nicaragua by the end of the 1970s and Guatemala and El Salvador in the 1980s. In the 1970s those responsible for Central America's economic management lost control of the basic mechanisms that produced the region's earlier stable balances and economic growth. The bourgeoisie, squeezed by the oligarchies and threatened by class competition or by the military's corrupt demand for patronage, neglected the macroeconomic factors at the very time when the terms of trade for the region's traditional products in the world market were favorable.

During the more artificial growth of the 1970s, the first significant extension of education and health benefits to the majority, and the establishment of patterns of consumption similar to those of Latin American countries with

TABLE 6.2
Public Debt, 1960-1984 (in millions of U.S. dollars)

Country	1960	1970	1978	1980	1982	1984
Guatemala	24.2	106.3	373.6	105.3	150.4	242.0
El Salvador	23.6	87.7	322.2	117.6	168.3	230.0
Honduras	14.0	90.1	591.1	151.0	180.0	225.0
Nicaragua	5.0	145.8	962.8	157.9	279.7	425.9
Costa Rica	26.3	134.2	962.8	318.3	349.7	405.0
Central America	93.1	564.1	3,212.5	850.1	1,128.1	1,527.9

Sources: CEPAL, *Centroamérica: Evolución Económica de la Posguerra* (Santiago, Chile, January 1980), and Coordinadora Regional de Investigaciones Económicas y Sociales (CRIES), *Estadísticas Centroamericanas* (Managua, Nicaragua, 1985).

TABLE 6.3
Balance of Payments, Current Accounts, 1979-1985 (in millions of U.S. dollars)

Country	1979	1980	1981	1982	1983	1984[a]	1985[a]
Costa Rica	-559.0	-663.0	-407.6	-252.6	-284.1	-216.5	-220.5
El Salvador	21.3	30.7	-250.2	-143.3	-65.2	-126.6	-50.9
Guatemala	-204.9	-163.9	-588.4	-380.2	-226.4	-382.0	-246.2
Honduras	-191.6	-316.7	-302.6	-215.1	-225.5	-298.4	-262.7
Nicaragua	180.4	-412.5	-554.2	-479.3	-562.1	-635.4	-834.8

[a]Inter-American Development Bank (IDB) estimates, provisional figures.
Source: IDB, *Economic and Social Progress in Latin America: 1986 Report* (Washington, D.C., 1986).

large middle classes, disguised the economic cancer that was undermining the system: the narrow inegalitarian base of the economies. The Central American countries (except for Costa Rica) were unable to effect economic and social reforms that could have made dependent capitalism politically viable, by creating middle classes large enough to sustain parliamentary regimes and civil societies of adequate sophistication to present an alternative to the armed struggle. The difficulty was evident in the military annulment of electoral victories by Christian Democrats and Social Democrats in El Salvador in the early 1970s. The fact that there was little industrialization prior to the 1960s partly explains the relative weakness of the middle class in these countries. In other words, Central America's societies missed the opportunity to emulate Latin American dependent capitalism, partly because their economies were smaller, but also because they had failed to diversify production beyond the primary agricultural phase during the long period of postwar economic growth.

The old dominant classes might be blamed for their failure to perceive or to act upon the national interest and to hazard diversification of their economic bases, as well as for their irresponsible use of capital during the boom years. After all, the crisis had emerged while they were managing

TABLE 6.4
Debt Service as Percent of Exports, 1960-1983

Country	1960	1965	1970	1976	1978	1980	1982	1983	Relative Increase (%) 1970-1979	Relative Increase (%) 1978-1983
Guatemala	1.7	4.9	7.4	1.5	2.9	2.6	6.8	11.0	-68	279
El Salvador	2.6	3.9	3.6	3.8	3.5	3.3	5.6	6.7	-3	91
Honduras	2.6	2.6	2.8	6.3	17.2	20.2	34.2	18.2	561	6
Nicaragua	4.3	4.2	10.4	12.2	14.3	11.9	43.7	20.0	37	40
Costa Rica	5.2	7.9	9.7	9.1	21.1	25.1	32.3	66.6	117	215

Sources: CEPAL, Centroamérica: Evolución Económica de la Posguerra (Santiago, Chile, January 1980), and CRIES, Estadísticas Centroamericanas (Managua, Nicaragua, 1985).

TABLE 6.5
Central American Fiscal Deficit, 1972-1984 (in millions of Central American dollars)[a]

Country	1972	1974	1976	1978	1980	1982	1984	Relative Increase (%) 1972-1980	Relative Increase (%) 1980-1984
Central America	167.6	221.6	457.9	560.7	1,360.0	1,433.1	1,810.1	711	29
	(2.7)	(2.5)	(3.8)	(3.4)	(6.5)	(7.0)	(7.0)		
Guatemala	53.4	40.7	137.9	8.9	352.1	405.7	360.8	559	2
	(2.5)	(1.3)	(3.2)	(0.1)	(4.5)	(4.7)	(3.8)		
El Salvador	12.5	37.2	77.3	109.6	213.9	268.8	25.5	1,611	-82
	(1.1)	(2.4)	(3.4)	(3.6)	(6.0)	(7.5)	(0.6)		
Honduras	30.4	24.9	65.0	111.8	198.5	339.1	323.3	552	63
	(3.6)	(2.4)	(5.1)	(6.2)	(7.8)	(12.2)	(10.1)		
Nicaragua	31.4	90.8	70.8	161.9	162.8	357.5	995.3	418	511
	(3.6)	(6.0)	(5.8)	(8.0)	(7.4)	(12.0)	(21.7)		
Costa Rica	39.9	28.0	106.9	168.5	432.7	62.0	105.2	984	-76
	(3.6)	(1.8)	(4.4)	(4.8)	(9.0)	(2.5)	(3.1)		

[a]Figures in parentheses indicate fiscal deficit as percent of GDP.
Source: Secretaría Permanente del Tratato General de Integración Económica Centroamericana (SIECA), Estadísticas macro-económicas de Centroamérica, 1971-1981 and 1980-1984.

TABLE 6.6
Rates of Inflation, 1977-1984

Country	1977	1978	1979	1980	1981	1982	1983	1984
Guatemala	12.6	7.9	11.4	12.3	13.7	0.2	5.4	7.4
El Salvador	11.8	13.3	15.9	18.9	19.0	11.7	20.0	21.7
Honduras	11.4	6.2	12.5	17.6	13.2	13.0	15.7	6.9
Nicaragua	11.4	4.6	48.2	35.3	23.9	24.8	30.9	--
Costa Rica	4.2	6.0	9.1	19.8	37.0	90.1	32.6	43.0

Sources: SIECA, Estadísticas macro-económicas de Centroamérica, 1971-1981 and 1980-1984, and CRIES, Estadísticas Centroamericanas (Managua, Nicaragua, 1985).

the economy in the long period of international growth. The functioning of capitalism on the periphery is, however, difficult for domestic investors. If, for example, coffee, sugar, and cotton producers had paid the large majority of rural workers wages adequate to cover their basic needs, and at the same time had paid taxes sufficient to sustain the structures necessary for long-term economic development, the producers would have gone bankrupt. The easiest solution was to use military power to prevent the structural changes required by the regional economies. The eventual result was a social and political explosion without the social cushion of a middle stratum that could have restrained the confrontation of classes. Instead, the emerging sectors of the middle class joined the armed insurrections in Nicaragua, El Salvador, and Guatemala.

Because the economies of the isthmus were so vulnerable to the cycles of the world capitalist economy, the Central American investor was less inclined than other Latin American businesspersons to invest in terms of national priorities. This tendency is apparent in four areas.

A. Investment efforts by the private sector have been low and declining. While the average rate of investment in Latin America in the period 1960–1980 was fluctuating between 20 and 25 percent, in Central America it fluctuated between 14 and 19 percent, according to a recent study by Programa Regional de Empleo para America Latina y El Caribe (PREALC).[5] Furthermore, private investment, which in 1950 was 70 to 80 percent of total investment, by 1980 had fallen below, sometimes substantially below, 50 percent in all Central American countries. Foreign investment also declined, dropping from 30 percent of total investment in the industrial sector in the 1960s to only 8 percent in the 1970s. Faced with this deteriorating situation, the state has increasingly had to assume the role of investor.

B. Not only did the dominant classes reduce their investments in the 1970s, they also paid minimal taxes. The state did not complement its new role as investor by introducing the necessary tax reforms. Each country's tax burden remained virtually stable at about 10 percent despite substantial increases in public spending (see Table 6.7). In particular, the industrial sector spawned by the Central American Common Market (CACM), which utilized large amounts of foreign exchange, remained exempt from taxation, a policy entailing an extraordinary sacrifice of fiscal revenues in all countries. By the end of the 1970s the majority of Third World governments, including those in Central America, were depending on international loans to augment public spending without resorting to new taxes, and these loans were often used for nonproductive investments. The resulting expansion of foreign debt began to accelerate rapidly in Central America in 1972 (see Table 6.2).

C. The investment that did take place was nonreproductive in the sense that modernization in both the industrial and rural sectors was not linked to past experience or to future prospects and that it did not enhance foreign exchange earning capacity. According to ECLA, the transformations realized were "minimally integrated either up or down."[6] That is, these investments did not give priority to using domestic raw materials, nor did they constitute

TABLE 6.7
Total Expenditure of Central Governments as Percentage of GDP

Country	1955	1960	1965	1970	1975	1980	1981	1982	1983	1984
Central America	10.6	11.2	11.3	11.6	15.8	19.3	20.2	20.4	23.3	23.9
Guatemala	9.5	9.3	10.6	9.9	12.5	15.2	16.9	14.4	12.1	10.9
El Salvador	10.9	12.2	10.9	10.3	13.4	17.2	19.8	20.5	28.0	22.1
Honduras	10.0	12.2	10.8	14.7	21.0	24.9	24.1	28.1	26.2	29.7
Nicaragua	12.4	11.1	11.2	11.8	19.4	29.5	32.4	37.4	56.4	55.1

Source: CEPAL, Centroamérica: Bases de una política de Reactivación y Desarrollo (Santiago, Chile, May 1985).

TABLE 6.8
Index of Minimum Wages in Selected Central American Countries, 1965-1979

Country	Minimum Industial Wages				Minimum Agricultural Wages			
	1965	1970	1975	1979	1965	1970	1975	1980
Guatemala	100	107	75	75	nd	100	89	79
El Salvador	100	117	87	95	100	94	86	80
Costa Rica	100	123	117	156	100	99	102	146
Panama	113	110	nd	100	93	131	nd	117

Note: nd = not determined.

Source: Programa Regional de Empleo para América Latina y El Caribe (PREALC), Modernización del mercado de trabajo y crisis en el istmo centroamericano, October 1985, p. 64.

a basis for the expansion of other economic activities. Furthermore, like other import-substitution industrialization projects, they failed to save on foreign exchange, partly because the cost of imported goods (sometimes for last-stage processing or assembly industries) more than made up for savings on former imports that were now produced locally. These investments merely converted foreign exchange into domestic currency. The industrial sector, which should have acted as a dynamic pole of capital accumulation, in fact played the opposite role of preventing the accumulation of national wealth. Supplies of foreign exchange which could have diversified the region's exports were channeled to industries such as Coca-Cola and those producing beer, cigarettes, and other items for domestic consumption.

D. The investments of the dominant classes indiscriminantly incorporated modern laborsaving technology (conserving a plentiful resource) and spent scarce resources in modernization that exceeded the region's possibilities for accumulation, generating neither employment nor foreign exchange in the Central American economies.

To recapitulate, the dominant classes, concerned mainly with profits, curtailed investments, and the investments they did make were damaging to the long-term health of the economy. When the state had to step in to replace these investors, it did so without increasing their taxes. Governments were thus forced to go into debt and run larger budget deficits to save their economies, in the process shattering the two most important economic macro balances. The region's foreign debt increased from $564.1 million in 1970 to $3.2 billion in 1978. Fiscal deficits rose by 1060 percent in the 1970s, from $122.9 million to $1.3 billion (see Tables 6.2 and 6.5). A vicious circle of inflation and monetary imbalances followed.

During the 1970s the economy had been held together by (1) a stable demand for Central American exports and (2) easy access to foreign credit. Increased foreign borrowing and budget deficits disguised the crisis, maintaining an artificial economic vitality. Favorable terms of trade helped avert an explosion. Another mechanism that postponed the crisis was a reduction in the wages of the poorest sectors between 1970 and 1980, especially in Guatemala and El Salvador (see Table 6.8).

By the end of the decade, however, the two major stabilizing factors had disappeared. The second oil shock of 1979–80 and the rapid deterioration of terms of trade (accelerated by the international recession and the high interest rates imposed by the United States) exacerbated the problems of the 1970s. With the recession, the demand for Central American products disappeared and their prices collapsed, particularly because the value of the exports was linked to the overvalued dollar. The jump in interest rates (from a traditional 7 percent to 8 percent and, in the worst instances, to 19 percent) made foreign loans and foreign exchange scarce, creating a major disequilibrium in the balance of payments and budget deficits and pushing all countries toward higher inflation and further currency devaluation.

Although the economic crisis of the 1980s represents a deepening of the same imbalances that had existed in the 1970s, the room for maneuvering to overcome the imbalances and to initiate reforms is now so narrow that the crisis is beyond control, leading to profound economic disorders.

2. From Economic Logic to Military Logic

Our second hypothesis is that with continuing warfare, economic logic gives way to an imposed military logic. This thesis has special validity in El Salvador and Nicaragua, where military budgets account for almost half of public spending. In El Salvador, basic social services have been cut as part of counterinsurgency policy, and the welfare of the armed forces has been emphasized over the country's economic needs. In Nicaragua, basic social services have also been cut and the assignment of cadres to the war zones impedes the promotion of mass organizations in the civil society, an effort that is crucial to counter the continuation of indirect U.S. intervention.

Although warfare has less impact on the economies of Honduras, Guatemala, and Costa Rica than on those of Nicaragua and El Salvador, these countries are nevertheless affected. The establishment of North American military bases in Honduras and the expansion of the Honduran army have profoundly changed the Honduran economy. In Guatemala the growth of militarism is evident from the increasing penetration by the armed forces into the government administration between 1982 and 1985. Costa Rica's neutrality has come under ever stronger pressure to yield to the establishment of a military force, as have also the social reforms initiated by the revolution of 1948, led by José Figueres. Furthermore, the debt crisis and budget deficits appeared in Costa Rica before they afflicted other Central American countries. The fact that the liberal reforms introduced in 1948 have not succeeded in protecting Costa Rica from the same external and internal imbalances that affect the rest of the isthmus is indicative of the long period of transformation and suffering which awaits the Central American people.

Given their history, Central American societies require more profound internal changes than the liberal ECLA-type reforms; above all, there must be changes in the way these countries participate in the international market to make them economically viable. All attempts to effect liberal reforms turn out to be unrealistic in a double sense: (1) the dominant classes and the military do not allow such reforms to be carried out; (2) more fundamentally, the reforms cannot guarantee the development and welfare of the Central American people. These two factors point to the weaknesses of the programs put forward by the centrist political parties, such as the Christian Democrats.

3. Subsidized and Geopoliticized Economies

Our third hypothesis is that the reinterpretation of the conflicts in Central America in an East-West framework has transformed the Central American economies into "subsidized and geopoliticized" economies. As noted above, in the 1970s the regional governments began to substitute foreign borrowing and deficit spending for investments by the dominant classes, thus initiating the subsidizing of their economies. The prolongation of the military conflict resulting from its geopolitical reinterpretation as an East-West confrontation and the sharpening of the economic crisis have deepened the subsidization process, but with foreign actors replacing the regional governments. If in the 1970s international finance capital, interested in recycling petrodollars, was the driving force of subsidy, in the 1980s a military-geopolitical logic prevails. External dependence has reached levels so irrationally high that, within this logic, a cutoff of or a substantial decrease in the flow of funds to any Central American country could bring about fundamental changes in its economic and political structures.

Guatemala, having maintained its own financial capacity, may be the exception to this rule, although its recent financial and fiscal decline suggests that its situation is similar to that of its neighbors. The only country in Central America to finance its own program of counterinsurgency, Guatemala finds itself in the same crisis partly because the business of a now generalized war and the military's management of the economy have generated not only rational costs, but also the irrational costs of corruption and the military's access to social class status. In Guatemala today, as in the other countries during the 1970s, the refusal of the national bourgeoisie to pay higher taxes forces the government to assume more debt, thus creating a fiscal crisis that could spill over into a deep socioeconomic crisis, as demonstrated in the popular uprisings beginning in August and September of 1985. The intransigence of the bourgeoisie over taxes is also driving Guatemala to increased dependence on U.S. aid,[7] which may bring its position on the Central American conflict closer to that of the United States. Only strong European financial support can halt this trend.

Eight Economic Tendencies in Central America

1. Economic Recolonization

External dependence in the form of subsidization of the Central American economies is growing rapidly. Whereas during the 1970s it was the growth of these economies which was subsidized, now larger amounts are required every year merely to slow the pace of economic contraction. The United States is the primary source of aid to Central American countries, except of course to Nicaragua. The political consequences of this financial involvement further aggravate the economic squeeze, leading to a process of economic recolonization or to the establishment of informal protectorates.

El Salvador is the most dramatic example of this process, as it represents a kind of Vietnamization of the Salvadoran economy, similar to the program carried on in that Southeast Asian country between 1956 and 1962, before the U.S. invasion. In 1985 the United States disbursed $744 million to El Salvador, an amount equaling 20 percent of the country's gross national product and roughly equivalent to the total expenditures of the Salvadoran government.

Although the United States disburses only about $300 million in Honduras, the effect is almost as strong as in El Salvador because the Honduran economy is smaller than the Salvadoran economy. Furthermore, the costs of maintaining U.S. bases, of undertaking frequent military maneuvers, and of funding the spending of U.S. soldiers stationed in Honduras, not included in U.S. aid funds, increase the amount of U.S. subsidization of the Honduran economy.

The heavy economic dependence, and the loss of sovereignty it implies, are most pronounced in El Salvador and Honduras, but a similar phenomenon obtains in Costa Rica, under the combined economic pressure of the International Monetary Fund (IMF) and the United States, as well as in Panama, owing to the IMF and the U.S. military pressure. The fact that Guatemala was unsuccessful in maintaining IMF support and is now receiving substantial U.S. aid marks its first advance into the ranks of informal protectorates in Central America.

The subsidization of the Nicaraguan government is the strongest in the region, but the sources of support are more diversified (Latin America, western Europe, and eastern Europe through the Council for Mutual Economic Assistance, or COMECON). The support has financed profound structural changes in Nicaragua's economy.[8] With its more diversified dependence, Nicaragua displays more independence vis-a-vis aid from Cuba and COMECON than other countries show with respect to North American aid, with the exception, up to now, of Guatemala.

2. Attrition of the Dominant Classes, Increasing Corruption, and the Nouveaux Riches

The prolongation of the conflict has weakened the former dominant classes. Their demoralization and uncertainty continue to be expressed in capital flight, by investments in services that mature quickly rather than in the productive sector, in their refusal to pay taxes to fund the war or to lower enormous budget deficits, and in the transfer of the economic crisis to the majority, adding to their suffering and making them more rebellious.

Increasing economic subsidization also precipitates intrabourgeois struggles over shares of North American aid. The corruption thereby generated spreads through a wide spectrum of society. The central banks gain access to foreign exchange which creates opportunities for capital flight, unremunerated exports, and overvaluation of imports. Programs sponsored by the Agency for International Development, despite efforts by the U.S. government, are tainted by corruption. The economy is fragmented into free-trade zones for the military. The increasing civil-military corruption permits the armed forces to take over customhouses, particularly those concerned with trading among El Salvador, Honduras, and Guatemala.

The recolonization resulting from subsidization tends to create a new class of wealthy people who have learned how to profit from the growing power of the military. Particularly noticeable is the growth of a new sector of highly sophisticated services that cater to the needs of international missions and the consumption patterns of the new wealthy class, which uses foreign exchange not for productive investment but rather with a *carpe diem* philosophy.[9] The old logic of the privileged minority is disappearing in the depth of the crisis and a new logic, more corrupt and less productive, has emerged.

3. Problems in Financing Recolonization

The bourgeoisie in Central America have no national plan or program, and the attitudes of the old dominant classes (uncertainty, disinvestment, capital flight, and relocation outside the region) and of the new rich (corruption and consumption) collide with the economic reactivation program advanced by the United States. In other words, there is no one to administer the dependent capitalist economy the United States is attempting to revive in Central America. Without a dependent bourgeoisie to defend its class privileges, the phase of indirect U.S. intervention enters into crisis. Each year larger subsidies are needed for the Central American economies, but the funds coming in are of necessity used for financing a war economy or providing welfare for its victims, such as the millions of refugees and displaced persons. Money from the United States is being poured into the bottomless barrel that today epitomizes the Central American economies.

The two cardinal sins, as seen in the halls of the U.S. Congress, are communism and welfare. If the Reagan administration cannot control corruption and create at least the image of reactivation (true reactivation remains decades away because of the continuing conflict), it is highly probable that Congress will not want to continue the subsidy. The contradiction between a "stingy Congress" and a project of "economic recolonization" whose costs rise every year will tend to deepen in the coming years.

At the root of the problem is the absence of an autonomous bourgeois program. The Central American bourgeoisie, instead of facing its own crisis, enjoys the comforts of life in the United States, sends its children to the best North American universities, and continues to withdraw its capital while waiting for the United States to eliminate the Salvadoran and Guatemalan guerrillas and destabilize the government of Nicaragua. Sooner or later Congress's impatience with these "lazy Latinos" will grow, but the alternative is even more disagreeable: while sons of the Central American bourgeoisie are studying in U.S. universities, American boys will die in the mountains of Central America. This is the same dilemma the United States faced in Vietnam.

4. Hyperurbanization and the Contraction of National Economic Space

Continuation of the military conflict provokes flight from country to city and from smaller cities to larger ones. This process of hyperurbanization contracts national economic territory, increases nonproductive overconcentration, and requires larger external economic injections to sustain it. The population shift is more intensive in El Salvador, Nicaragua, and Guatemala, but the deterioration of country-city exchange has affected Honduras and

Costa Rica as well. In El Salvador, the population of such cities as San Miguel and Sonsonate doubled between 1980 and 1985.

Hyperurbanization creates a false impression of intense economic movement. For example, extensive construction activity in San Miguel, San Salvador, and Santa Ana, and the dramatic growth of highly sophisticated services in San Salvador, suggest boom conditions in El Salvador. Yet cotton production has been drastically cut and coffee farms are disappearing from the area around the capital.[10]

5. Increasing Erosion of Central American Integration

One of the reasons for the formation of the Central American Common Market was to attenuate downturns in the international market for commodity exports which cause the stagnation of economies as small and as vulnerable to the world market as those of Central America. Although intraregional trade grew from 6.5 percent of total trade in 1960 to 23 percent in 1979, the increase was damaging to the foreign exchange generated by the agroexporting sector and by foreign borrowing.[11] Now, in face of the worst international market downturn to hit Central America, instead of mitigating the crisis, CACM trade has shrunk to 50 percent of the 1980 level and to 18.5 percent of the region's total trade.

The fundamental problem is the integrationist sector's extreme dependence on imports from the same international market. Given this dependence, in ECLA's estimation, "economic interdependence among the five countries has tended to convert itself into a mechanism for transmitting recessive economic forces,"[12] and thus it exacerbates the crisis. The increasing erosion of CACM is foreseeable, not only for the reasons indicated, but also because the United States is paying its costs and has increasingly assumed direct responsibility for the Central American economy. As it is clear that the CACM does not benefit Central America, alternative solutions are being sought.[13]

6. Effect of the Crisis on the Poor

The fall of per capita income to the levels of the 1960s in the countries suffering most severely from the armed conflict, and to the levels of 1970 in the others, means an enormous increase in poverty. ECLA estimates that, in the 1980s, 63.7 percent of the population is living in poverty and that 41.7 percent is living in extreme poverty. PREALC's data are incomplete (covering only Costa Rica and Guatemala), but they indicate that in these two countries the poorest 20 percent has been further impoverished by the crisis, whereas the bourgeoisie and the upper middle class have benefited most in relative terms.[14]

In particular, the series of devaluations in El Salvador between 1984 and 1986 struck especially hard at those who were already bearing the brunt of extreme poverty in the region. In El Salvador, where direct taxes on income and wealth have fallen, the government has attempted to avoid complete dependence on U.S. aid by raising indirect taxes, thereby disproportionately increasing the burden on the poor. Subsequent efforts by the Duarte government to raise taxes of the wealthier sectors were actively resisted by these groups. In Guatemala, the refusal by the wealthy classes to defray the cost of the crisis, and the attempt to force even more suffering on the poor by cutting social welfare subsidies, led to unexpected street riots in August and September of 1985. Likewise, the new wave of labor union disputes and strikes (including strikes by public employees) in El Salvador is attributable to the impact of the inflation that has struck the Salvadoran economy in the 1980s.

Worsening social tensions of similar type and origin are foreseeable throughout Central America. The region not only lacks a bourgeoisie capable of responding to the U.S. program of reactivation; it also suffers because its bourgeoisie and its governing officials act without regard for the people. The implication is that U.S. hegemony is being threatened by a military challenge born of the very people that the United States and its proconsuls continue to scorn.

7. Increasing Emigration from Central America

Military conflict has precipitated the migration of Central Americans to the United States by way of Mexico. Most of them are seeking to escape from the misery caused by the crisis. The poor borrow from members of their families already established in the United States. Even at the low wages paid to undocumented migrants in Los Angeles, a youth can earn in three days the monthly salary of a Salvadoran professor. In the same three days of manual labor an immigrant can earn three times as much in Los Angeles as a Salvadoran farmworker earns in a month.

It is no wonder that Los Angeles has become "the second-largest Salvadoran city"; New York and Washington compete with Santa Ana for third place. Officially received remittances in El Salvador from relatives outside the country equal approximately $125 million (the country's most important source of foreign exchange, after coffee exports and U.S. aid). This type of family support is estimated to run from $300 million, or 39 percent of El Salvador's total exports, to more than $1 billion, which exceeds the proceeds from exports and from total U.S. aid. Such transfers create wide disparities in standards of living, even among the poorest classes.[15]

8. The Informal Urban Sector (IUS)

Several factors set up the IUS as a future field of battle in the Central American economy. They include the increasing isolation of Central American urban centers from their rural hinterlands and from trade with the rest of the isthmus, the U.S. project of export outside the region, and, above all, the growth of the informal urban sector in the large cities in a context of strong devaluation and inflation. The IUS is experiencing extreme pressure; as it was growing through migration to the cities, its average income was proportionately diminishing, making it particularly volatile. This sector emerged as revolutionary both in Cuba and in Nicaragua; it failed to bring down the Peruvian government in the insurrections of 1978–79 only because it lacked an armed vanguard. The Guatemalan riots of 1981 and 1985 erupted most violently in the barrios, where the IUS is strongly represented.

For these reasons the IUS emerges as the social force most sought after by both reactionary and revolutionary political forces. The informal urban sector was in fact the principal theme of a recent meeting of Central American business organizations held in San Pedro Sula, in Honduras, which affirmed that survival of the private sector depended on taking the IUS into account. The materials prepared for this meeting, promoted by Henry Kissinger, depict the IUS as resistant to Sandinista planning and as an ally of businesspeople throughout the region.

Summary

As seen in the discussion of the eight tendencies that the economic crisis may follow, the prolongation of the conflict tends to deprive the Central American economy of its residual autonomy, reducing it to a function of U.S. geopolitics. It tends to marginalize the old Central American dominant classes, leaving the region without a national bourgeois program. It fosters economic recolonization, further aggravated by corruption and by the division of the countries into free-trade zones among political actors.

Nevertheless, another tendency of enormous import is simultaneously at work in Central America: the poverty-stricken masses seem to be developing a critical economic consciousness. The severity of the crisis has raised consciousness about the economic problem and its causes throughout Central America. This sort of questioning by the majority marks a political and cultural watershed of central importance in the region.

Decades of economic growth followed by what may be decades of recession and misery are producing a profound economic awareness. The stable economic growth between 1950 and 1978 allowed the masses to lift their heads in hopes of a better life. Then, just as the earthquakes of the 1970s in Nicaragua and Guatemala unveiled the bitter economic reality that the poorest 20 percent of society earns only 4 percent of the national income, the sharpening of the crisis between 1978 and 1986 precipitated a prolonged earthquake in the social consciousness of the people of the region.

Notes

1. The new historical subject refers to the traditionally exploited sectors of Central American society—peasants, rural and urban laborers, workers in the informal urban sector, indigenous populations, and in some instances women and youth—who through organization and mobilization have been transformed into political protagonists in the current conflicts in Central America.

2. For an analysis of the economic specificity of Central America, see Eugenio Rivera Urrutia Anasojo and José Roberto López, "Centroamérica Política Económica y Crisis" (San José, Costa Rica: ICADIS-CRIES-DEI, January 1987).

3. Richard Fagen/PACCA, *Forging Peace: The Challenge of Central America* (New York: Basil Blackwell, 1987), suggests a new paradigm for regional development.

4. Comisión Económica de América Latina (CEPAL), *Bases de una política de Reactivación y Desarrollo* (May 1985).

5. PREALC, "Modernización del Mercado de Trabajo y Crisis en el Istmo Centroamericano" (October 1985).

6. Comisión Económica de América Latina (CEPAL), *Bases de una política de Reactivación y Desarrollo* (May 1985).

7. Editors' note: In fiscal year 1987–88 the U.S. Congress granted Guatemala $117 million in military aid. In March 1987 the Reagan administration requested $40 million in supplemental aid for fiscal year 1987–88 and $144 million for fiscal year 1988–89.

8. These changes include the distribution of land to the peasants in the form of cooperatives or individual holdings, the diversification of international markets to include the socialist countries and Latin America, the initiation of relations with India and China while maintaining traditional relations with Europe, Japan, and Canada. For further information on the structural changes in Nicaragua see Rose J. Spalding, *The Political Economy of Revolutionary Nicaragua* (Boston: Allen and Unwin, 1987); Thomas W. Walker, ed., *Nicaragua in Revolution* (New York: Praeger, 1982), and his *Nicaragua: The First Five Years* (New York: Praeger, 1985); and Abraham F. Lowenthal, ed., *Latin American and Caribbean Contemporary Record*, Vol. V: chapter on Nicaragua (New York: Holmes & Meier, 1987). (Editors' note: See also chapter by Michael Conroy and Manuel Pastor, Jr., in this volume.)

9. The concept of *carpe diem* is based on a poem by the Roman poet Horacio, which manifests the philosophy of living for today, although tomorrow "comes the deluge."

10. Editors' note: See chapter by Ricardo Stein in this volume.

11. PREALC, *Modernización*.

12. CEPAL, *Bases de una política*.

13. Editors' note: For a more positive, albeit critical, assessment of the Central American Common Market, see chapter by Edelberto Torres Rivas in this volume.

14. PREALC, *Modernización*.

15. See Segundo Montes, "La Crisis Salvadoreña y las Consecuencias de una Repatriación Masiva de Refugiados en los Estados Unidos," Boletín de Ciencias Económicas y Sociales (San Salvador), X, 1 (January–February).

7

The Central American Crisis and the Common Market

Edelberto Torres Rivas

The serious economic problems and political crises afflicting the Central American countries have revived the debate on the Central American Common Market (CACM), instituted more than twenty-five years ago as a program of regional cooperation and development. Can the economic and political crises be attributed to a failure of the CACM to fulfill its original objectives? Is it indeed accurate to say that the CACM was a failure? If so, was it a failure in the implementation of its program or in the conception itself?[1]

Assessments of the Central American Common Market range from the optimistic vision of the technician, who perceives problems as amenable to technical solutions, and the catastrophic view of the reformer, who focuses on deep-rooted structural problems requiring profound socioeconomic changes. For the former, conceptualizing the Common Market as a regional cooperation effort to liberalize intraregional trade, the CACM was a success. For the latter, the inability to eliminate structural inequalities within and among countries, or the external trade dependence characterizing their relationship with the rest of the world, makes the Common Market a failure.

Both assessments are partly correct, and both are misleading. While the first may be superficial in ignoring the goal of reducing external dependence, which regional cooperation was to achieve, the latter is unrealistic because it imputes failure to non-existent strategies aimed at internal structural change and ignores those changes that did occur in industrial structure and regional economic cooperation.

As some form of regional cooperation is necessary for the eventual recovery and development of the Central American economies, a reassessment of the CACM experience, taking into account both its negative and positive

Translated by Nora Hamilton, Department of Political Science, University of Southern California, Los Angeles.

features, is essential. And such an assessment must proceed from an understanding of the nature and limits of economic integration among the Central American countries. Economic integration was initiated gradually in the 1950s through a series of agreements for bilateral exchanges between different sets of countries, but it did not take a regional form until the 1960s. The arrangements never constituted integration in the strict sense, for two reasons. First, economic integration in a region such as Central America is possible only on the basis of complementarity in production and export, which clearly did not exist in Central America. Second, regional economic integration should ideally produce internal effects and homogenize local markets. The purpose of the Common Market was to establish certain levels of collaboration among the Central American countries through the exchange of non-competitive manufactured products. No one expected the CACM to homogenize the internal structural inequalities of the Central American countries, as a broad project of regional integration would have implied. Thus, the term economic integration, as used in this chapter, should be understood in the more limited sense of economic cooperation.

In this limited sense, which is the perspective of the technician, the program was successful through the mid-1970s. It is thus a mistake to attribute the current political crisis of the region to the poor functioning of the economy or to the failure of the Common Market. Various studies have demonstrated that between 1950 and 1975, the period preceding the emergence of popular movements of armed protest in Nicaragua, El Salvador and Guatemala, the combined Central American economy grew by 5 percent annually;[2] at certain periods and for some countries the rate of growth was even higher.

Nonetheless, by the mid-1970s three countries of the region were undergoing a political crisis which developed into what has been termed[3] a mass based armed crisis of the traditional political order. Although the Central American economy was already suffering from the rise in petroleum prices (1972–73), subsequent financial difficulties, and a weakening demand for agricultural exports (1975), it was only after 1980 that the economic crisis was definitively felt in all its ramifications, constituting a new factor in the weakening of Central American economic integration. Strictly speaking, then, the political crisis preceded the economic crisis; the roots of the former must be sought not in economic paralysis but in the direction, style, and limitations of the development of the previous decades.

Some Elements of Integration History

The development of the Central American Common Market was characterized by a profound disjuncture between the somewhat idealistic proposals of ECLA (United Nations Economic Commission for Latin America) and of other regional academic institutions, on the one hand, and the political and economic conditions in the Central American countries, on the other. ECLA, in its initial proposals for regional integration, assumed that the economy had its own impetus, unconnected with political institutions, and that it could therefore be reoriented and made more predictable. Integration as a utopia was originally predicated on the possibility of regional planning.

Although the program for Central American economic integration assumed an independent economy and planning at will, the conditions which made this program possible were not economic. Most important, the Central American governments were composed of mutual friends who manifested a high degree of political homogeneity.[4] Despite diverse economic points of departure, inter-governmental compatibility presupposed a desire for economic growth with shared costs. The model of economic growth promoted in the region was import substitution industrialization (ISI), the domestic production of previously imported industrial goods, with the diversification of export agriculture. In the environment of the 1950s industry was synonymous with modernization, just as years before it had been the railroads that created the illusion of progress.

In the European experience the point of departure for economic integration was highly industrialized societies whose cooperation would assure higher levels of growth. In 1950 the Central American economies were backward and were just emerging from a long period of stagnation. The Central American countries were in fact agrarian societies that had barely begun the progress of capitalist modernization. Some Central Americans believed that urgent structural changes (agrarian reform, for example) were necessary before a program of regional integration could be implemented. At this point political factors, based on the prevailing class structure, enter the picture. The political domination of landowners/exporters and of backward social sectors was total. The oligarchy never permitted the implementation of social reforms, and with the postwar economic reactivation it simply benefitted from conditions it had neither foreseen nor created.

Today it is evident that the purpose of the Common Market was not to introduce the structural changes demanded by leftist forces; nevertheless it did facilitate changes in the total society. These changes did not have the desired social and political effects, however, and the present crisis is largely the result of the orientation or the style of economic growth promoted.

Despite the importance of political compatibility of the Central American governments, the model of economic growth was not centered in the state, as has mistakenly been assumed, but in the private sector. It was based, in the first instance, on a pact between the agrarian and industrial sectors which precluded agrarian reform as a means of expanding the internal market. The introduction of an industrial base was seen as a platform that would make it possible to take advantage of a wider regional demand without disturbing agrarian ownership or broadening internal markets.

The process of economic growth was directed by private enterprise, with private interests represented and guaranteed in multilateral meetings, in institutional organisms, and in all the circles where problems relative to the Common Market were decided. The role of the state was always a subsidiary one. The active presence of a bourgeois-business fraction served not only to orient economic cooperation toward its own goals but also to achieve organic integration of business interests by establishing business organizations at the national and regional levels, a process completed by 1980. Of all social groups, these organizations are best able to exert pressure, and today are strong enough to paralyze any initiative by a national state.

In effect, the program of cooperation now known as Central American economic integration was the result of a tacit agreement between business— national and especially foreign—and the states of the region. In fact, state economic policy was designed to protect the private sector in numerous ways, ranging from customs barriers to tax exemption, to create financial as well as fiscal incentives. The combination of protective measures intended for a newly emerging industry was converted into a "modus vivendi" between the public and private sectors.[5] The measures adopted by the governments favored the dynamic of accumulation beyond the level possible for the expanding market. Consequently, in the relation between the state and the private sector, politics was openly placed at the service of the latter. In less elegant terms, the government fully capitulated to the pressures of private, and especially foreign, interests.

This model of politically stimulated and protected capitalist growth was made possible not only by the nature of political alliances but also by short-term external factors which demonstrated the extraordinarily open and vulnerable character of Central American societies. Foreign capital flowed into the region in the form of direct or associated investment, transfers of technology (generally obsolete in the countries of origin), and the broadening of brand consumption, made possible by the expansion of the mass media. The capacity of exports to finance imports was sustained, in spite of some critical moments, largely by agro-livestock diversification and increased volumes of sale.

The favorable economic conditions of the initial period can probably not be reproduced. The most important, as noted above, was the flow of resources from abroad—through foreign capital and the increased volume and higher prices of agricultural exports. There funds did not go to agriculture or services, as in the past, but to industrial investment. The terms of trade were also favorable, and the capacity to import increased more than could reasonably have been expected. It was thus the recovery of export trade in the early 1960s which most favored the establishment of the Common Market.

These economic and political circumstances must be taken into account in examining the causes of the present disarray in Central America. Other factors cannot compensate for their absence, demonstrating that when the dynamism of the external sector was exhausted it was never replaced by an internal regional potential.

As institutional and economic measures established in this favorable climate have been extensively described elsewhere, they are only quickly reviewed here. The major commitment was to develop a free trade zone. The creation of a tariff-free economic space required the imposition of a regional customs barrier, the common tariff. When the General Treaty was signed in 1961, 81 percent of the products from the participating countries were subject to free trade; the proportion increased to 96 percent in 1971. Abolishing tariffs, a relatively easy undertaking, gave immediate impetus to the trade and transport sectors and, less quickly, to the industrial sector. Intraregional exports increased at an average rate of 29 percent throughout the 1960s; beginning in 1970, the growth was more modest and less regular, especially because of the break in relations between Honduras and El Salvador (a result of the war between the two countries in 1969) and the international recession of 1974–75. Nevertheless, the value of intraregional trade continued to rise, reaching its highest level of more than $1 billion in 1980. In 1985 this figure was estimated to be just above $500 million, a 50 percent drop in five years that demonstrates the commercial dimensions of the crisis. (See Table 7.1.)

The proportion of intra-regional trade in total exports from Central America also increased dramatically. When the General Trade Treaty was signed, trade among the Central American countries was 6.9 percent of the total; it rose to 26.1 percent in 1970.[6]

As pointed out earlier, the assessment of the success or failure of the Common Market during the 1960–1980 period depends on the differing perceptions of the reformer and the technician. The reformer, who evaluates success on the basis of structural changes, such as reducing inequality or increasing social development, is inevitably disappointed. Such changes were precluded in Central America from the beginning—a result of the pact between the agrarian oligarchy and industrial sector and of the control exercised by private capital, both national and foreign, over the state. These private groups were further strengthened by the growth of the 1960–1980 period, as well as by their increased organization and cohesion at both national and regional levels.

The technician, however, who judges success on the basis of measurable changes, such as industrial growth rates and an increase in intra-regional trade, could be well satisfied with the results achieved by 1980. The increase in demand caused by the geographic broadening of the market was a major stimulus to import-substitution industrialization, which also benefitted initially from favorable external factors, especially the growth in agro-livestock exports and the rapid increase in foreign investment and loans. Nevertheless, the importance of external factors demonstrated the continued vulnerability of the Central American economies to external economic conditions, a vulnerability that was increased, rather than lessened, by the twenty-year experience.

Structural Changes in Industry

The mixed effects of the Common Market experiment are also evident in the types of changes that occurred in industry and the limitations on those changes. On the one hand, all countries of the region experienced a

142

TABLE 7.1
Central America: Intra-Regional Exports, FOB, 1970, 1975, 1980-1985

Year	Central America	Guatemala	El Salvador	Honduras	Nicaragua	Costa Rica
1970	286.3	102.4	73.8	18.0	46.1	46.1
1975	536.4	168.2	141.8	26.6	92.6	107.2
1980	1,129.2	403.7	295.8	83.9	75.4	270.3
1981	936.8	355.5	206.5	65.9	70.9	238.0
1982	765.5	320.1	174.2	51.9	52.9	167.2
1983	766.6	308.7	164.9	61.3	33.5	198.2
1984[a]	706.9	291.4	157.2	49.4	37.1	171.8
1985[b]	538.0	227.8	106.1	29.7	21.3	153.1

[a]Preliminary figures
[b]Estimates of SIECA
Source: Inforpress Centroamericana, No. 718 (Guatemala City, 4 December 1986).

dramatic industrial upsurge, reflected in the types of intra-regional exports, which transformed them from agricultural societies into more complex economic structures. On the other hand, as suggested above, the program of import substitution industrialization had little impact on the inequalities within and among the countries of the region, and it created an industrial structure that was excessively vulnerable to the ensuing economic and political crises. The reciprocity between regional trade expansion and industrial development in the 1960s and 1970s is evident both in the significance of industrial products in intraregional trade and in their changing quality. In the 1960s, the most important products in trade were nontraditional industrial exports, mainly non-durable consumption goods (food, textiles, clothing and shoes), cosmetics, and pharmaceutical products. Later, in the 1970s, the pattern gradually changed as intermediate products (glass and glass products, industrial chemicals, cardboard and metal mechanical products, and others) became important.

The dynamism of the industrial sector in the twenty years ending in 1980 is evident in its annual growth rate of 7 percent, decisive evidence of changes wrought in a sector which had been artisan until the industrial process was well underway.[7] The decade of the 1960s was indeed a golden age of regional economic growth: the total industrial product increased by 8.4 percent annually. Growth in the 1970s was less dramatic but it maintained an annual average of 5.5 percent.[8]

The production of non-durable consumption goods also increased and the products were diversified appreciably, but intermediate and metallic and machine industries expanded at rates greater than 9 percent. Because intraregional trade was based on manufactured products, the potential demand in Central America, rather than local markets, was the major incentive for entrepreneurs. From the beginning, 25 percent of industrial production was distributed to other Central American countries, and in some instances the proportion was larger, reaching more than 63 percent of the total export of manufactured goods within the region by the end of the 1970s. In this period Central American countries also began to export their products to countries outside the region, although in smaller quantities.

As integration implied neither the equalization of productive structures nor industrial complementarity, national advantages differed from one country to another according to their respective starting points. In its "moment of glory" Guatemala was the major exporter in the Common Market (with chemical products, textiles, processed foods, and glass products). It was also the most diversified producer and exporter. Prior to the war with Honduras, El Salvador exported most of its industrial products through the Common Market, especially various kinds of textiles, shoes, and clothing, as well as plastic products and cardboard boxes and packaging. The war with Honduras, and subsequently the civil war, ended El Salvador's advantages. Costa Rica, which had been in third place as regional supplier, increased its participation to 21 percent in 1976, especially with the sale of chemical products, machinery, and metal products, as well as textiles and clothing. Because of the lack of national specialization, however, the list of products exchanged among the Central American countries is essentially the same for each.

All this is now history which many hope will repeat itself; in the meantime it constitutes an important phase in the accumulation of manufacturing experience. Today neither the volume nor the quality of production is the same. And although the industrial growth of the 1960s and 1970s did initiate significant changes in industrial structures, including the completion of import substitution in the basic sectors of industry and even some diversification into intermediate industries, these changes did not have the desired effects.

This failure is a consequence of the way in which measures promoting industrial growth were implemented. The first measure, the Agreement on the Central American System of Integration Industries (1958), was proposed to facilitate the selective promotion of industries of regional scope. Explicitly, it was expected to create a complementary productive structure with new, nontraditional industries, with economies of scale greater than those already existing, and with reasonable national control. From the start, the Central American countries did not take advantage of this agreement; in fact, its effects were nullified when the General Treaty went into effect in 1961.[9] The agreement was adamantly opposed by the U.S. Agency for International Development (AID), and local entrepreneurs who feared statism regarded it with suspicion. The failure to apply the 1958 integration industries agreement is critical to understanding why the Common Market never aimed at the structural homogenization of the region.

The failure of the Central American integration agencies to develop a coherent regional industrial policy could be blamed for the ineffectiveness of the 1958 agreement. But national industrial policies were also lacking in each country of the region. The Central American Treaty of Fiscal Incentives for Industrial Development, applied belatedly (after 1968), had been preceded by disparate legislative efforts to promote industry. The treaty summed up these national experiences, allowing exemptions from import duties (primary products and capital goods) to firms at their inception and for long periods thereafter. But comparable benefits to nearly all existing firms, and requests for indiscriminate protection, lowered the competitiveness of the industrial market; entrepreneurs became accustomed to profits well above average and disproportionate to their investment and efforts. Undoubtedly the generous fiscal incentives limited the resources the state could collect in the form of taxes.

Since Central American private capital was not only limited but also timid about making medium or long term investments, the financing of new industry became a major problem, and there was strong competition among governments to attract foreign capital. Just as there was never a regional industrial policy, neither was there a common policy on direct foreign investment. In the absence of such a policy, the freedom of movement of foreign capital became almost anarchic, demonstrating the absence of nationalism and bourgeois consciousness among political and business elites.

Regional competition in textile and chemical products, for example, gave the impression that they were national manufactures trading in a dynamic regional market, whereas they were simply various products of transnational firms which transferred their international rivalry to the small Central American space.

The U.S. Department of Commerce estimates that the total accumulated foreign investment in Central America had reached nearly $900 million by 1979, of which $630 million was U.S. capital.[10] More recently it has been calculated that foreign investment rose to one billion dollars in 1980. By this time, however, it was surpassed by international bank lending, and the private international debt became decisive in comparison with investment.[11]

The absence of a regional policy for foreign capital, along with the large influx of foreign investment and loans, worsened the impact of the economic and political crises of the 1980s. When the character of the enterprise permitted, foreign companies pulled out of the region, and the drop in exports left the Central American governments unable to pay interest on debts accumulated earlier during periods of growth.

The policy of import substitution industrialization (ISI) also had mixed results in Central America. It gave a notable push to Central American industrial growth, especially in the first years, and paralleled a decrease in the import coefficient (industrial inputs imported relative to those of domestic origin). But subsequently the situation changed. In some industrial sectors the import coefficient increased and production slowed. Although no technical evaluation of this process has been conducted, the policies of import substitution have in fact substituted the import of intermediate goods for the import of consumption goods, thus increasing the vulnerability of the economy.[12] This pattern has been the experience of other Latin American countries (import coefficients which fall and then recover, reflecting an initial decline in the import of industrial inputs relative to total inputs followed by an increase in these imports). This experience demonstrates the need for an economic policy responsive to the nature of imports as well as to the degree of elaboration of what is produced in relation to what is imported. This relationship reflects the development (or absence) of forward and backward linkages—the extent to which domestic products are used in producing other products (forward linkages) and draw upon domestic resources or stimulate the production of other inputs (backward linkages). In turn, forward and backward linkages are the best criteria for determining achievements in industrialization, the accomplishment of real structural changes, and the extent of economic homogenization.

The issue of the degree to which import substitution produces backward and forward linkages is related to the debate on last stage industries. The pejorative concept of last-stage industrialization (in which virtually all inputs are imported and simply assembled or packaged by the domestic industry) is sometimes mistakenly applied to any industrialization that requires imported inputs. The polemic derives from a phenomenon common to both: an increase in imports of primary materials and semifinished industrial goods used for local production. One may ask: what is national about an industry in which the productive processes are merely the packaging, assembling, or diluting of inputs from abroad? The decisive factor is the degree of value added locally in elaboration of the final product: the heavier the dependence on primary materials and semifinished goods from abroad, the weaker the industrial development.

Although a detailed study of the productive structure established by the Common Market is still lacking, there is no evidence of sectoral integration or of the effect of backward and forward linkages. To the extent that Central American industrialization is last-stage industrialization, this can be explained by the virtual absence of regional and national industrialization policies, and by the failure to apply those principles that did exist, combined with the prominence of foreign capital in Central American industrialization. This simple industrial structure in turn explains why numerous firms, impelled by the strong winds of the economic crisis, are now packing up their belongings and looking for more tranquil climates elsewhere.

The project of the Common Market was a program of industrialization supported by a combination of favorable external conditions, state incentives, and initiatives of foreign capital, associated in some degree with national capitalists. After twenty years, the result was the creation of a valid industrial base and the introduction of some changes in industrial structure, such as diversification into intermediate industries. In general, Central America ceased to be a predominantly agrarian society and demonstrated its ability to satisfy the internal demand for intermediate consumption goods. Import substitution was nearly completed in the basic sectors of industry, and consequently, perceptible changes were evident.

The industrial project, however, was not based on agrarian restructuring through the redistribution of either land or rural income. Industrial firms were established and productive technology spread, but sectoral integration was not achieved nor was there evidence of the effect of backward and forward linkages. Although some of the changes are undoubtedly definitive, others are more ephemeral. The present crisis has led to deindustrialization, whereby firms are easily transferred to other areas, although again, as data are lacking, the extent of this process cannot be precisely determined.

The Crisis: Regional Disintegration?

In order to understand the implications of the integrative process, it is not enough to go back to its origins and initial achievements. The political and economic crisis in Central America demands consideration of the present and of future possibilities. By no means is there a prospective funeral; only a serious illness, caused especially by the powerful virus from abroad.

Central America is the Latin American area most affected by the economic crisis; it is also an area where policies of stabilization can be least successful. Since 1980 Central America has not only been stagnating economically, but it has also been paralyzed by a political and military entanglement involving almost every sector and country, requiring large amounts of military expenditures and bringing the region to the brink of war. Every indicator—industrial growth, trade, agricultural production, etc.—is negative relative to 1979 figures. The region has been impoverished to levels that statistically reflect a fifteen-year retrogression: per capita income in 1986 was the same as in 1971. In Nicaragua and El Salvador, the decline has reduced the economies to levels of twenty years ago.[13] The product per inhabitant of Central America has declined for the eighth consecutive year and, whereas the gross domestic product of Latin America increased by 3.4 percent in 1986, in Central America it stagnated at 0.3 percent.

The economic and political crisis is a disintegrating factor in that it makes regional cooperation difficult and inhibits efforts toward national articulation in individual countries. As a result, several elements favoring integration have disappeared. The assumed homogeneity among the political leaders of the five countries has ended. Agricultural exports do not produce enough foreign exchange to strengthen industrial development. Moreover, intraregional trade has sharply decreased, due less to difficulties in producing than to difficulties in trading. As noted above, trade within Central America has dropped from one billion dollars in 1980 to an estimated $500 million in 1985 and its share of total trade has been reduced from an average of 25 percent to less than ten percent.

Foreign investment has retreated completely from Central America; in its stead is the foreign debt, demanding service that was never even imagined in the 1960s and 1970s, when advances, royalties and dividends on foreign investment were being paid. At the end of 1986 the total external debt was $16.8 billion, entailing service payments that, if they could be paid at all, would amount to an annual outlay equal to approximately 17.3 percent of the exports of the five countries.[14] Low international market prices for the primary products exported by Central America depress the capacity to import. The bleeding of foreign exchange to cover the minimum interest on the debt has depleted internal savings, never abundant to begin with.

The concentration of income and social wealth in Central America enabled entrepreneurs to become permanent exporters of capital. The small millionaire entrepreneurial groups, with little commitment to national or long-term industrialization, financed their speculative transactions and imports of consumption goods with foreign capital. The fact that only a small portion of internal savings have been channeled to immediate productive employment is the outstanding cause of foreign indebtedness. The political crisis, which creates insecurity for current investment, and especially the historical propensity to send capital abroad, explain the large amount of resources deposited by the Central American bourgeoisie in foreign banks.[15]

The disintegrating tendencies of the period of crisis have been accentuated by pressures from abroad, particularly from the United States. The relationships developed among the Central American countries through two decades of economic efforts are being destroyed for political reasons, although the destruction is attributed to the difficulties associated with the recession.

New proposals, for example, the Caribbean Basin Initiative and especially the recommendations of the Kissinger report (released in January 1984) on economic issues, are based on the isolation of Nicaragua and direct bilateral relations between other countries and the United States. Some Central American business groups closely linked to parties of the extreme right assume that these bilateral relations offer the only solution to the economic crisis, given the unlimited market in the United States. The protectionist actions of this market in recent years demonstrates, however, that the U.S. market is not unlimited but it is indeed becoming increasingly closed. The closing of the U.S. market has affected the Caribbean Basin Initiative (CBI), a series of economic measures designed to encourage the production of non-traditional exports by Central American and Caribbean countries chiefly for the U.S. market. In its early years, the CBI stimulated only a few Central American exports even though Central America has been the major beneficiary after the Dominican Republic.[16] One difficulty has been that not all exports can enter the United States without paying tariffs, but the principal problem is quotas and non-tariff barriers. In addition, the emphasis has been on products that interest the United States and not on those important for Central America. The CBI also enables U.S. agencies to incorporate themselves, even more directly than in the past, in Central American business organizations.

Despite apparently strong tendencies toward regional disintegration, spurred by the crisis and by reactions of foreign and domestic groups to it, certain events in the past two years have given new impetus to integration. In fact, such events have once again confirmed the existence of a desire for regional cooperation, never really absent. In December 1984 the governments of Costa Rica, El Salvador, Guatemala, and Nicaragua subscribed to the Agreement on the Tariff and Customs System, which established normative conditions for a new common tariff. The new tariff reduces differences in protectionist policies and makes conditions in the different countries more homogeneous, enabling Central America to negotiate as a bloc with the rest of the world.[17]

Two further initiatives are important, although their results are still uncertain. First, the agreement of cooperation signed with the European Economic Commission, although initially no more than a declaration of good intentions, may well be converted into an effective support for integrationist initiatives provided the regional political will of the Central Americans is strengthened. Second, the constitution of the Rights of Central American Imports (DICAS) complements the existing systems of payments, which are presently in crisis due to the lack of foreign exchange, by resolving difficult exchange problems and avoiding the direct use of foreign exchange in intraregional trade.[18]

There are, in fact, no internal tendencies toward disintegration. The great majority of intellectuals and politicians believe that disunity is not a viable option, that national economic strength stems from regional strength, and that no isolated strategy can be successful in the long term. The Common

Market experience has resulted in a high degree of economic interdependence which could serve as a basis for new development initiatives.

Options for Confronting the Crisis

The resumption of economic growth in Central America is not possible under the policies of stabilization even if they are successful, as they have not been in any country of the region. What is needed is regional integration on a new basis, at the same time taking advantage of the cooperation already established through the Common Market.

It is essential in the search for cooperation that the state assume a more prominent role relative to both the domestic private sector, now weakened by excessive capital export, and to foreign capital, which has taken flight due to the political crisis. As a first step, internal markets must be strengthened and a real regional complementarity must be created, a type of Central American division of industrial development.

The obstacles to the implementation of a new regional integration policy are formidable. First, the policy presupposes a political homogeneity among the Central American countries which does not now exist. Second, among other external factors, there must be improvement in the terms of trade or a reformulation of extraregional trade, even though the latter cannot be expected to regain the dynamic role it played in the early years of the Common Market. Third, the policy presupposes vigorous support by international capital, for which the outlook is still very negative.

Finally, the political and ideological factors operating in the international environment, such as the isolation of Nicaragua and proposals for direct bilateral relations with the United States, must not be underestimated. Still, the national economies of the Central American countries would undoubtedly be responsive to a stimulus for regional cooperation, once international pressures have been reduced or perhaps eliminated.

The future of Central America in the post-crisis period cannot be predicted, as it is impossible to foresee the future international division of labor. Even united and armed with a vigorous political resolution, the countries of the region face serious difficulties. But if Central Americans are allowed to control their own destiny, cooperation among the countries can be successfully reinitiated on new foundations, taking advantage of the past Common Market experiences and of the existing impetus toward regional integration.

Notes

1. Editors' note: The Central American Common Market (CACM) refers to an experiment in economic cooperation—sometimes referred to as economic integration—undertaken by five Central American countries: Guatemala, El Salvador, Honduras, Nicaragua and Costa Rica. Beginning in the 1950s, it included the reduction and ultimately the virtual elimination of tariffs among the five countries in an effort to facilitate trade among them as well as investment in infrastructure (electric power, communications) and in manufacturing industries. The CACM was negatively affected

by the brief war between El Salvador and Honduras in 1969, which led to the breaking of relations, including trade relations, between the two countries, and by the more recent economic and political crises. Nevertheless, trade among the five countries is still higher than it was before the Central American Common Market was established.

2. Comisión Económica para América Latina (CEPAL), *El crecimiento de la economía centroamericana en la postguerra* (Mexico, 1978), Table 1.

3. Among the numerous works on this subject, see especially the publications of ICADIS, and Edelberto Torres Rivas, *La crisis del poder en Centroamérica* (San José, Costa Rica: EDUCA, 1982).

4. G. Rosenthal, "Algunas Lecciones de la Integración Económica en América Latina: el Caso de Centroamérica," in *Comercio Exterior*, 12 (Mexico City, 1983): 1144ff.

5. Benjamin L. Crosby, *Crisis y Fragmentación: Relaciones entre los Sectores Público-privado en América Central*, Occasional Papers, Florida International University, no. 10 (May 1985): 11.

6. CEPAL, *El crecimiento*.

7. The disintegration of artisan manufacturing is a forgotten chapter in the history of Central American economies. At the beginning of 1960 artisan production was 34.4 percent of industrial production; by the middle of the 1970s it had dropped to 19 percent. The census of industries are not necessarily comparable, however. Firms are classified by number of workers; under a certain number the firm is classified as artisan, on the assumption that the low number of workers corresponds to a limited division of labor.

8. CEPAL, "Industrialización en Centroamérica, 1960–1980," *Estudios e Informes de la CEPAL*, no. 30 (Santiago, Chile, 1983).

9. A. Guerra Borges, "Hechos, Experiencias y Opciones en la Integración Económica Centroamericana," presentation at ICADIS-CRIES conference, San José, Costa Rica, May 1986: p. 35.

10. G. Rosenthal, *The Role of Foreign Investment in the Central American Common Market* (Guatemala City, 1970).

11. The total Central American exposure of the eight largest U.S. banks (which normally represent 75–80 percent of total U.S. bank exposure) had reached $1.6 billion by 1978.

12. Luis R. Cáceres, *Integración Económica y Subdesarrollo en Centroamérica* (Mexico City: FCE, 1980): p. 195.

13. M. A. Gallardo, *Centroamérica: la crisis en cifras* (San José, Costa Rica: FLACSO-IICA, 1986), Cuadro no. 1, p. 49.

14. CEPAL, "Balance Preliminar de la Economía Latinoamericana en 1986," *Notas sobre la Economía y el Desarrollo*, no. 438–439 (December 1986).

15. Calculations of the amount of capital flight from Central America between 1977 and 1984 range from $1.7 billion to $3.8 billion. See Banco Centroamericana, *La Fuga de Capital en Centroamérica*, 197.84, Plan 040/EE (10 Ver. 1/30 June 1986).

16. Exports to the United States from Central America (excluding Nicaragua) increased by an average of 13.6 percent in 1983 and 1984. Of the 1984 total of $1,690,000,000 in exports, 14 percent adhered to the formula of the CBI. Henry Gill, "Aspectos comerciales de la iniciativa estadounidense para la Cuenca del Caribe," *Capítulos del Sela*, no. 9 (January–June 1985).

17. The unilateral decision of Costa Rica to enter GATT (General Agreement on Trade and Tariffs) represents a potential weakening of efforts toward regional cooperation.

18. Traditionally intraregional payments are handled by the Central American Chamber of Compensations (CACC), which deducts the balances of each country and makes payments in dollars. The CACC was in financial straits in 1982 due to the unmanageable accumulation of balances. For a useful summary of this issue see J.A. Fuentes, *La Integración Económica Centroamericana: nuevas perspectivas a partir de la turbulencia* (USAC, Cuadernos de Investigación, 1986), p. 29.

8

The Hidden War:
Guatemala's Counterinsurgency
Campaign

Gabriel Aguilera Peralta

In the early 1980s the Guatemalan army was facing defeat by the revolutionary forces, which had been gaining strength since 1975. The insurgents' military operations had spread to most of the country and began to be felt in the capital and in major economic zones. The regular army suffered repeated setbacks and the authority of the state was progressively weakening, disappearing altogether in certain areas of the country. The rebels had also made progress in building alliances with centrist sectors and social democrats, augmenting the legitimacy of their struggle. At the same time, the government under Romeo Lucas García had contributed to the crisis of legitimacy and political isolation of the regime through increased repression and official corruption, further undermining its war effort.

The international situation also seemed to favor the revolutionaries. The policies of the Carter administration in the United States, the triumph of the Nicaraguan revolution, and the development of the internal war in El Salvador seemed to open the way for profound changes in Central American societies. Under the circumstances, the insurgents so confidently anticipated a military success that one faction came to consider June 1982 as the probable date of victory.

By 1985 the situation had been reversed. Beginning in mid-1981, the army developed a series of offensive campaigns, progressively implementing successive stages of the counterinsurgency war. These included the concentration of the population in strategic hamlets ("model villages"), grouped into larger complexes known as development poles, and its organization into pro-government militias ("civil patrols"). This strategy succeeded in changing the correlation of forces in favor of the army, which tactically

Translated by David Ayón, Department of Political Science, University of California, San Diego.

defeated the insurgency, although the war has not been definitively ended and the conditions that led to its emergence still exist.

The purpose of this article is to delineate the elements of the Guatemalan army's counterinsurgency strategy, examine the factors underlying its success, and point out some of the limitations on this success. It concludes with some reflections on the possible directions of events in the future.

The Logic of Counterinsurgency in Guatemala

The Guatemalan army's counterinsurgency strategy in the 1980–1985 period was not original. Since World War II, regular armies in other countries have repeatedly applied modern counterinsurgency principles in the effort to control internal insurgencies, succeeding in some instances (Malaysia, Kenya, Venezuela) and failing in others (Algeria, Vietnam, Nicaragua). The principal sources of counterinsurgency doctrine for the Guatemalan army were the United States and Israel.

The basic tenet of counterinsurgency doctrine is the need to confront the insurgency not just militarily but also politically. Given the characteristics of guerrilla warfare, regular forces may indeed be unable to win on the battlefield, but military blows inflicted upon guerrilla forces can have a political effect, leading to their slow disintegration. In other words, the political aspect of the war is primary. Aside from geopolitical factors, the victory or defeat of the regular forces depends on their ability to maintain an adequate balance between the political and military elements of this type of warfare. It follows that the central emphasis of counterinsurgency strategy cannot be purely military, although this aspect may predominate during a particular phase. The global or comprehensive character of this concept is based on a political appreciation of the insurgency and the consequent effort to structure a multiple response, embracing political, economic, ideological, and even international—political or diplomatic—as well as military approaches.

A second basic concept of counterinsurgency doctrine is the necessity to control the population, which constitutes the support base for the insurgent forces. This control should not be understood as solely coercive; it also demands the voluntary adherence or consent of the population whose support is sought. The concept is epitomized in the slogan "to win the hearts and minds of the people," which holds that it is necessary to provide rewards or offer material and/or spiritual incentives to the targeted population.

From this second concept—the need to control the population—flows the strategy of bringing the environment in which the people live under the spatial, social, and economic control of the government in order to diminish or cut off the possibility that they may support the guerrillas. To win it over, the population should receive material incentives in its reordered environment. Furthermore, some of the people—or all of them, if possible—should be incorporated into the military struggle against the insurgents, giving them an active role in the war so as to consolidate their allegiance to the government.

In Guatemala, internal war has erupted repeatedly over the past twenty-five years, and is usually dated from an uprising of a part of the Guatemalan army in November 1960. Although this revolt was motivated by nationalism and by factors relevant to the military as an institution, the insurgent struggle developed and spread in response to the socioeconomic and ethnic inequalities of Guatemalan society and the exclusionary and repressive character of its political system. The prolongation of the war enabled the Guatemalan army to gain valuable experience and to refine its counterinsurgency strategy in both content and style.

During the initial period of the war in the 1960s the Guatemalan army suffered a number of setbacks at the hands of a guerrilla force, despite the latter's military and, especially, its political weaknesses. By the end of the decade, however, the army, guided by U.S. military advisors, had succeeded in forging a counterinsurgency strategy which it directed against guerrilla fronts in the northeast region of the country. Search-and-destroy operations were aimed at the guerrillas' strategic forces; coercive, extralegal mechanisms were used to gain control of the population; elements of the population were incorporated into paramilitary groups with vigilante characteristics; and a civic-military action plan was devised to introduce material improvements in the region at war.[1]

Although the insurgents were defeated they were not extinguished, probably because the socioeconomic and political injustices that led to their emergence not only persisted but even worsened. Both sides reorganized and gathered strength during the first half of the 1970s. The revolutionary *foquistas* (adherents of the *foco* guerrilla strategy developed on the basis of the Cuban experience) of the 1960s subsequently adjusted their approach and expanded their military-political strategy in the next decade, obtaining a foothold among the country's indigenous majority. Between 1969 and 1975 the army, for its part, trained several cohorts of officers in internal war, reequipped its troops, redeployed in preparation for the coming struggle, and sharpened its intelligence capabilities.[2] By the early 1980s the Guatemalan army was second only to that of Colombia in its preparation for irregular combat in Latin America.

In 1975, despite this preparation, the army slowly began to suffer reverses and to lose control of territory to the guerrilla forces. The various insurgent organizations, relying on thousands of combatants and hundreds of thousands of supporters,[3] extended their influence, with varying levels of intensity, to nearly three-fourths of the Guatemalan territory.

By mid-1981 three guerrilla organizations had reached a high level of military development.[4] The Ejército Guerrillero de los Pobres (EGP; Guerrilla Army of the Poor) was active on seven fronts nominally covering two-thirds of the country's territory; the most important of them were the Ho Chi Minh in Quiché, the Ernesto Che Guevara in Huehuetenango, and the Augusto César Sandino in Chimaltenango. The Organización del Pueblo en

Armas (ORPA; Organization of the People in Arms) was active principally in the departments of San Marcos, Quetzaltenango, Sololá, and part of Retalhuleú and Suchitepéquez. The Fuerzas Armadas Rebeldes (FAR; Rebel Armed Forces) was active mainly in Petén. All the organizations carried out military actions in the capital city.

In this period the insurgents seem to have had the allegiance, in varying degrees, of a substantial part of the population, especially of the indigenous peasants, but the total number of their regular combatants apparently did not exceed 6,000. The army, besides its approximately 17,000 regulars, could count on several thousand more from the security forces. It therefore lacked the numerical superiority needed to confront the guerrillas adequately; it was hampered, moreover, by the overextension of its troops as it attempted to deal simultaneously with guerrilla activity in all parts of the country.

The rebels, operating from zones where they had popular support and bases of organization, attacked moving targets and harassed fixed targets. They also carried out numerous operations of propaganda and sabotage. Owing to their lack of heavy weapons, problems with their communications systems, and inefficient organization of joint maneuvers, their militry operations tended to be small in scale and the casualties they were able to inflict on the army were absorbed, albeit with difficulty. Nevertheless, guerrilla activities succeeded in wearing down the government, and a vacuum of state power began to characterize the zones of armed conflict. In 1981 the guerrillas occupied about forty important settlements, including one provincial capital. According to the insurgents' analysis, "In the first half of 1981, in effect, the guerrilla war entered fully into the phase of generalized war. Political-military organizational development, the gaining of combat experience, the systematization of new irregular tactics and the acquisition of significant lots of armaments allowed the revolutionary movement to take qualitative leaps of a partial and local nature. The enemy lost the initiative on practically all fronts."[5]

Were the rebels really in a position to take power in 1980 and 1981? The question is debatable. In retrospect we can see that in military terms they still had not created regular forces, nor had they really "liberated" any territory. They could, however, count on massive support in certain regions, and with enough time and adequate resources they might well have organized these supporters into an alternative army.

Sociopolitical factors may have been more important than purely military factors in the guerrillas' success between 1975 and 1981. The successive governments of the 1970s were characterized by high levels of corruption, the use of repression as a mechanism to maintain social control, and electoral fraud. In general they were closed to the social and democratic demands emanating from the society. By mid-1981 the government could no longer count on substantial internal or external support and seemed incapable of developing either military or political initiatives. Its sole reaction to the situation was intensified repression, which produced thousands of victims but had little effect on the insurgents and simply hastened its own political deterioration.

In this period the state seems to have weakened more rapidly than would have been expected from the effect of guerrilla activity alone; if that deterioration had continued the state would probably have entered into a definitive crisis. Internal wars are different from conventional wars, and it is not unusual for rebels, even though markedly inferior in strictly military terms, to achieve victory under certain political conditions. The triumph of the insurgents in Cuba in 1959 and in Nicaragua in 1979 are examples.

Initially the army's responses to the political deterioration of the government of President Lucas García were purely military. The improvement of the intelligence apparatus enabled the army to dismantle important guerrilla bases in the capital city in June 1981. In November General Benedicto Lucas mounted a general counteroffensive in the department of Chimaltenango, where the insurgents, particularly the EGP, had increased their activity. As the department was near the capital, they hoped to cut communications between Guatemala City and the western provinces where the war was for the most part concentrated. The army's attack was launched on November 25 by close to 5,000 troops, a number sufficiently large to weaken its reserves and its garrisons in other parts of the country. Had the guerrilla forces been better coordinated they probably would have counterattacked in other areas and strengthened their position. Even so, the offensive had little success in inflicting casualties upon guerrilla military units, which tended to flee the confrontation and redeploy. The army was able, however, to demolish local bases of rebel support and to start organizing its own bases, establishing a model that would be more fully implemented later.

But the country's political problems could not be resolved under the existing government, whose loss of legitimacy was accelerated by the fraudulent general elections in March 1982.[6] A military coup in that month brought General Efraín Ríos Montt to power; subsequently he was overthrown in the August 1983 coup that brought General Oscar Mejía Víctores to the presidency. These governments created the conditions necessary for the development of a global counterinsurgency strategy. This strategy, drawn up by the Centro de Estudios Militares on the order of the high command, is laid out in the Guatemalan army's *Plan Nacional de Seguridad y Desarrollo* ("National Plan for Security and Development") of April 1982.[7] The *Plan Nacional* details a political-military strategy which was implemented through operations instituted in three phases:

1. Victoria 82, a predominantly military phase, entailing an offensive against the principal guerrilla fronts, their strategic forces, and their civilian support base.
2. Firmeza 83, a military phase continuing the offensive against the opposition's strategic forces while also incorporating population control by concentrating the people in strategic hamlets.
3. Encuentro Institucional 84 and Estabilidad 85, the predominantly political phase in which electoral processes were initiated to provide

for the election of a civilian government in an effort to reestablish
political legitimacy.

The Military Operations

The first guerrilla assessments of the military offensive that followed the
Chimaltenango attack cast doubt on its chances of success.[8] After the coup
d'état of March 1982, however, the offensive continued under the rubric of
Victoria 82, now within the framework of a broad political reconstruction.
The objective of the offensive was not only the recovery of governmental
control over disputed areas but also the destruction of guerrilla military
units: "The mission is to destroy the guerrilla forces. The control of territory
is a means to this end, but never an end in itself." At the same time, the
"mind of the population is our principal objective."[9] The army continued
its operations throughout 1982, primarily attacking the departments of
Quiché and Huehuetenango and, to a lesser extent, Petén and San Marcos.
Its objective, as in the Chimaltenango offensive, was to destroy the guerrillas'
bases of support.

The social cost of the Victoria 82 offensive was high. Intelligence work
had enabled the army to locate and therefore attack the principal villages
supporting the guerrillas. Although some of them had a rudimentary self-
defense organization, they were not prepared to fight against helicopter-
transported troops. The military actions, seemingly directed indiscriminately
against all inhabitants, affected noncombatants such as children and the
elderly. On occasion the army adopted a scorched-earth tactic, which included
the destruction of buildings and of fields ready for sowing and the killing
or dispersal of livestock and domestic animals. The policy of militarily
attacking the guerrillas' bases of civilian support follows the logic of
counterinsurgency:

> . . . the diminution or destruction of the organization of support will be the
> primary objective of the cleanup and retention operations. It [the support]
> cannot be neutralized or destroyed by combat action against guerrillas, but
> such action can leave the organization defenseless, allowing it to be identified
> and destroyed by the population and resource control forces.[10]

Only approximate statistics are available to calculate the war's effects in
the combat zones during the offensives of 1981 and 1982. The army estimates
that 440 towns, villages, and hamlets were destroyed.[11] Other sources
estimate that immediately after the military operations one million people
were displaced or had to flee, becoming internal refugees. In addition, close
to 150,000 people fled to Mexico as refugees. Early estimates placed the
number of deaths at 10,000 to 20,000,[12] but later figures, probably based
on more reliable data, indicate that between 50,000 and 75,000 people died
or disappeared as a result of the war in the altiplano in the 1980–1984
period.[13]

The purely military effects of the offensives, in terms of the number of engagements recorded and the casualties suffered by both sides, are even harder to estimate, given that the figures offered by the belligerents are contradictory and probably exaggerated. It is likely, however, that from the end of 1981 to the end of 1982 close to 150 engagements of various types took place in the affected zones. Official statistics claim that 636 insurgents were killed, whereas army casualties numbered only 105;[14] according to guerrilla sources the army lost 503 dead (no figures were given on their own casualties).[15] These data, though only indicative, point to two conclusions: (1) the high number of actions and the relatively low number of deaths suggest that the engagements were mainly combat by infantry patrols; (2) there is a marked disproportion between military casualties and the civilian casualties mentioned earlier.

At the end of 1982 President Efraín Ríos Montt announced victory for the army. In at least three previously contested areas of guerrilla activity (the departments of Chimaltenango, Quiché, and Huehuetenango) local guerrilla support networks had been destroyed and government authority reestablished. As most of the regular insurgent units seem to have eluded government attacks, however, the army's strategic offensive had not achieved all its objectives. For the insurgent movement, the 1981 and 1982 offensives marked a serious military reversal and dissipated the possibilities of the short-term victory it had visualized a year or so earlier.

The tactical defeat suffered by the revolutionaries had several causes. First, the tasks of organizing the population for war, and of agitating for and building a popular movement to support the war and ultimately to engage in insurrection, were not coordinated. Although the high point of the popular struggle in both countryside and city was reached between 1978 and 1980, the highest levels of military development were not achieved until 1980–1981. The disparity in timing was not solely a consequence of the social dynamic, for the counterinsurgency, foreseeing that the two levels of rebellion might peak simultaneously, managed to disarticulate the popular movement organized in 1978–1980. Second, the various rebel movements had not achieved the unity that would have allowed maximum use of their military resources. Although together they constituted an alternative army in formation, their lack of coordination permitted the counterinsurgency forces to attack them separately. Third, a sector of the revolutionary forces, lacking a realistic appreciation of the correlation of forces, overestimated its own capacity while underestimating that of the army. Thus the 1981 order to generalize the guerrilla war throughout most of the country seems to have been premature; the guerrillas apparently lacked the necessary logistical and organizational structures for such a step.

Finally, the rebels had no adequate response to the political aspect of the counterinsurgency strategy. Even when this aspect was obviously hampering the coordination of forces, the insurgents, viewing it as simply an aspect of psychological warfare, continued to downplay its strategic importance. Even so, the army failed to accomplish the military destruction of the armed popular groups. The guerrillas' strategic forces are still continuing their operations, having demonstrated a greater than expected capacity to withstand blows and, presumably, to correct their military-political strategy. Consequently, the guerrilla war is not over, nor does a conclusion seem near at hand.

Socioeconomic and Psychological Operations: Population Control

Model Villages and Development Poles

An important principle of internal wars is to relocate and concentrate part of the population so as to separate it from the insurgent forces. The purpose is to, "(a) cut off the population's support for the guerrillas, (b) discover and neutralize the insurgents' organization and activities in the community, (c) provide the population with a physically and psychologically secure environment."[16]

The aim is not simply to move people into specific communities. It is essential to organize their daily lives under elaborate controls and subject them to psychological warfare. For the most part, these controls are based on intelligence-gathering operations that investigate "people's thinking on insurrection, individual movement, open and secret meetings, out-of-the-ordinary acquisitions of goods, guerrilla propaganda, mass reactions to government measures, location of the guerrillas' secret agents, [and] information on combat." A second aspect includes the rationing of provisions "to avoid having a good part of them end up with the guerrillas," and the "control of vital necessities such as food, fuel, oil, lubricants, and ammunition" and of the movement of persons and vehicles.[17]

Psychological operations seek to influence the population's behavior. People's reactions to the measures outlined above—rationing of foodstuffs, searches, limitations on movement, surveillance—mean that a psychological operation is needed to convince them that these measures are absolutely necessary and due to the actions of the guerrillas and their collaborators.[18] At the same time an attempt should be made to provide favorable conditions for the concentrated population, so the strategic hamlets cannot be likened to concentration camps. This dual vision of military and developmental needs is embodied in the organization of development poles.[19]

The concentration of the rural population in the war zones, officially dubbed "zones in conflict," and in strategic hamlets, initially called "model villages," began during the Victoria 82 offensive. In the course of the Firmeza 83 offensive, the effort to concentrate the population in regions called "Poles of Development and Services" intensified. At the beginning of 1985 five poles of development covered areas of the departments of Huehuetenango, Quiché, Alta Verapaz, and Petén, with a total of 52 strategic hamlets and a population that probably surpassed 20,000. There were plans to develop hamlets in the departments of Sololá and Chimaltenango.[20]

The poles of development were established in areas of conflict; some model hamlets were built in the same places where villages had been destroyed. The population of the hamlets included some of the original inhabitants and some from other areas. Immediately after the destruction of communities in the region, perhaps hundreds of thousands of campesinos fled to and remained in the mountains. The army and the patrols it subsequently formed have persistently searched these wooded areas, locating encampments of displaced persons and steering the inhabitants to the model hamlets. The recovered groups are commonly portrayed as having been "prisoners" of the guerrillas or as surrendered followers of the insurgents.[21] Apparently some of the people living in the mountains continue to elude the military and to resist its efforts to resettle them.[22]

Some of the model villages are similar to the reeducation camps in other areas that have experienced internal war. The inhabitants of such camps are tightly controlled and are subjected to ideological indoctrination, with public rituals featuring repentance by old insurgent militants; they submit to heavy schedules of ceremonies, talks, discussions, group dynamics, and the like, apparently aimed at a change of consciousness. Possibly displaced persons who have militant revolutionary histories are taken to these camps.[23] In the other model hamlets, the pattern of organization and daily life corresponds to the more usual pattern in other counterinsurgency experiences: close control of all kinds of activity aimed at preventing any type of support for the insurgents; ideological work; and the provision of services that will materially improve the standard of living—electric power, potable water, communications, health services, education, means of transport, access to land, and technical assistance.

It is too early to assess the army's success with the develoment poles, as the project is still in the developmental phase. According to field studies, the achievement of established objectives has varied: in some hamlets the inhabitants have satisfactory services and access to land, whereas in others living conditions are still precarious.[24] What stands out in every instance, however, is the formidable dimensions of the problem. If we assume the figure of a million internal *desplazados*, it would seem that the poles, which have barely integrated 20,000, have had little impact. Cost is also a factor limiting extension of the project. Although precise figures are lacking, official calculations place the cost of a hamlet such as Ojo de Agua in the development pole Triángulo Ixil at Q344,251.05.[25] A network of poles incorporating a substantial number of the *desplazados* would take ten years to complete at an estimated cost of a billion quetzales.[26]

If successful, the poles of development program could lead to substantial social change in the affected indigenous campesino population. The program seeks to create a large number of small property owners imbued with a capitalist mentality, which would generate loyalty for the regime. The substitution of export crops for traditional subsistence crops would break down the isolation of the subsistence campesinos, rapidly incorporating them into mercantile and material credit channels. All these procedures together might hasten ethno-cultural change among indigenous campesinos.

But aside from the question of costs, there are structural limits to the fulfillment of this objective. In the majority of the development poles the state has taken over the land of the destroyed communities or has bought or rented property. The land is distributed in individual lots, sometimes with property titles. But distribution is a slow process affecting only a portion of the settlers in the model hamlets. It is highly improbable that the army will find a solution to Guatemala's agrarian problem, which has been a fundamental cause of the country's social ills and of the rebellion itself. To date the army has been unable to carry out an agrarian reform and lacks the resources for alternative programs providing for the purchase of land or for colonization on the scale needed. Nor has it the capacity to resist pressures from the oligarchy, which rejects any change in patterns of land tenancy. Agrarian reform is likely to continue on a very modest scale which cannot significantly enhance campesino life.

Military Organization: The Civil Patrols

In internal wars the institutional forces, in addition to concentrating the population in selected communities, often seek to organize the people militarily to support the government. The objective is both military—to create local militias more familiar with the terrain who can assume local defense tasks, freeing regular troops from that function—and political—to bring part of the population militarily to the government's side, further alienating it from the rebels.

As noted earlier, during the first stage of the war in 1960–69, in the eastern region of Guatemala, civilians were recruited to serve as army auxiliaries in paramilitary corps. These corps, however, resembled vigilante groups charged with local repression, and were probably the origin of the secret anticommunist groups that carried out numerous extrajudicial executions. During the administration of Lucas García, militias called Patrullas de Autodefensa Civil (PAC; civil defense patrols) began to be formed; one of the first was the Zaragoza *ladino* cavalry, which appeared at the end of 1980. Soon, however, within the framework of Victoria 82 the army began to form patrols on a massive scale, utilizing the population concentrated in the strategic hamlets. The organization of patrols was later extended throughout the country, although they are more numerous in the war areas. At the beginning of 1985 official statistics cited 900,000 *patrulleros* in the country as a whole, an extraordinarily high number that amounts to almost 12 percent of Guatemala's population.

Although officially the PACs are voluntary, testimonies and observations from the field indicate that participation may in fact be forced.[27] All male adults and occasionally young women are expected to take part. The duties basically consist of twenty-four-hour patrols around the community every ten or fifteen days. Commonly some 10 percent of the population of these communities is permanently mobilized. The objective of this kind of territorial defense is to monitor the movement of persons and to guard bridges, roads, and other fixed positions in order to make the mobilization of the insurgents and their contact with the civilian population more difficult. When the army carries out operations in PAC areas, it usually mobilizes dozens of patrols as auxiliary mobile troops, allowing one or two army companies to be accompanied by thousands of *patrulleros*,[28] who then function as auxiliaries in combat.

The PACs are usually under the immediate command of individuals whose loyalty to the government is proven, such as military commissioners (local agents of the army). Their arms vary; in combat zones they are often equipped with infantry firearms, but the large majority of PAC members are reputedly armed only with hunting and target rifles or even with clubs and ropes. It is estimated that no more than 2 percent of the PACs are supplied with modern weapons. PACs in war zones are better organized, equipped, and controlled than those in other parts of the country, where the organization is more embryonic and tends to have a preventive and preemptive role.

It is difficult to establish the PACs' military prowess; their contact with the guerrillas is rare, since the latter pursue a policy of avoiding confrontation with the *patrulleros* and seek instead to work with them politically. Various sources report low morale among the *patrulleros*, who see PAC service as an additional burden and participate only because they fear being tagged as subversives. There have been reports, however, that some PAC units serve with enthusiasm and even take part in extrajudicial executions.[29]

The PACs also have a political role, acting as another means of control by permitting the detection of affection for or disaffection from the government on the basis of participation in the militias. Another political objective is to create a spirit of opposition between the civilian population and the guerrillas through armed encounters. As there are few known experiences in which militias have been organized on the scale of those in Guatemala, no valid comparisons can be drawn. It is still too early to judge their effort, but the strictly military benefits hardly seem to justify the scale of the mobilization.

The National System of Interinstitutional Coordinators

The most comprehensive structure in the new triangular form of state-society relations is the National System of Interinstitutional Coordinators, a complex administrative system that parallels the existing governmental structure. Like the poles of development and the civilian patrols, it follows precedents in counterinsurgency strategy used by ad hoc territorial and administrative organizations. Government functions come to depend on the armed forces as a mechanism that permits both tighter control of the population in insurgent regions and pursuit of public and private development policies within the framework of counterinsurgency. The administrative-military mechanisms established by Israel in zones of Palestine seem to have been the immediate reference for the model employed in Guatemala. The Guatemalan precedent is the structure established after the earthquake of 1976, through which the Committee for National Reconstruction and the

National Emergency Committee centralized public and private resources for reconstruction under the direction of army officials.

To implement counterinsurgency and population control in accordance with the Victoria 82 offensive, the armed forces had sought to channel and centralize resources needed for the reconstruction and development of zones destroyed in the war. Among several plans drawn up during the presidency of General Lucas García was the Eastern Social Action Plan (PASO), which the president rejected with his characteristic lack of interest in reformist policies inherent in any counterinsurgency strategy.

The administration of General Ríos Montt, however, carried out the Program for Assistance to Areas in Conflict in successive phases known as Fusiles y Frijoles ("rifles and beans") and Techo, Trabajo y Tortilla ("roof, work, and tortilla"), as well as the policy of "food for work" in building the strategic hamlets. In the course of the Firmeza 83 offensive the National System of Interinstitutional Coordinators was implemented, though it has undergone several modifications before reaching its present form.

The system establishes four administrative levels under the army. They are responsible for designing and executing development programs from the national level down to the hamlet, using resources from government ministries, decentralized organizations, and private development agencies. At the top is the National Interinstitutional Coordinator under the direction of chief of staff of national defense; below are departmental interinstitutional coordinators, the municipal interinstitutional coordinators, and finally the local development committees. Each level consists of a board in which ministries, decentralized organizations, representatives of neighborhood groups, cooperatives, and the like participate. A representative of the army, usually a G-5 official (development and civilian affairs), plays a part in each interinstitutional coordinator.[30] The official purpose of the coordinators is to improve the design and execution of development policies, with the goal of benefiting the provincial or rural population, and to improve the administration of resources—a task the army believes it is better equipped to carry out than other state institutions.

The national interinstitutional coordinators, the poles of development, and the civil patrols control a vast region of Guatemala under a specific concept of development and forms of social relations and within a framework of concrete socioeconomic plans. This concept posits a model of rural development based on the substitution of export crops for crops destined for the home market, such as corn. Military leaders visualize a future for the Guatemalan *altiplano* of chains of modern farms producing for export and organized to stave off insurrection.[31]

Political Operations

By the late 1970s electoral fraud and government manipulation of political parties had weakened the political process in Guatemala. By 1981 the extreme repression practiced by the Lucas García government had reached the center of the political spectrum, including parties of Christian democratic and social democratic inspiration, the labor and popular movements, as well as sectors of the Catholic church. The result was the disarticulation, almost the elimination, of moderate social and political elements that play a mediating role in the political process. Important sections of political and popular leadership, which under other circumstances would have established their own centrist project, were pushed toward revolutionary positions, culminating in an alliance with the revolutionary forces in the Democratic Front against the Repression (FDCR), created in 1979. Thus government policies had caused an extreme polarization of society. The armed opposition had begun to develop an authentic alternative to government policies, incorporating the demands of highly diverse social groups. Hegemony was passing to the armed organizations, which were politically, though not military, in a favorable position to assume power.

The Lucas García government was oblivious to this situation. The problem, however, was clearly perceived by the military command, which after the coup d'état of March 1982 developed the strategy of "political opening" to resolve it. The fundamental objective was to reincorporate the middle sectors. Subsequently, the Ríos Montt government modified the standards governing political parties, stimulating their formation or reemergence; it also initiated contacts with centrist sectors of the opposition. Eventually Ríos Montt was accused of attempting to manipulate the political opening to his personal advantage, which contributed to his overthrow.

Under the succeeding presidency of Mejía Víctores and throughout the Firmeza 83 and Encuentro Institucional (Institutional Reencounter) 84 offensives, the government issued new electoral rules. Elections for the National Constituent Assembly took place in 1984, and two rounds of general elections in 1985 culminated in December in the election of a civilian president, Vinicio Cerezo of the Christian Democratic party. The operation Institutional Reencounter achieved its ends. The middle sectors that had been opposed to the government were reincorporated into the political process. The presidential election was not manipulated, control of the government was indeed in contention among participating parties. Voter turnout was high, and abstention from voting, though fluctuating around 40 percent in the three elections, was the lowest since 1958.[32] The vote favored centrist political forces,[33] and the president-elect won percentages of the vote in both rounds which had not been achieved since 1944 and 1958.

The opposition tied to the insurgent forces maintained that the elections were held in the context of repeated and gross violations of human rights and of army control of a substantial part of the electorate; it also noted the high levels of abstention (including disqualified and blank ballots).[34] It is evident that given the war, part of the population accepted the electoral outcome, while another part—difficult to quantify—apparently continued to consider violent forms of struggle legitimate. Nevertheless, the new government, invested with the legitimacy of having been constitutionally elected by a large vote, found itself in a better political position to prosecute the war than any that had preceded it. Whereas from a military perspective the election was an important aspect of counterinsurgency strategy, the parties that entered the contest saw it as a step toward the democratization of the country.

The new Christian Democratic government is seeking to implement a development project based on pacts with different social groups and to expand its autonomy vis-à-vis the military. From the counterinsurgency viewpoint, the objectives of the war made it necessary to allow a civilian government to take power so as to legitimize the state. The civilian authority, however, comes into conflict with the military's need for hegemony over society in certain areas because of the war effort. Examples of the tension thereby engendered have surfaced in the civilian government's efforts to place the System of Interinstitutional Coordinators under its control (via the Ministry of Development) and its cautious attempt to improve human rights. In June 1986, for example, the Army Chief of Staff, General Hector Gramajo (subsequently Minister of Defense), made statements to the press indirectly criticizing the Minister of the Interior of the new Christian Democratic administration for attempting to extend its control over the police force in order to control abuses and human rights violations. This was one of the first public clashes between the Army and the civilian members of government, and illustrates the extreme difficulties the new government confronts in resolving such questions.[35]

The International Situation and Counterinsurgency

The Guatemalan army's counterinsurgency strategy was largely selfgenerated and self-sustained. Participation by successive U.S. administrations, especially in the supply of arms and in pilot training, was not particularly significant. The interruption in the provision of military aid by the Carter administration, owing to the abuse of human rights, continued to have political effect—alienating certain Guatemalan right-wing groups from the United States—even when allies of the United States, in particular Israel and Taiwan—supported the Guatemalan army's counterinsurgency effort. Nevertheless, the counterinsurgency strategy in Guatemala clearly served the U.S. strategy in Central America. The solution sought by the United States in El Salvador—the combination of military advances, elections as a political weapon, substitution of a civilian government for a military one, and a reformist program—has been applied in Guatemala with little participation by the United States and, consequently, with little political cost to the White House.

At the same time, the coincidence of interests between the Guatemalan and U.S. governments has not been total. Guatemala's foreign policy under the military government, continued by the current civilian government, officially calls for neutrality and normal relations with Nicaragua, thereby distancing itself from the U.S. policy of hostility toward the Sandinista government. The Guatemalan policy probably stems in part from resentment toward the United States dating back to 1954, when a mercenary army organized by the Central Intelligence Agency overthrew the government of President Jacobo Arbenz Guzmán, an episode interpreted in Guatemalan military thought as a humiliation suffered by the army at the hands of a force organized by foreigners. The interruption of military aid by the Carter administration in 1977 heightened the resentment. In addition, a realistic assessment of the demands of the internal war, which requires all the resources of the armed forces, makes the Guatemalan military reluctant to become involved in international conflicts. Sectors of the industrial bourgeoisie are also anxious to keep open the Nicaraguan and Central American markets. These considerations reinforce President Vinicio Cerezo's international perspective and help to explain the persistence of a policy now called "active neutrality." Nevertheless, this policy is subject to intense pressures from the Reagan administration; based as it is on pragmatic considerations, the policy could change when Guatemala's needs for more economic and military aid make such a shift expedient.

Conclusion

Between 1980 and 1985 the Guatemalan army conceived and implemented a counterinsurgency strategy that allowed it to improve substantially its military and political position vis-à-vis the insurgents. The multifaceted and complex strategy was not accepted in its entirety by the dominant class or even by sectors within the army itself. Its execution was characterized by advances and retreats. The military sector pushing it attempted to impose it both by force and by persuasion and did not hesitate to use repressive measures against either the dominant class or its own members in the process. From a theoretical perspective, the army as an institution seems to have acted in the interests of the state, with a broader vision of class interest than that held by fractions of the dominant class. The military could not always achieve its goals, however, and sometimes had to retreat before the oligarchy, as when the latter opposed the agrarian policies of the Ríos Montt government and the attempts at tax reform by the Mejía Víctores government. It also encountered difficulties in its efforts to open social and political space, simultaneously seeking participation by and control over popular sectors, as evident in the hunger riots in Guatemala City in August and September 1985. Still, the army did succeed in imposing its strategy and achieving its short-term objectives.

With respect to longer-term objectives, however, the counterinsurgency strategy did not resolve the country's conflict, nor did it solve the fundamental problems that gave rise to the war. The counterinsurgency perceives these problems and is attempting to find a solution, but the possibility of changing Guatemalan society without fundamental reform of land tenure patterns and patterns of social relations is remote. The basic issue is the viability of reformism in Guatemala. Although a country with ample economic resources can improve conditions for a sector of the population under the banner of counterinsurgency without redistributing property and income, this is not the situation of Guatemala and it is unlikely that measures being undertaken will achieve the desired goals on the scale envisioned.

Guatemala's model of accumulation rests on the superexploitation of labor, and the base of that model—agricultural and agro-industrial production—depends on the availability of vast reserves of labor for the harvest. One potential effect of the army's activity in radically disrupting the patterns of life and production in the *altiplano* region is to reduce the availability of *minifundista* land and thus accelerate the process of proletarianization. This process could make available to Guatemala's dominant sectors a vast reserve of labor, even more controlled and less autonomous than before. But it would bring other problems, as the superexploitation of this labor force has made the *minifundio* necessary for its reproduction. To assume that this drawback could be compensated for by raising agricultural pay rates and augmenting social benefits through services planned for development poles is to ignore the characteristics of the system of domination. It is the rigidity of the classist and racist patterns of social domination that have made such measures as moderate changes in agrarian property ownership (recommended by AID in 1980) unworkable, even though they might eventually alleviate social pressure in the rural areas. The basic contradiction between the reformist aspects of modern counterinsurgency and the refusal by dominant sectors to accept any reform for any reason has not yet been resolved.

The effects of rural counterinsurgency in Guatemala could in fact turn out to be the opposite of those sought by the armed forces. Analyses of revolutions in peasant countries in different epochs have yielded the hypothesis that it is those masses that have been stripped of their land and their traditional forms of life—but not incorporated into other forms of work and life—that join revolutionary movements most readily and with the strongest determination. The few empirical data available for Guatemala indicate an acceleration of the process of pauperization, but not proletarianization, in the *altiplano* in the late 1970s and early 1980s, a period coinciding with the growth of insurgency.

It is also possible that elements of the counterinsurgency social model, such as the system of Interinstitutional Coordinators, will be questioned and limited by the civilian government, which may attempt to reintegrate them into the normal administration as regional councils for rural development. It is not likely, however, that the armed forces will relinquish control of fundamental areas of government and society. Nor is an end to the internal warfare foreseeable in the medium term. This type of conflict does not usually end with a single dramatic event, such as a battle; instead, it winds down over a prolonged period. There are ways of detecting that popular support for an armed struggle has weakened and that a nucleus of revolutionaries has become progressively isolated, eventually fighting alone without realistic possibility of winning or the capacity to alter or influence the life of the society. The Malayan insurgents, though defeated in the 1950s, continued to fight for nearly twenty more years, even after their country had achieved independence. Conversely, there may be indications that the power of a state, and the will of its armed apparatus and the dominant class to fight, have diminished, as demonstrated by the Somoza government in Nicaragua in the first half of 1979.

At present, however, neither of these tendencies is discernible among the combatants in the internal war in Guatemala. Consequently it is likely that the struggle will persist through the next half decade. During that period either of the contending parties may advance or intermediate forces may accumulate sufficient strength to constitute a viable alternative. In the meantime there is no evidence that the contradictions that gave rise to the Guatemalan conflict are near resolution.

Notes

1. For an analysis of the first phase of the internal war in Guatemala, see Richard Gott, *Rural Guerrillas in Latin America* (London: Penguin Books, 1973), Part One; Robert Lamberg, "Guatemala: Marx contra Marx," in *Die Castristische Guerrilla in Latinamerika*, Verlag für Literatur und Zeitgeschehen (1971); Gabriel Aguilera, *La violencia como fenómeno político en Guatemala*, CIDOC (Mexico City, 1971).
2. See "La cuestión militar," *Opinión Política* 2 (Guatemala City), January–February 1985.
3. The army estimates that by 1980–1981 the insurgents could count at least 260,000 supporters ("Discurso del Señor Jefe del Estado Mayor de la Defensa Nacional, General de la Brigada Rodolfo Lobos Zamora," in *Polos de desarrollo* [Guatemala City: Editorial del Ejército, 1985]).
4. Four insurgent organizations made up the *Unidad Revolucionaria Nacional Guatemalteca* (URNG) in 1982, including a sector of the communist *Partido Guatemalteco del Trabajo* (PGT). The party sectors were unable to develop militarily, however, and in 1985 the URNG reorganized itself around the three more important organizations.
5. "La cuestión militar."
6. The fraud perpetrated in that month's elections was mentioned as one of the motives given for the March 1982 coup d'état by its organizers (see "La proclama emitida por los golpistas el 23 de Marzo de 1982).
7. Guatemalan Army, *Plan nacional de seguridad y desarrollo* (Guatemala City: Centro de Estudios Militares, 1 April 1984).
8. Organización del Pueblo en Armas, "Elementos característicos del momento actual: Expresiones especiales de una crisis final" (Guatemala City, January 1982).
9. Estado Mayor del Ejército, Palacio Nacional, Guatemala City, "Appendix H" (standing order for the development of anti-subversive operations) of "Plan de campaña victoria '82," cited in George Black et al., *Garrison Guatemala* (New York: Monthly Review Press, 1984).
10. United States Army, Escuela de Guerra Especial, "Guía para el planeamiento de la contrainsurgencia," FM-31-176 (Fort Bragg, NC, n.d.).
11. "Discurso del Señor Jefe del Estado Mayor."
12. Luisa Frank, et al., *Indian Guatemala: Path to Liberation* (Washington, DC: EPICA Task Force, 1984).
13. Chris Krueger, et al., *Security and Development Conditions in the Guatemalan Highlands*, (Washington, D.C.: Washington Office on Latin America, 1985).
14. Figures from the Guatemalan press of the period, which mainly reproduced official communiqués.

15. Figures are given in insurgent publications of the period, especially *El informador guerrillero del EGP.*

16. "Guía para el planeamiento."

17. Andrés Cassinello Pérez, *Operaciones de guerrillas y contraguerrillas* (Madrid: COMPI, 1966); "Guía para el planeamiento."

18. "Guía para el planeamiento."

19. Officers give their candid views on the role of the develoment poles in *Guatemala: Acción cívica militar en la guerra contrainsurgente* (Guatemala City, 1985). This document, which contains a summary of interviews with military officers, is, in my opinion, authentic.

20. "Mensaje del jefe del Estado General Oscar Humberto Mejía Víctores al pueblo de Guatemala sobre importantes aspectos de su labor gubernativa," *El Gráfico* (Guatemala City, 12 January 1985); and Krueger, et al., *Security and Development.* Other estimates, however, place the number of inhabitants of the development poles as high as 600,000 (see "Más de medio millón de personas asentados en polos de desarrollo," *Diario de centroamérica* [Guatemala City], 11 March 1985).

21. "Discurso del señor jefe del Estado Mayor."

22. On these groups, called Comunidades en Resistencia, see Iglesia Guatemalteca en el Exilio, *La montaña nos ha enseñada* 5, No. 1 (March 1985).

23. In particular, the hamlet of Acamal has been referred to as a reeducation camp. For contrasting views of this hamlet see the descriptions by Krueger et al., *Security and Development,* and the United Nations Economic and Social Council, "Informe sobre la situación de los derechos humanos en Guatemala, preparado por el relator especial, Vizconde Colville de Culross, de conformidad con el párrafo 14 de la resolución 1984/53 de la comisión de derechos humanos," Doc. E/CN.4/ 1985/19, 14 March 1984.

24. Krueger et al., *Security and Development.*

25. "Discurso del señor jefe del Estado Mayor."

26. "Primer plano: General Federico Fuentes Corado," *El Gráfico* (Guatemala City), 9 September 1982.

27. Ricardo Falla, "Genocidio en Guatemala," in Tribunal Permanente de los Pueblos, Sesión Guatemala (Madrid: IEPALA, 1984).

28. "Persiguen a subversivos," *Prensa Libre* (Guatemala City), 19 November 1983.

29. On the PACs see Frank et al., *Indian Guatemala,* "Milicia india persigue a la guerrilla en Guatemala, *El Imparcial,* 6 January 1983; "Hombres y mujeres ingresan a autodefensa civil," *Prensa Libre,* 30 April 1983; "Patrullas civiles y el voto," *El Gráfico,* 25 May 1984; "En Taxisco juramentan a patrullas de defensa civil," *Prensa Libre,* 23 April 1984; "Juramentaron comités de seguridad y emergencia," *Prensa Libre,* 3 December 1984; Comité Guatemalteco de Unidad Patriótica, "Alto al genocidio de un pueblo en lucha," 1983; Falla, "Genocidio en Guatemala;" Krueger et al., *Security and Development;* Gaspar Ilom, *Guatemala: El fracaso de la contrainsurgencia y la nueva dictadura* (Guatemala City, 1983).

30. On the Interinstitutional Coordinators see *Guatemala: Mayor coordinación de las coordinadoras interinstitucionales, Inforpress Centroamericana* 620, 12 June, 1984; Richard Allan White, *The Morass* (New York: Harper Books, 1984); Krueger et al., *Security and Development;* Movimiento Cooperativista Guatemalteco, *Boletín Informativo,* October 1985; "Iglesia Guatemalteca en el exilio," *Publíquese y cúmplase, las coordinadoras interinstitucionales,* 5, No. 2, (1985); "Discurso del señor jefe del Estado Mayor."

31. Army officers' comments on the development of Guatemala are in "Transforming the Indian Highlands," *Latin America Regional Report* (London, 6 May 1983), and in *Guatemala: acción cívica militar.*

32. The abstention rate had increased from 33.2 percent in 1958 to 65.2 percent in 1978. The abstention rate in the 1984 elections and the two rounds of elections in 1985 were 41.21 percent, 38.71 percent, and 39.8 percent, respectively. See Hector Rosada, *Guatemala 1984. elecciones para asamblea nacional constituyente,* Cuadernos de CEPAL, 2 (San José, 1985), and data of the Tribunal Supremo Electoral, "Resultados oficiales eleccionarios," *Prensa Libre,* 10 December 1985.

33. The two parties of the center together received 58.88 percent of the total vote; the five right-wing parties, 37.68 percent; the left-wing party, 3.42 percent.

34. According to this argument, of a total of 2,753,572 voters registered by the Supreme Electoral Tribunal, 953,816 did not go to the polls for the second round. To these must be added 127,913 disqualified ballots (*nulos*) and 24,588 blank ballots, for a total of 1,106,317 or 40 percent of the electorate. The Supreme Electoral Tribunal gives a lower figure because it does not include null and blank ballots in the category of "abstentionism." See "El abstencionismo marca la última vuelta electoral en Guatemala," *Cerigua* 94 (2–9 December 1985).

35. Editors' note: Several of these trends have been reinforced in the first two years of the Cerezo government, which appears to have reached an understanding with the military regarding the institutional coordinators structure. While the military still maintains control in the zones of conflict, the Cerezo government is converting the coordinators in other regions into bases for the Christian Democratic reformist project. But Cerezo, like the leaders of the military governments which preceded him, continues to be frustrated by private sector resistance to reform. The implementation of the ambitious counterinsurgency strategy of the Guatemalan army—particularly the phase of economic and social reforms—has been limited.

9

Exporting Democracy: The Unanticipated Effects of U.S. Electoral Policy in El Salvador

Terry Karl

The Reagan administration has sought to export democracy through the promotion of elections in Central America, and it actually began to claim outright success in this endeavor with the 1984 victory of José Napoleón Duarte in El Salvador. But such claims have been widely disputed in political and academic circles. If, on the one hand, elections in El Salvador have been praised as the symbol of the instauration of a democratic regime, on the other they have been strongly condemned as pure "demonstration elections" or the antithesis of democracy.[1] Given that the series of elections held between 1982 and 1985 cannot be fully understood until the political transition is complete and reliable data become available, how should these contending analyses be weighted?

In order to shed light on this question, it is important to discard the notion that elections in themselves constitute democracy. They can mark a major step forward in a broader process of democratization if they contribute to extending civil rights under a liberalized authoritarian regime or if they foster political equality, participation, accountability, and contestation. They can, however, also impede democratization, especially if they are used as a means of limiting basic individual and collective rights to levels that do not constitute durable guarantees of citizenship. Moreover, carefully staged elections may merely ratify existing power arrangements and serve to legitimate subsequent intervention by a foreign power to protect a threatened regime. Under these circumstances, the introduction of an electoral process

A more extensive version of this article, entitled "Imposing Consent: Electoralism versus Democracy in El Salvador," originally appeared in Paul W. Drake and Eduardo Silva, eds., *Elections and Democratization in Latin America, 1980–1985* (University of California, San Diego: Center for Iberian and Latin American Studies, 1986), pp. 9–36.

may actually prevent the successful forging of the basic socioeconomic and political compromise that permits democracy to endure.

First and foremost, the significance of elections in a period of transition should be assessed in light of their contribution toward forging the basic social pact or fundamental compromise that necessarily underlies any democracy. Elections that antedate this sort of broad agreement between contending forces are vulnerable to persistent challenges and may be expected to result in instability and future repression. It does not follow, however, that such contests can be dismissed as mere shams, even under conditions of authoritarian rule or civil war. They still may assume real significance regardless of the original intentions of those who call them. Such elections can shape politics in several ways: they may narrow options for actors on the extremes of the political spectrum, provide changes in the strategies of all political actors, encourage moderation or the demobilization of participants, and shift the agenda toward the definition of specific rules of the game which may delineate the extent of democratization in the future. Yet holding elections under these conditions may also increase the uncertainty inherent in any regime transition and may produce unlikely and unexpected results that backfire on the very actors who called for elections in the first place.

An examination of three elections in El Salvador—to choose the Constituent Assembly in 1982, to name a president in 1984, and to elect a legislature in 1985—reveals the fallacy of the Reagan administration's claim that democracy has been successfully introduced into El Salvador. In effect, the strongest impact of these electoral contests has been to permit escalation and prolongation of the war while preventing the negotiations that might have resulted in a fundamental social pact for a new regime. Nonetheless, these elections have evolved into something more significant than the antidemocratic demonstration exercise that may have been intended by their convokers and expected by some of their sharpest critics.

Blocking Negotiations:
The Imposition of an Electoral Strategy in 1982

The decision to hold elections in El Salvador in 1982 during a civil war was rooted primarily in a foreign policy crisis in the United States and only secondarily in events taking place in El Salvador. These elections were thus qualitatively different from those that had periodically legitimated military rule in the past.[2] Following the classic model of demonstration elections, the 1982 contest was imposed by the United States in order to improve the international image of the ruling Salvadoran junta as well as to deflect strong pressures for a negotiated settlement between domestic power contenders. The administration of President Ronald Reagan believed that giving a democratic cast to the junta would facilitate pursuit of a military victory against the Democratic Revolutionary Front/Farabundo Martí Front for National Liberation (FDR-FMLN) and block the spread of revolution in Central America. Specifically, elections in El Salvador could assuage a U.S. public that had grown skeptical of alliances with repressive Third World regimes and thereby free Congress to allocate sufficient funds to maintain the Salvadoran government.

Cleaning up the image of the military hard-liners who held power in El Salvador was not easy. Having blocked the electoral victory of reformist candidate José Napoleón Duarte in 1972, they had successfully restored their traditional alliance with economic elites in 1980 by overturning a short-lived progressive military-civilian junta which had taken power in October 1979. The 1980 junta's fierce repression of peasant, worker, church, and party groups helped to unify these organizations into a national front, the FDR-FMLN. State-directed violence against the FDR-FMLN, reformists, and apolitical bystanders reached the astonishing rate of more than 1,000 political murders a month—including the archbishop of San Salvador, five major FDR leaders, numerous union leaders, and four U.S. churchwomen— and soon provoked the outbreak of a full-scale civil war.

Despite strong repudiation of the bloody regime by most European and Latin American countries, President Jimmy Carter's administration supported the Salvadoran military but insisted that some degree of reform accompany increased assistance. The Carter administration forced the military to accept a partnership with its despised enemy, the Christian Democratic party, to promulgate land reform, and to appoint José Napoleón Duarte as president of the ruling junta.[3] After some initial hesitation about backing Duarte, the Reagan administration took an ever stronger stance. Ignoring the nationalistic (and even anti-Soviet) sentiments of the majority of the opposition,[4] it argued that Cuba and the Soviet Union were the source of revolutionary turmoil in the region and pledged to draw the line against communism in the hemisphere in El Salvador. This meant lending full U.S. support to the junta's efforts to defeat the surging rebellion.

This decision was unpopular. As state-sponsored political assassinations continued to mount through 1981, condemnation of U.S. backing for the Salvadoran regime increased, both internationally and domestically. In response to rising public concern over the army's involvement in death squad activity as well as the growing potential for direct U.S. intervention, the Congress began to restrict the administration's policy of seeking military victory by tying foreign aid legislation to a presidential certification of the curtailment of human rights abuses and the promotion of socioeconomic reform. Although the administration issued a white paper to defend the militaristic thrust of its policies in the name of anticommunism, Congress repeatedly threatened to cut funds to El Salvador. In 1981 the FDR-FMLN came out in favor of negotiations to end the war, an initiative tentatively supported by Duarte and the Christian Democrats. Meanwhile, Mexico began a series of diplomatic activities calling for negotiations, which ultimately culminated in the Contadora peace initiative in 1983. The Reagan administration's persistent refusal to support such a dialogue soon became a major obstacle to mediation efforts between the Duarte government and the FDR-FMLN, and diplomatically isolated the United States.[5]

Inside El Salvador, the Christian Democratic party faced similar isolation. Although Duarte had firmly defended the decision of the Christian Democratic party (PDC) to join the military junta, approximately one-fifth of the PDC's membership left the party in March 1980, declaring that they could not "participate in a regime which has unleashed the bloodiest repression ever experienced by the Salvadoran people."[6] Most of the disaffected PDC members joined the FDR-FMLN. By 1981 Duarte's obvious inability to control the military, to contain the growing strength of the FDR-FMLN, or to protect the members of his own party from repression created new tensions in the party. Because their alliance with the military had resulted in the worst of both worlds—responsibility for repression and waning authority, the Christian Democrats began to search for a way out of a political predicament.

Holding elections—the Reagan administration's response to the problem—provided a policy answer for both the United States and the Christian Democratic party. Thus it is not surprising that in July 1981 the U.S. called for "prompt, free and open elections."[7] Elections, Assistant Secretary of State Thomas Enders explained, were an alternative to negotiations between the government and the rebels and would provide the only political solution acceptable to the United States; the Reagan administration would not condone any form of compromise with the Salvadoran opposition. Although the primary function of the elections was to block growing pressure for a negotiated settlement, they were also integral to the overall strategy for winning the war. From the beginning, preparations for voting were coupled with increases in U.S. military aid to "make the guerrillas realize that they cannot win by force of arms," a pattern that would prevail in future elections.[8] The government deliberately excluded the FDR-FMLN, a force representing hundreds of thousands of Salvadorans, through repression so extreme that it prevented any open FDR-FMLN political activity (see Table 9.1). This exclusion was also reinforced by the legal framework of the electoral process.[9]

In the view of the Reagan administration, elections had the additional advantage of democratizing a domestically repugnant ally.[10] The electoral process would force the antidemocratic alliance of coffee growers and the military—led by Roberto D'Aubuisson, a man closely associated with the leadership of El Salvador's death squads—to organize itself into a political party and begin to play by somewhat more predictable rules. Indeed, in 1981, these forces formed ARENA (The National Republican Alliance), a new party financed largely by coffee growers and based upon ORDEN (the Nationalist Democratic Organization), a paramilitary organization established by the right. U.S. officials also believed that elections would serve as a consensus-building mechanism to consolidate a center-right alliance between the National Conciliation party (PCN), traditionally the party of the military, and the PDC, an alliance that could be used to isolate the left.

The electoral results of the contest among ARENA, the PCN, and the Christian Democratic party surprised the planners. Because the PDC was

TABLE 9.1
Deaths Attributable to Political Violence Immediately Before the
1982 Elections in El Salvador

Month	Press Reports	Legal Aid Office Reports
January	279	466
February	361	532
March	438	526
Total	1,078	1,524

Note: The figures given are lowest (first column) and highest
(second column) estimates for the period.

Source: U.S. Certification Hearings, 1982, Vol. II, p. 487,
cited in Edward S. Herman and Frank Brodhead, *Demonstration
Elections: U.S.-Staged Elections in the Dominican Republic,
Vietnam, and El Salvador* (Boston: South End Press, 1984), p. 145.

a mass-based party that had won an electoral victory as recently as 1972, ARENA represented the interests of the landowners, and the rightist vote would be split between ARENA and the PCN, U.S. policy-makers had anticipated an overwhelming victory for Duarte, the popular former mayor of San Salvador. Instead, although they won 35 percent of the total vote to ARENA's 26 percent, the Christian Democrats failed to gain a majority in the new, sixty-seat Constituent Assembly. U.S. political engineers had failed to take into account the PDC's lack of a strong rural base as well as the tendency to vote *oficialista*, or for the party most closely associated with the military, especially in the context of widespread political terror. Indeed, ARENA and the PCN proved strongest electorally in areas tightly controlled by the armed forces.[11]

The unexpected strength of the right threatened to undo the planned demonstration effect of the elections because the ultraright, headed by D'Aubuisson, announced that it would form a governing alliance with the PCN that would exclude the Christian Democratic party. The Reagan administration, realizing that a government led by D'Aubuisson would be a public relations disaster endangering future U.S. military aid, pressured the Salvadoran armed forces to deny the presidency to D'Aubuisson. After prolonged political wrangling, the army high command informed both Duarte and D'Aubuisson that neither of them would be provisional president and instead appointed Alvaro Magaña, a businessman, to the post. The right-wing alliance, furious at the United States, elected D'Aubuisson to the presidency of the Constituent Assembly and adopted legislation to annul much of the U.S.-promulgated land reform. In the end, the 1982 elections made it necessary for the army to appoint a president that had not even been a candidate, and led to the dismantling of land reform, an increase in foreign involvement in El Salvador's affairs, and the perpetuation of a civil war. Subsequent revelations of fraudulently inflated voter turnout even raised questions about the credibility of election procedures.

Although the elections had done little to advance democratization or reform, they did serve their function for the United States. Criticisms of administration policy dwindled in the wake of media enthusiasm over lines of voters, and Congress increased total aid to El Salvador by almost 100 percent. Direct military aid more than doubled between 1981 and 1982, permitting a sharp escalation of U.S. involvement in the war. As a secondary effect, the elections temporarily disorganized the FDR-FMLN. Opposition leaders gave conflicting instructions to their supporters to boycott the elections, spoil ballots, or engage in armed sabotage against the electoral process. The FDR-FMLN achieved some success in these tactics: estimates of the abstention rate hovered around 20 percent, and the number of spoiled or invalid ballots reached 12 percent.[12] But the new electoral strategy of the United States caused temporary disunity among the left while effectively placing a new barrier in the path of El Salvador's rebels.

Striking Bargains with the Right: Political Pacts and the 1984 Elections

A period of intense political turmoil followed the 1982 elections. Because the elections had preceded a basic political accommodation that established clear-cut rules of the game for the conduct of politics in El Salvador (even if only between the center right and the ultraright), conflict broke out immediately in the newly formed Constituent Assembly. Although the competition for votes had forced ultrarightists to organize themselves into a political party, ARENA, it had done little to diminish the ultraright's reliance upon terrorist tactics to resolve political disagreements. As tension mounted between the Christian Democratic party and the parties tied to the military (ARENA and PCN), the country became virtually ungovernable. Faced with a political paralysis which threatened the conduct of the war against the FDR-FMLN, the United States brought El Salvador's political parties together to make explicit agreements on which to base the rules for their future coexistence.

On 3 August, 1982, all of the parties that had participated in the 1982 elections signed the Pact of Apaneca, an agreement modeled after the 1958 Pact of Punto Fijo, which had marked the instauration of a democratic regime in Venezuela.[13] The Salvadoran accord, which established a government of national unity to regulate relations between the ultraright and the center right, had several basic features: (1) the parties agreed to establish a transitional political commission as a mechanism for governing until the 1984 presidential elections;[14] (2) they established a formula for power sharing between the ultraright and the center right by agreeing to use the results of the elections as a general guideline for dividing up all local posts of influence; (3) the parties pledged to lower the level of interparty disputes and to refrain from attacking the executive branch, particularly the president; (4) they set a timetable for the next stage of the transition by setting March 1983 as the deadline for writing a new constitution and March 1984 and March 1985, respectively, for presidential and legislative elections.

Civil war interrupted the temporary breathing space that followed formation of the government of national unity.[15] By 1983 fighting had increased tremendously in scale and was clearly shifting in favor of the FDR-FMLN. In January the FDR-FMLN carried out more than 181 military actions, culminating a highly successful offensive and demonstrating its ability to attack over a broad area of the country. This offensive, coupled with strong international criticism of human rights violations committed by the right, exacerbated existing divisions in the military and eventually precipitated a dispute within the army high command over the merits of a hard-line versus a semireformist course. Internal army conflicts were settled through a delicate compromise, but three factions had clearly emerged: an ultraright group closely linked to the coffee growers and opposed to reform; apolitical military technicians trained by the United States; and nationalists who favored widespread reform.

The governing political parties were also deeply divided. Their major disputes centered on land reform and, to a lesser extent, other economic reforms. Because the new constitution would establish the parameters of future land reform, a full-blown political crisis erupted in the Constituent Assembly during the drafting of that document. ARENA and the PCN, after having dissolved their coalition in January 1983, reunited to block completely or to limit the key phases II and III of land reform. When the Agency for International Development applied pressure to protect the reform during a close vote on constitutional language, the ultraright countered with death squad threats as part of its "legislative" tactics. Meanwhile, the PDC defended the third phase of the reform, mobilizing peasants to march into San Salvador. In a compromise mediated by the U.S. embassy, the assembly adopted two vague constitutional articles permitting former landowners to buy back their land and in effect providing the legal framework to quash the second phase of land reform. This action threatened the heart of the reform, which had been designed to break up the oligarchy's control of lucrative, medium-sized coffee farms and to create cooperatives for the landless. Since land reform was the key to ending the civil war and ensuring future democratization, the new constitution laid the foundation for further destruction and instability.[16]

The Reagan administration's policy on El Salvador faced similarly bleak prospects in 1983. Despite the temporary success of the 1982 elections, pressure to support a negotiated settlement in El Salvador increased in the United States, particularly because the alternative seemed to be the domestically unpopular prospect of direct military involvement. Harris polls conducted in the United States during 1982 and 1983 consistently demonstrated that 79 to 85 percent of respondents opposed the introduction of U.S. troops into El Salvador. Congress began to withhold funds from El Salvador, cutting a $60 million aid request in half to protest the lack of progress in the investigations of the deaths of four churchwomen and other citizens of the United States. By November 1983 Reagan was forced to take the embarrassing position of defending an openly repressive regime when he vetoed a bill that renewed human rights certification requirements on El Salvador as a condition of supplying aid to the regime.

Again, the Reagan administration chose elections as the means to alleviate a growing domestic policy crisis. In an attempt to ward off a major battle with Congress, the administration urged the Salvadoran government to advance the date of its presidential elections to demonstrate its commitment to reconciliation and democratic rule. Roberto Meza, the Christian Democratic representative to the Central Electoral Council, explained that U.S. envoy Richard "Stone told us, 'If you do the elections this year, we will give you all the money you need.'"[17] When technical difficulties prevented any acceleration in the election schedule, the United States began devoting its energies to producing a desirable outcome. Because an electoral victory for Roberto D'Aubuisson would permanently jeopardize congressional approval of aid and the pursuit of a military victory against the FDR-FMLN, the United States threw its influence into gaining the public relations advantages of a win by Duarte's Christian Democratic party.

In the six months preceding the presidential vote, the Reagan administration openly pursued a strategy of reining in the ultraright while enhancing Duarte's candidacy. The Central Intelligence Agency (CIA) gave financial support to the Unión Popular Democrática (UPD), a confederation of unions associated with the Christian Democratic party, which became Duarte's main electoral base. Although other parties also seem to have benefited from U.S. spending, the Reagan administration clearly favored the Christian Democratic party over the relatively well-financed ARENA.[18] In the end, the United States poured more than $10 million into the Salvadoran elections for electoral technology, the administration of the elections, and even the air fares of international observers. Despite a number of legal and administrative foul-ups, these actions brought the desired outcome: in a runoff election, Duarte won 53.6 percent of the vote compared to D'Aubuisson's 46.4 percent.

The chief result of the 1984 election, like that of 1982, was a major escalation of the war, made possible through a dramatic increase in U.S. aid (see Table 9.2). Duarte's victory marked a shift of government power from the extreme right, represented by ARENA and part of the military, to the center right, represented by the Christian Democratic party, part of the National Conciliation party, and part of the military. This shift, which began with the imposition of an electoral strategy in 1982, created a new image of the Salvadoran government, one that could justify growing U.S. involvement. Seduced by Duarte's democratic credentials, Congress began

TABLE 9.2
U.S. Military Assistance to El Salvador (in millions of dollars)

Year	Amount
1979	.04
1980	5.9
1981	35.6
1982	81.3
1983	81.3
1984	196.5
1985	132.5[1]

[1]Through April; further funding requested.
Source: Central America Research Institute, Berkeley, California.

moving to authorize additional military aid for El Salvador less than twenty-four hours after the runoff election. During the next five months the Reagan administration won approval for more military aid to El Salvador—$61.7 million for fiscal year 1984—than had been granted in the preceding four years combined.[19]

The leap in U.S. funding transformed the character of the war in El Salvador. What for the Salvadoran military had begun in 1980 as a civil war over socioeconomic reforms and political rights had by 1984 become a full-blown, foreign-directed conflict to defeat the FDR-FMLN. The United States, in addition to arming and training the military, began supporting aerial bombardments of the countryside and daily reconnaissance flights; it increased the technological sophistication of the war by introducing highly destructive AC-47 gunships and a large helicopter fleet; and it funded the army's expansion from 12,000 to 50,000 troops. Eventually American military personnel became openly involved in combat-related activities. Although these changes gave the Salvadoran military a strong technological advantage over the FDR-FMLN, the deepening U.S. engagement also accelerated the army's loss of political influence vis-à-vis the United States. Having grown completely dependent upon U.S. aid, the Salvadoran military (traditionally a fiercely nationalistic force) could no longer afford to act with its customary level of political autonomy.

The 1984 elections thus marked a turning point for foreign intervention in El Salvador. But, ironically, they also had the unintended secondary effect of making the range of permissible political expression wider than at any time since the outbreak of the war. Even though the FDR-FMLN was still excluded from the elections, the preelectoral atmosphere in 1984 provided a sharp contrast to that of the 1982 campaign. By placing restrictions on the terrorist activities of the ultraright, the Reagan administration helped to create a political opening in which labor and peasant unions, human rights groups, and other critics of the regime could become significantly more vocal. Open strikes, prohibited since the ferocious repression of 1980–81, broke out in the Social Security Institute, the Salvadoran Teachers' Union, the textile industry, and several financial institutions. These strikes, along with occasional street demonstrations, continued throughout 1984 and 1985. The growing militancy of labor strengthened the UPD, the most important peasant and labor federation permitted to operate without repression. As a result of its growing strength, the UPD was able to strike a bargain with the Christian Democrats, who agreed to support labor demands and dialogue in exchange for electoral support.

This resurgence of the popular movement was not surprising. By 1984 the living conditions of a majority of Salvadorans had become desperate: more than 50,000 people had died during the civil war, and a staggering 27 percent of the population had been displaced from their homes;[20] between 1979 and 1983 real minimum wages declined by 65 percent and consumption levels fell nearly 50 percent; almost 80 percent of the population was unemployed or underemployed.[21] Polls conducted before the March elections revealed that 70 percent of Salvadorans saw the war and the economy as the country's principal problems. A striking 51.4 percent supported dialogue with the FDR-FMLN as the best way of resolving these problems, openly expressing the view of the opposition. Only 10.3% favored annihilating the FDR-FMLN through a military victory.[22] Even with the smallest political opening, these views were bound to find expression in the electoral arena.

The restrictions placed on the ultraright in the 1984 elections gave Salvadorans their first meaningful, albeit limited, electoral choice. Although the contests took place between the same key political contenders that had participated in the 1982 campaign, this time the parties had strikingly different platforms. At one end of the spectrum, ARENA strenuously opposed economic reforms, particularly agrarian reform, and any kind of dialogue with the FDR-FMLN. It demanded a purely military resolution of the war. At the other end, the Christian Democratic party, impelled by an increasingly vocal constituency, called for agrarian reform, the disbanding of the feared Treasury Police, prosecution of the death squads, and a dialogue with the FDR-FMLN which might draw it into the municipal elections of 1984. Duarte's election represented the victory of this sharply defined vision over that of the right.

Thus the end results of the 1984 election were profoundly contradictory. To the extent that voters were free to choose—given the exclusion of the FDR-FMLN and the failure of 33 percent of the electorate to vote—the majority of Salvadorans endorsed an agenda of peace, a more equitable distribution of land, termination of human rights abuses, defense of the right of association and an opening toward the FDR-FMLN. Yet these preferences stood in direct contrast to the new round of military escalation made possible by the election.

Negotiations, War, and the
Political-Electoral Cycle in the 1984 Elections

The 1984 elections created a painful political dilemma for the new Duarte government. On the one hand, the regime was at the mercy of a U.S.-backed military establishment that viewed negotiations as weakness in the face of Soviet-inspired communism and pressured the government to preside over a military solution to El Salvador's problems. On the other hand, the Salvadoran people had given Duarte a mandate to end the war through negotiations and to proceed with reforms. The government's responses to these contradictory positions followed political rhythms that moved in tandem with the country's electoral cycle. Prior to the legislative elections of March 1985, the regime attempted to circumvent the United States, the army, and the private sector in order to implement short-term popular policies which appealed to a broad constituency. After the elections, it bowed to the forces that kept the government in power.

The new president immediately announced that he would strive to create a climate of security which could eventually permit the opposition to participate in elections. Four leading rightist officers, including Col. Nicolás Carranza (head of the Treasury Police) and Col. Denis Morán (implicated in the murder of two U.S. labor advisors), were transferred to posts outside El Salvador; both were known supporters of D'Aubuisson and suspected leaders of death-squad activity. In addition, Duarte dismantled the widely feared Treasury Police and took command of the security forces away from the regular army, thus bringing security matters under closer government supervision. In this restructuring, Duarte removed ultrarightists and replaced them with conservatives in charge of the police, an obvious boon to the Christian Democrats. The military's reaction was cautious. "If it stops here, it is okay," one high commander publicly warned. "But if it continues, it could become worrisome."[23]

The government's concessions to its base did not extend to the economic sphere.[24] Declining exports, severe economic sabotage, soaring unemployment, and strong pressure from the Reagan administration to strengthen the private sector intimidated the Christian Democratic administration, keeping it from taking action against the interests of El Salvador's economic elites. When the right-dominated National Assembly dismantled the last remnants of the pending land reform program, the government made no serious attempt to fight the move; on the contrary, the Christian Democrats tried to demobilize their angry peasant base. The UPD accused Duarte of failing to live up to his preelection commitments and threatened to withdraw its support from the government before the rapidly approaching legislative elections. Pushed by its party base, the Christian Democratic government attempted unsuccessfully to fight U.S. proposals to devalue the colón and implement an austerity program, measures that would strengthen the right and weaken the PDC prior to the elections.

By late 1984, as legislative elections approached, the Christian Democratic party's goal of "completing Duarte's power" by obtaining an electoral majority in the legislative elections seemed seriously endangered. In its first six months the Duarte government had achieved no demonstrable progress toward peace or economic recovery. The FDR-FMLN had adjusted to the postelectoral military escalation by settling in to fight a "prolonged war of attrition" intended to inflict casualties on the army, sabotage the economy, and encourage the resurgence of a popular movement in the cities.[25] The number of strikes and labor stoppages aimed at raising wages and initiating dialogue rose precipitously, and Christian Democrats often joined such actions. Meanwhile, the government faced the continuing threat that a coup by the right or a victory by the left would either topple the elected regime or provoke U.S. intervention. Christian Democratic officials, believing that their political position could only deteriorate over time, grew more desperate by the day. Pushed from all sides, the party leadership began to insist that negotiating with the opposition was the only viable means of consolidating future electoral support.[26]

While electoral pressures inside El Salvador intensified, demands from the United States temporarily diminished. Preoccupied with its own reelection and stunned by Nicaragua's acceptance of peace negotiations sponsored by the Contadora countries, the Reagan administration could not afford to oppose publicly any attempt to reach a peaceful settlement of El Salvador's conflict. Duarte understood that the Salvadoran military and the Reagan administration—the two leading forces historically opposed to negotiations— needed him in order to extract aid from a skeptical U.S. Congress. For the moment, at least, they could not openly resist a peace initiative. After surprisingly little consultation with the United States, Duarte gambled on his own indispensability; in a dramatic speech to the United Nations, he invited the FDR-FMLN to the town of La Palma to join in a dialogue with his government.

Despite the popular outpouring of euphoria which greeted the meeting between rebel forces and the government, the political process promoting a negotiated solution to El Salvador's civil war soon ground to a halt. Talks at La Palma and Ayagualo revealed sharp differences between Christian Democratic and FDR-FMLN visions of democratization and reform and generated little hope that the left would participate in the 1985 elections. The Duarte government maintained that the essential conditions for democratization were already in place: human rights violations had been brought under control; the antidemocratic practices of the armed forces had been curtailed; and the power of the landowners had been broken. The rebels could therefore put down their arms, abide by the 1983 Constitution, and immediately enter the electoral process. The FDR-FMLN rejected this view. According to the rebels, the power of the country's traditional elites and the death squads that backed them remained intact: land reform had been blocked and no army officer had faced either trial or punishment for the deaths of Salvadoran citizens. Their plan called for a new constitution, reorganization of the army, and formation of a new government in advance of new elections.[27]

Subsequent actions by the U.S. government deepened the divisions among El Salvador's power contenders. After the Republicans' 1984 landslide victory removed political restrictions on the government's El Salvador policy, the Reagan administration began taking positions that effectively undercut the peace process. Besides refusing to support negotiations, the administration encouraged an escalation of the war in the days following the La Palma talks and sought to weaken the political forces calling for dialogue. Worried by the leftist tilt of mass organizations allied with the Christian Democratic government, U.S. officials fomented a split in the UPD and subsequently created a new, less reformist union which openly competed with Duarte's labor base. Unable to pressure the Duarte government into adopting an austerity program, they began to talk publicly of the desirability of a victory by the right in the 1985 elections "to give balance to El Salvador's democracy."[28] In addition, the CIA withheld its traditional financial support for the Christian Democrats' electoral campaign. By early 1985, differences over economic policy had strained relations between the United States and its PDC allies almost to their limit.

The Reagan administration's attitude toward dialogue and its subsequent criticism of the Duarte government encouraged right-wingers to renew their political challenge. The army, disabusing the government of its illusions of civilian control over the military, refused to abide by Christmas truce agreements between President Duarte and the rebel leaders. The high command subsequently set extremely narrow parameters on the president's freedom to negotiate and made compliance with these limitations a condition of its support for the government. It ruled out any formal cease-fire, declared that the executive had no authority over purely military matters, and insisted that any future settlement had to be based strictly on the 1983 Constitution, a document written mainly by the ultraright. Without assistance from the United States, the Duarte government could do nothing to win greater flexibility or exercise control over the military. "This is not our army," a cabinet member admitted.[29]

In March, as these complex tensions escalated, the Christian Democratic party swept the legislative elections by an unexpectedly wide margin. It gained a small majority in the sixty-seat legislature, thus overturning the right wing's veto power, and it won control of more than 200 of El Salvador's 262 municipalities. Although the issue of negotiations was carefully kept out of the campaign, Duarte had unquestionably gained popularity through his peace initiative. In addition, the Christian Democrats benefited from a combination of other factors: their control over the resources of the bureaucracy, the electoral neutrality of the army, certain changes in electoral laws, the tendency of Salvadorans to vote *oficialista*, and deep divisions within ARENA.[30]

On the surface, the 1985 legislative elections represented the culmination of the Christian Democratic party's bid for power. For the first time the party controlled both the executive and the legislative branches. Even more impressive was a dramatic televised expression of support, immediately after the vote, from the entire High Command of the Salvadoran armed forces. Given its popular mandate and its apparent control over the central institutions of the state, it seemed that the PDC finally could effectively implement its program of democratization and agrarian reform which had been blocked since 1980.

Nevertheless, the electoral scene suggested by the Christian Democrats' 1985 victory was deceptive. Although the party had won by a surprisingly large margin, the election was marred by a sharp decline in voter turnout. Of the 2.7 million voters eligible to participate, less than 1 million actually voted, a third fewer than had voted in the 1984 election. Approximately 17 percent of the ballots cast were spoiled or invalid. The failure to vote apparently reflected either sympathy for the FDR-FMLN or disillusionment with the government. Because President Duarte could no longer blame his policy failures on right-wing control of the legislature, this trend was bound to increase in the future, unless the Christian Democrats could deliver on their campaign promises of peace, land, political rights, and jobs.

It seemed unlikely that these promises could be fulfilled. Despite a series of elections, power still resided with contending forces which had not formally participated in the electoral process and which owed no permanent allegiance to the Christian Democratic government: the United States and the Salvadoran armed forces on the one hand, and the FDR-FMLN on the other. Each side could exercise a powerful veto over government policy, for neither of the central issues facing the country—the economic crisis and the war—could be resolved without their cooperation. With the elections out of the way, the political-electoral cycle began to reverse itself. The PDC, which had initiated peace talks to placate its electoral constituency, now began to shift to the right as its members sought to placate the United States, the armed forces, and the private sector.

The army high command promptly clarified the parameters of acceptable policy space for political and military matters. It would support the construction of a formal democratic order, even one dominated by Christian Democracy, as long as Duarte kept to the letter of the conservative 1983 Constitution and limited dialogue with the FDR-FMLN to the procedural aspects of leftist participation in future elections. The military thus effectively prevented Duarte from negotiating an end to the civil war, the formation of a new government, or the integration of El Salvador's two armies. In an important speech on Soldier's Day, General Vides Casanova emphasized another condition of the army's acquiescence in an electoral regime: continued U.S. military and economic aid.[31]

The parameters of economic policy were also largely preestablished for President Duarte. Because the economy had become completely dependent on U.S. aid during the civil war, Duarte began to cede ground to the United States and traditional Salvadoran elites. In measures contrary to the PDC's campaign promises of 1984–85, his administration devalued the colón, gave huge incentives to coffee growers, and channeled a major portion of development funds into the traditional private sector. Emboldened by their access to an extraordinarily high level of U.S. funds, the elites renewed their pressure against a negotiated settlement or a political opening and in favor of an eventual military victory over the FDR-FMLN. Thus, by winning control of the executive and the legislature during a civil war, the Duarte administration now had the most to lose.

Conclusion

The introduction of elections has not brought democracy to El Salvador. Rather than resulting from a prior compromise among domestic power contenders to establish rules for conflict resolution or the parameters of policy, the elections have been imposed by a foreign power during an uncertain regime transition and a bloody civil war. Thus they cannot be considered "founding" elections which mark the instauration of a democratic polity. Yet neither are they purely demonstration elections, aimed exclusively at influencing an external constituency. Although the 1982 electoral contests might fit that characterization, the subsequent series of elections, taken together, have had a significant impact upon internal policy processes.

Most important, they have prolonged a stalemated civil war. Elections have made possible enormous flows of U.S. aid which rule out a short-term defeat of the Salvadoran armed forces. Meanwhile the strength of the FDR-FMLN prohibits the restoration of the old regime. The Reagan administration/Salvadoran government and the opposition can thus veto each other's preferred outcomes and produce a protracted war rather than the necessary basic agreement on such fundamental issues as the share of power to be exercised by the opposition, the extent of socioeconomic reform, particularly land reform, the fate of the contending armies, and accountability for past terrorist activities.

Thus far, electoralism has seriously impeded such compromises, though it cannot be said that elections per se have failed to produce any progress toward democratization. The elections from 1982 to 1985 have narrowed political options for the ultraright by somewhat reducing its reliance on paramilitary groups, led to coalition formation between the center right and the right, widened the range of permissible contestation, and encouraged the formation of rightist parties. But elections have not moderated the behavior of the left because the left opposition has been excluded from electoral participation through repression. This policy has been pursued precisely because the FDR-FMLN is likely to receive substantial support (often estimated at well over 30 percent)[32] in an open political contest. Without the participation of the opposition, however, elections, no matter how frequent, cannot channel conflicting interests into peaceful contests. To the extent that external forces continue to impose elections to facilitate the conduct of the war and thereby prevent any agreement with opposition forces, the overriding consequence of elections will be to impede the accommodation that must precede democratization.

U.S. policy, however, has also produced results that were neither anticipated nor welcomed by those who conceived the strategy. Foreign designers of

El Salvador's democracy have frequently found, to their dismay, that events and people have a propensity toward unpredictability which eludes political engineering, particularly in the context of a political transition. The 1982 demonstration elections, staged to clean up the public image of the Salvadoran regime in the United States, resulted in intervention to prevent a reputed leader of death squads from being elected president. The 1984 elections, aimed at shifting power inside El Salvador so as to win military aid from the U.S. Congress, unexpectedly produced a peace platform from the winning candidate, the first actual negotiations between warring forces, and a political opening for labor agitation. The 1985 elections, intended to create a stable balance of power between the ultraright and the center right, instead brought the clear victory of the latter, which in turn has made the Duarte administration accountable for progress toward peace and reform.

The ultimate impact of an electoral system on democratization may be as unpredictable as these outcomes. But in the meantime, after three elections in four years, El Salvador continues to suffer endemic violence, political exclusion, and ever-growing social inequalities—unhappy results that have been perversely aggravated by the U.S. attempt to export democracy.

Notes

I would like to thank the Tinker Foundation and Harvard University for their financial support of my research in El Salvador, Mexico, Venezuela, and Washington, D.C. in 1983-84.

1. See Edward S. Herman and Frank Brodhead, *Demonstration Elections: U.S.-Staged Elections in the Dominican Republic, Vietnam, and El Salvador* (Boston: South End Press, 1984).

2. For a history of elections in El Salvador, see Cristina Eguizabal, "El Salvador: Elecciones sin democracia," *Polémica* 14–15 (March-June 1984). For overviews of El Salvador before the October 1979 junta, see Stephen Webre, *José Napoleón Duarte and the Christian Democratic Party in Salvadoran Politics, 1960–1972* (Baton Rouge: Louisiana State University Press, 1979); Enrique Baloyra, *El Salvador in Transition* (Chapel Hill: University of North Carolina Press, 1982); and Tommie Sue Montgomery, *Revolution in El Salvador: Origins and Evolution* (Boulder, CO: Westview Press, 1982).

3. For a description of these events and an analysis of the Carter administration's policy in El Salvador, see Martin Diskin and Kenneth Sharpe, "Facing Facts in El Salvador: Reconciliation or War," *World Policy Journal* (Spring 1984): 517–548; Raymond Bonner, *Weakness and Deceit: U.S. Policy and El Salvador* (New York: New York Times Books, 1984), p. 167; and James Dunkerley, *The Long War: Dictatorship and Revolution in El Salvador* (London: Junction Books, 1982).

4. On the ideology and roots of the Salvadoran opposition, see Tomás R. Campos, "El papel de las organizaciones populares en la actual situación del país," *ECA*, 34:343 (October-November, 1979): 934–946; Italo López Vallecillos and Victor Antonio Orellana, "La Unidad Popular y el surgimiento del Frente Democrático Revolucionario," *ECA*, 35: 377–378 (March–April 1980): 183–207; and Robert Leiken, "The Salvadoran Left," in *Central America: Anatomy of a Conflict*, ed. Robert Leiken (New York: Pergamon 1984), pp. 111–131.

5. In 1981 the archbishop of San Salvador, Rivera y Damas, received a tentative go-ahead from Duarte and the FDR-FMLN to attempt some form of mediation in

El Salvador. He also gained critically important backing from the Socialist International, International Christian Democracy, and the pope. During a meeting with U.S. Vice President George Bush, however, he was informed that the United States was not interested in the initiative. After the meeting the archbishop wrote to Bush: "The United States must clearly indicate that it is in favor of a political solution through negotiations or such negotiations will not occur in El Salvador . . . the U.S. role is essential in pressuring the military to accept a political solution" (see Bonner, *Weakness and Deceit*, p. 285). For a discussion of the role of Latin American countries in El Salvador, see Terry Karl, "Regional Powers and Central American Peace: Mexico, Venezuela, and the Contadora Initiative," in *Confronting Revolution: Security through Diplomacy in Central America*, ed. Morris J. Blachman, William M. LeoGrande, and Kenneth Sharpe (New York: Pantheon, 1985).

6. Bonner, *Weakness and Deceit*, p. 173. Héctor Dada, former leader of the Christian Democratic party, confirmed these events in a personal interview (Mexico City, August 1984).

7. *New York Times*, 17 July 1982; see also "El Salvador: The Search for Peace" (Washington: U.S. Department of State, Bureau of Public Affairs, 16 July 1981). Interviews with an official of the U.S. State Department's Latin America Bureau (Washington, 1983) and with a political officer in the U.S. embassy in El Salvador (San Salvador, October 1983) also support this interpretation.

8. *Latin American Weekly Review*, 27 July 1981, p. 2. Before the 1984 vote, for example, the Reagan administration succeeded in wringing major concessions from Congress as part of its "comprehensive plan to secure the elections," even though the FDR-FMLN had pledged not to disrupt the voting process. These concessions included permission to fly observation planes over combat areas, to conduct maneuvers near the Salvadoran border, and to rearm U.S. advisors. See "El Salvador: Elections Amidst War," *Central America Bulletin*, May 1984, p. 2.

9. The Provisional Law for the Formation and Registration of Political Parties required that a new party submit the names and addresses of at least 3,000 members, conditions that were impossible to meet in a context of death-squad activity aimed at political dissidents. Several parties, including the PCN, the MNR, and the UDN (the latter two are members of the FDR-FMLN), were exempted from this requirement and automatically registered, but the FDR-FMLN saw the law as an attempt to split their organization (see Herman and Brodhead, *Demonstration Elections*, p. 118).

10. Confidential interview in U.S. State Department (Washington, September, 1983); interview with political officer in U.S. embassy (San Salvador, October 1983); interview with José Miguel Fritis, IVEPO (San Salvador, October 1983).

11. Although the available data on voting patterns in the 1982 and 1984 elections are not completely reliable, support for ARENA was generally strongest in rural areas with long traditions of direct control by the military, in militarily contested areas, and in the wealthier sectors of San Salvador. Interviews with José Napoleón Duarte and an ARENA party official (October 1983) and with a Christian Democratic party official (April 1985) support this analysis.

12. Baloyra, *El Salvador in Transition*, pp. 171–173.

13. See Tomás R. Campos, "El Pacto de Apaneca, un proyecto político para la transición," *ECA* (September-October 1982). This pact was so heavily influenced by the Venezuelans that it borrowed some of the actual language from the Pact of Punto Fijo.

14. The Political Commission, headed by President Alvaro Magaña, included the three vice presidents of the country (one each from the PDC, the PCN, and ARENA); the minister of foreign relations (Fidel Chávez, a Christian Democrat with close ties

to the private sector); the minister of defense (General José Guillermo García); the president of the Constituent Assembly (D'Aubuisson); and one representative each from the PCN (the traditional party of the military) and the PPS (a small party of the right). The Christian Democrats, heavily outnumbered, requested another representative but were rebuffed. Duarte did not sign the agreement and kept a low profile. Interview with Minister Fidel Chávez Mena (San Salvador, October 1983).

15. This description of the military situation is based on interviews conducted in El Salvador in October 1983. See also Terry Karl, "After La Palma: The Prospects for Democratization in El Salvador," *World Policy Journal* (Spring 1985): 315–316.

16. *Christian Science Monitor,* 5 August 1983; *New York Times,* 19 September 1983; *Los Angeles Times,* 19 September 1983.

17. *Miami Herald,* 19 March 1983. The United States was also deeply involved in the selection of the PDC candidate. Some embassy officials favored the candidacy of Fidel Chávez Mena, a younger PDC leader with close ties to the private sector. Duarte managed to secure the candidacy by a narrow vote after a precampaign fight which threatened to divide the party. Interview with José Napoleón Duarte (San Salvador, October 1983); interview with U.S. embassy official (San Salvador, October 1983).

18. The United States used IVEPO, a Venezuelan conduit, to aid the Christian Democrats. Supposedly a public relations firm in San Salvador, IVEPO received at least $2 million in direct funds from the CIA and the Konrad Adenauer Foundation of West Germany to finance Duarte's campaign. Interview at IVEPO (San Salvador, October 1983); *Boston Globe,* 4 May 1984; *Time,* 21 May 1984. This money provided the Christian Democrats with ample resources to match the well-financed campaign of ARENA. See Ricardo Chacón, "Las campañas de los partidos," *ECA* (April–May 1983): 229–252.

19. For a complete description of the growth in military aid, see "U.S. Policy towards El Salvador," *Central America Bulletin,* January 1985, pp. 4ff., and "United States Aid Escalates Salvadoran War," *Central America Bulletin,* June 1985, p. 4.

20. U.N. High Commission for Refugees, Instituto Histórico Centroamericano, Washington, 1984.

21. See Segundo Montes, "Condicionamientos socio-politicos del proceso electoral," *ECA* (April–May 1983): 188. For a description of economic conditions in El Salvador, see *NACLA Report on the Americas* 18:2 (1984).

22. These polls, although of obviously limited reliability because of the atmosphere in which they were conducted, are nonetheless one of the few indicators of public opinion in El Salvador. See Ignacio Martín-Baro and Victor Antonio Orellana, "La necesidad de votar: Actitudes del pueblo salvadoreño ante el proceso electoral de 1984," *ECA* (April–May 1983): 255–256.

23. *New York Times,* 25 May 1984, 31 May 1984.

24. For a description of the differences over economic policy between the Christian Democratic party and the U.S.-allied private sector, see "Duarte's Difficulties Grow as Elections Near," *Central American Bulletin,* January 1985, pp. 1ff.

25. Interview with Joaquín Villalobos, commander of the FDR-FMLN (Morazón Province, El Salvador, April 1985).

26. Eduardo Molina, a PDC leader, expressed the sentiments of the party when he said: "There is no military solution to our conflict now, unless it is a military victory by the guerrillas. . . . If we continue to attempt to resolve the conflict militarily, we will lose. Only a dialogue and eventual incorporation of democratic elements of the left into our ranks offer any exit for us now." (*Christian Science Monitor,* 8 March 1984, 30 March 1984).

27. Transcript of presidential press conference (San Salvador, 16 October 1984); see also FDR-FMLN Political-Diplomatic Commission, "La Palma: A Hope for Peace" (November 1984).

28. *New York Times*, 12 May 1985; interview with political officer, U.S. embassy (San Salvador, April 1985).

29. Interview with Duarte administration cabinet minister (San Salvador, April 1985).

30. Interview with PDC leader Adolfo Rey Prendes (San Salvador, April 1985); interview with Hugo Barrera, former member of ARENA (San Salvador, April 1985).

31. "Discurso del Ministro de Defensa, Gral. Vides Casanova, con motivo del Día del Soldado," *Proceso*, 13 May 1985, pp. 7–9.

32. Estimates of support for the FDR-FMLN vary widely. Former U.S. Ambassador Pickering claimed that the opposition had the support of about 2 percent of the country, whereas the opposition itself claims majority support. Informed observers in academic circles generally use a figure of approximately 30 percent, but these estimates will remain informed guesses until there is open political contestation in El Salvador. Interview with U.S. Ambassador Pickering (San Salvador, April 1985).

10

Civil War, Reform, and Reaction in El Salvador

Ricardo Stein

The period following the election of José Napoleón Duarte in 1984 has been characterized by a deepening of the political and military conflict in El Salvador, with little prospect of a solution. Among the most important characteristics of this period have been the strengthening of both the Salvadoran armed forces and the guerrilla forces of the FMLN (Farabundo Martí Front for National Liberation), signifying a prolongation of the war; the continuing deterioration of the economy; the increasing political isolation of President Duarte; and the renewed mobilization of urban opposition, especially labor.

Between 1979 and 1983, at least three identifiable political agendas were being put foward by groups vying for power. The first was that of the FMLN-FDR (Democratic Revolutionary Front), supported by a coalition of social and political forces, including organizations of labor, peasants, students, and professionals. The FMLN-FDR program called for a thorough socio-economic restructuring and supported revolution as the only means to achieve it. The second agenda, that of AID (U.S. Agency for International Development), and the third, that of the oligarchy, did not differ strategically with respect to the FMLN-FDR; their objective was, and is, to defeat the insurgents and to break up the alliance that supports them. Yet a number of secondary contradictions led to substantial bickering and infighting between those supporting the U.S. agenda and elements of the oligarchy. In the 1979–1983 period these contradictions were expressed in conflicts over reforms and the conduct of the war.

The U.S. agenda was partly implemented by the military-Christian Democratic junta which came to power in March 1980 and enacted an agrarian reform program, nationalized domestic private banks, and estab-

This article is an edited version of a presentation given by Ricardo Stein on 21 February 1986. The notes and update section have been added by the editors of this volume.

lished government control over foreign trade—all reforms that were adamantly opposed by the oligarchy. Conflicts over conduct of the war concerned the level of repression against civilians by military and security forces and the ineffectiveness of the army's offensive strategy.[1]

In 1984 the picture changed. Strategic objectives vis-à-vis the FMLN-FDR were the same, but the election of Duarte substantially reduced the internal contradictions among those in power. One reason was Duarte's effectiveness in convincing the U.S. Congress to provide military and economic aid to El Salvador, thus benefiting both the armed forces and the private sector.

By the end of 1985, however, the historical differences among political factions had deepened, and the precarious equilibrium established by the election of Duarte in May 1984 is heading rapidly for a breakdown. The weakening or collapse of the alliance, however, will not reduce the uncertainty about the future or lead to resolution of the crisis.

The situation in El Salvador as of spring 1986 may be described as possessing a number of clearly observable characteristics:

1. The military situation has been characterized by a "dynamic equilibrium" since mid-1982 in spite of a substantial reaccommodation of strategy and tactics on both sides. This equilibrium, which should not be confused with a stalemate, essentially means that neither side is capable of overcoming the other in the foreseeable or the forecastable future or of militarily weakening the other sufficiently to impose negotiating conditions on it. As both sides still perceive the possibility of military victory, they regard dialogue, or negotiations, as an auxiliary rather than a central element of strategy.[2]

2. A series of economic decisions, pushed by the Reagan administration, has been directed primarily to the objective of financing the war, but also to laying the groundwork for a new economic model. This model would privilege a certain segment of capital and in effect would mean abandoning reforms previously enacted with the important exception of government monopoly over export of traditional crops.

3. Social discontent has grown because of the deterioration of living conditions for the large majority of the population, in turn a consequence of the deepening of the economic crisis. The grievances have been exacerbated by governmental procedures in confronting protests and organized demonstrations. A tendency toward contraction of the existing political space for dissension and of the forms in which it can be manifested has been accompanied by a retreat or rollback in the limited progress achieved in human rights.

4. Political erosion of support for President Duarte's government has opened spaces for the political recovery of the left, politically weakened since the 1979 coup.

5. Finally, the Salvadoran government is almost totally subordinated to the Reagan administration, which has become an external over-determinant imposing limitations and conditions on processes in El Salvador from the perspective of its own interests. (This U.S. involvement is particularly evident

in what has been referred to as low intensity warfare. Low intensity can be defined only from the perspective of the United States, in terms of managing the war, and probably of facing less criticism from U.S. opposition. In El Salvador, of course, the intensity is very high.)

Military Impasse

Strategic and tactical modifications, which began in 1984, have dramatically altered the conduct of the war in El Salvador. First and most important, the parameters of the war are now conceived differently. The prospect is for a prolonged war; no one, not even in the most optimistic assessments, talks of a war that will end in the near future.

Second, the army has made substantial improvements, not only in size but in its methods of operation; it is a more proficient army today. Still, a question remains: Is the progress sufficient to enable the army to deal with the enemy it faces? The answer is not necessarily in the affirmative. What is changing the whole dynamic of the war is the strategic reevaluation of the FMLN, which since early 1984 has been operating on the assumption that to go for a military victory would be the fastest way to defeat of the revolution. The FMLN has responded to the increased efficiency of the Salvadoran army by reducing the size of its units and dispersing them throughout the country, reconcentrating them for large-scale operations. It has also succeeded in expanding its activities to all fourteen departments of El Salvador, including those in the western part of the country.

One element in the deepening of the war is the effect of firepower used against the civilian population. Beginning in mid-1984, the Salvadoran army stepped up its search-and-destroy missions against concentrations of the civilian population believed to be supporters of the FMLN. Villages were bombed or strafed with helicopter gunships; ground forces then moved in, destroying homes, crops, and livestock and removing villagers who had not fled, usually to refugee camps in the cities. Although these maneuvers succeeded to some extent in displacing the civilian populations, success was often temporary, as those who had fled returned to the villages when the danger had passed. The effect of these army tactics on the guerrilla forces themselves was minimal.[3]

The increased level of intensity of the war today is not necessarily evident in statistics. The number of confrontations between the FMLN and the army may have dropped (probably by 25 percent), and the number of dead may be lower, but the number of wounded has increased dramatically. The army contends that at least 40 percent of all its casualties are attributable to mine fields laid by the FMLN; that is, a substantial number of its casualties are inflicted by indirect confrontation.

From the government's perspective, the crucial variable, identified at least since mid-1984, is logistics. The assumption is that in a war of attrition (as the conflict is now being defined) the side best able to resupply its forces enjoys the logistical advantage and, consequently, the long-run advantage.

The FMLN, however, contends that logistics at this moment are not the most critical variable, and that by dispersing its forces it can neutralize this advantage as defined by the government. They do not need to be logistically resupplied in the terms conceived by the government, because a group of fifty has fewer logistical requirements than a fighting unit of 500.[4]

Another element is that territory in a war like El Salvador's may be a serious liability. To the statement that in the past year the FMLN has lost control of territory one should introduce the nuance that it has lost territory but not necessarily control. The issue of control has been put forward by the FMLN in the thesis of dual power. The FMLN asserts that it has dual power because it is able to control the political and administrative processes in particular concentrations of population without the government army being able to dispute that control. The army may periodically disrupt ongoing political and social processes in these areas, but it cannot alter the new political reality emerging there. In at least 54 or 55 municipalities either the FMLN exercises total control or the officially elected authorities serve as administrators for FMLN political organizations, with the knowledge of the government. In a third situation, officially elected municipal authorities have to concentrate in provincial capitals because they are unable to remain in the municipalities.

In short, the upgrading of the Salvadoran military has not altered the balance of power between the armed forces and those of the FMLN-FDR. As long as both parties continue to believe that a military victory is a real possibility, the prospect is prolongation of the war.

Economic Deterioration

The Salvadoran economy entered into a crisis in the late 1970s. The gross domestic product decreased by nearly 21 percent between 1979 and 1985, and fixed capital investment by the private sector dropped from 20.1 percent to 8.8 percent of GDP between 1976 and 1985. As the population increased by 2 percent annually the deterioration in per capita product has been even more violent; in 1985 per capita output was 50 percent below that of 1979. Real wages for agricultural workers fell 60 percent between 1979 and 1985 and those of workers in industry, trade, and services by nearly 45 percent. Unemployment is officially recognized to be over 30 percent, and unemployment and underemployment together probably affect two-thirds of the population.[5]

The two major factors in the current economic crisis are the international recession and the effects of the war. The world market prices for El Salvador's three major commodity exports—coffee, cotton and sugar—declined in the early 1980s; between 1979 and 1982 El Salvador's coffee exports dropped from 1,688 million colones to 1,006.5 million; cotton exports from 211.5 million to 112.9 million, and sugar exports from 67.1 million to 39.7 million. The prices of all three commodities revived subsequently, but while coffee prices continued to recover the prices of sugar and cotton have again declined or fluctuated, and cotton production in El Salvador has been drastically reduced.

On 20 January 1986 Duarte introduced an economic package that for the first time provided a coherent formulation of Christian Democratic economic policy at all levels—fiscal, monetary, exchange—including prices and wages. The economic package included a devaluation of the colón from 2.5 to 5 to the dollar; taxes on luxury imports and a temporary tax on "extraordinary" profits accruing from increased prices for coffee on the international market; increased interest rates and expanded restrictions on government credit; an increase in wages for public employees while encouraging the private sector to raise wages by 10 to 15 percent; and a freeze on the prices of goods and services.

The implementation of this package was accompanied by a change in political discourse. For the first time the government called war the number one priority of the country and required all citizens to make sacrifices to help finance the war. This pronouncement marked a significant reversal of Duarte's electoral promises. Having campaigned mainly as a candidate for peace, he was now openly asserting that winning the war was the prime objective, and that everybody was responsible for financing it. He also recognized that the war was not concentrated only in the eastern or the northern part of the country but now affected the entire nation. Thus Duarte was implicitly contradicting military assertions that the guerrilla movement was almost under control.

The economic package was attacked by all sectors, including the right wing, which took advantage of Duarte's political weakness. The right, however, was more critical of the rhetoric of the government, which had blamed rightwing groups for raising prices and creating economic problems that, compounded by the war, had made the economic package necessary in the first place. With the exception of the coffee growers, however, who bitterly resented the government taking advantage of increased coffee prices through its control of foreign trade, the effects of the package on the private sector were minimal.[6]

It was, in fact, around the main policy instruments of the economic package that the new organic expressions of capital began to develop—including both political expressions like Patria Libre, a new right-wing political party,[7] and FUSADES (Fundación Salvadoreña de Desarrollo Económico y Social), an economic think tank that almost literally translates AID memoranda from English into Spanish. There is in fact an almost one-to-one correlation between the regional model in El Salvador, as proposed by AID, and the formulations by FUSADES.[8] The modernizing and most progressive elements of capital in El Salvador—families traditionally engaged in industry—are associated with FUSADES and the new model.

The new model is based on the Caribbean Basin Initiative (CBI) and centers on the development of nontraditional exports for markets in the rest of the world outside the Central American Common Market (CACM) and particularly those in the United States. According to this model, El

Salvador's potential lies in the production of goods requiring intensive labor which must also be of high quality in order to be competitive on the world market. Projected as an alternative to the strategy of import substitution industrialization which prevailed with the formation of the CACM in the late 1950s and early 1960s,[9] the new model would utilize El Salvador's abundant supply of labor by specializing in labor-intensive production of export items. AID and the Inter-American Development Bank are devoting substantial resources to FUSADES and to private sector groups interested in export-oriented production.

The Resurgent Labor Opposition
and the Political Isolation of Duarte

As noted above, the living conditions of the Salvadoran population have been deteriorating since 1978. What is significant now is a new thrust toward political organization for the first time since 1981, when organized urban opposition virtually disappeared, due to intense repression by military and security forces. Thus, for the first time since 1981, the economic crisis has the potential of becoming a political crisis.

Beginning in 1984, the labor movement has developed a new strategy of organization, breaking away from its former vertical structure and shifting to a horizontal structure. In February 1986 several confederations, including organizations that formed part of the base of the Christian Democrats, joined together to form the Unidad Nacional de los Trabajadores Salvadoreños (UNTS, National Unity of Salvadoran Workers).[10] The disaffection of organizations previously supportive of the Christian Democratic government may be explained not only by deteriorating economic conditions but also by Duarte's failure to fulfill promises made during his presidential campaign, including an end to repression, prosecution of human rights violators, and negotiations with the FMLN-FDR in an effort to find a political solution to the war. The UNTS and its member organizations have been at the forefront of mobilization efforts and have been constant and vociferous critics of government policy. The FMLN clearly supports this development, but its support does not imply that the FMLN was responsible for it or that it controls it.

The implication of this process for social and political mobilization has been of considerable concern to the government, which has attempted to foster organizations that would strengthen the Christian Democratic party and to divide unions that have traditionally opposed the government.[11] In spite of this, as noted above, a significant sector of labor abandoned the traditional base of the Christian Democrats and this abandonment is probably the most important element of Duarte's political erosion.

Duarte has also encountered serious difficulties with the military since the kidnapping of his daughter in September 1985, when sectors of the military and of the right wing accused him of placing his personal concerns above the national interest. After forty days of negotiations his daughter was released, along with twenty-three Christian Democratic mayors the guerrillas had been holding, in return for the release of twenty-six political prisoners and a safe conduct for ninety-six wounded guerrilla fighters to leave the country. The negotiations, as well as their outcome, brought the FMLN considerable national and international visibility and recognition; at the height of the process fourteen countries were dealing with the FMLN as a party to the negotiations.

In effect, President Duarte has become the captive of his strength. In 1984 he came to power as a leader who could raise money for a program that was not necessarily his own, believing that his ability to obtain military and economic aid from the U.S. Congress would enable him to carry out his own projects. Duarte soon discovered, however, that the heavier his reliance on external sources, the less effective he was in controlling the money he received. Internally he is totally trapped, having to acquiesce more to the right than ever, moving the entire political process further to the right.

One question that has not been addressed is: Who actually obtains power? In the context of the electoral process, the major beneficiary has been the armed forces. If any legitimation has been achieved by elections it is the legitimacy of the armed forces. They are broadly recognized as the agents of transition and the guarantors of the political process, whether or not it is democratic, and whether or not it is viewed from a counterinsurgency perspective. This is a crucial aspect, because it goes back to the power issue. Whatever is argued about whether or not there is more political space, what its limits are, power stays in the same place. The alliance of the United States, capital, and the armed forces has been reestablished.

The Role of the United States

As U.S. military aid has facilitated a quantitative and qualitative change in the Salvadoran armed forces, so economic aid has been essential to keep the economy from collapsing. In 1985 U.S. economic assistance financed 43 percent of El Salvador's imports of raw material, capital and intermediate goods, and services and 25 percent of public sector expenditures. The bulk of this aid has come in the form of economic support funds, which have a double advantage: dollars are given to the Salvadoran government which sells them to the private sector for colones. The private sector supposedly uses the dollars to import goods needed for production; the colones are spent for projects agreed upon by the government and AID, including war-related expenditures (such as restoration of services destroyed by the war and for programs for displaced persons) and for economic programs benefiting the private sector, particularly those promoted under the new economic model discussed above.[12]

Although economic and military aid has given the Reagan administration considerable control over the Duarte government, the United States has not been able to gain control over events in El Salvador. The administration has, however, established a working policy that is able to cope with unanticipated results. The measure of a policy's success is not whether the desired results are obtained, but whether the policymakers can accommodate to failure to get those results. The Reagan administration has been notably accomplished at coping with unexpected outcomes.

Nevertheless, the power of the United States is limited. It does have veto power, but that power gives it little room to maneuver. At most, what the United States has been able to impose is a very brittle stability, meaning that anything at any moment can send it out of control. This delicate balance is the predicament in which El Salvador finds itself.

In conclusion, El Salvador is trapped in a no-win situation; it is going nowhere. Internal forces are moving, but the limits on their direction seem to be rigidly set. Without an external impetus, such as a change in U.S. policy, El Salvador is condemned to entropy.

Clearly the revolutionary moment in Central America has passed. That is not to say that the revolution has been defeated, although it has suffered a tactical setback in Guatemala. In El Salvador, the FMLN has acknowledged that a military victory is not possible in the immediate future, that even if it were it would not necessarily be desirable, given the geopolitics of the region, and that the situation confronting the FMLN is much more complex and difficult to overcome than the situation it faced in 1979. It has fewer possibilities for alliances, particularly outside the labor movement or the deprived sectors of Salvadoran society. The spheres of power in the United States are closed, politically and ideologically, to consideration of negotiations, and the international constellation that was favorable to the FMLN in the past is less so today. In a sense, the FMLN has the capacity to continue fighting but lacks the capacity to impose the utopian model presented in 1979, or even to achieve a dialogue. The paradox is that at the moment in El Salvador, the FMLN is the major defender of reformism and the agent most responsible for reform, even though the original purpose of reform was to contain the FMLN. The geopolitics of the region has made it impossible for El Salvador to become another Nicaragua. And the first group to recognize this situation is the FMLN itself.

Update: June 1987

Events over the past fifteen months seem to be deepening the tensions and contradictions described above.

1. The earthquake of October 1986 left more than 1,500 dead, 10,000 injured, and 250,000 to 300,000 homeless and caused an estimated $1.5 billion to $2 billion in damages. In addition to increasing the misery of the poorest sectors of the population of San Salvador, those most affected, the earthquake compounded the country's economic problems and further weakened support for President Duarte, whose response to the disaster was widely denounced as inadequate.[13]

2. In the middle of 1985 the military introduced an ambitious program for economic reconstruction, United to Reconstruct, calling upon all sectors

of society to support the war and to aid reconstruction efforts and initiating a government-controlled resettlement program in zones previously controlled by the FMLN. The program was designed to favor progovernment sectors among the displaced and to sponsor development projects in the resettled areas which would create zones of economic growth and political stability.

Aside from the lack of sufficient funds, several other factors have limited the success of the resettlement effort. First, the requirement that those resettled under military auspices join civil patrols to combat the guerrillas has been resisted by some prospective candidates for resettlement because of support for the FMLN or fear of guerrilla retaliation. Second, in many cases, the FMLN has retained a presence in or has been able to enter areas allegedly cleared of guerrillas by the military. Finally, even before the announcement of the United to Reconstruct campaign, displaced families were returning to their villages, either on their own or under the auspices of the Catholic church and national and international religious and humanitarian organizations, a process that has accelerated in 1986 and 1987 despite military efforts to block it.[14]

3. In the meantime, the economic situation has continued to deteriorate: the price of beans increased by 150 percent between January and December 1986, and at the end of the year the government deficit was 900 million colones ($180 million). As part of the United to Reconstruct campaign, the government and the armed forces called upon the private sector and wealthy classes to help support the war effort, resulting in the introduction of a second economic package, this time geared to high and middle income groups. In October 1986 the PDC-controlled Legislative Assembly approved a war tax on all income above 100,000 colones ($20,000) and in December it approved an income and property tax (with the right wing parties abstaining). The new package was vociferously opposed by the right, which boycotted the assembly (making it impossible to pass the budget, which requires a two-thirds vote) and formed a new organization, Movement for National Action (MAN), which has demanded Duarte's resignation. The right also called for a work stoppage for 22 January 1987, which was 70 percent effective. Duarte was also under pressure from labor and other popular groups objecting to the projected use of new taxes to support the war effort and fearing the costs would be transferred to consumers in the form of higher prices. In February 1987 the Supreme Court declared the war tax unconstitutional, and subsequently the Duarte government reduced other taxes, to the benefit of high income groups and the private sector.[15]

4. A series of unsuccessful FMLN attacks in the departments of San Miguel, Morazán, La Unión, San Vicente, and Chalatenango, including the assault on the heavily fortified El Paraiso military barracks in Chalatenango on 31 March 1987 as well as the stepped-up FMLN activity in the capital city of San Salvador, have led to a reassessment of the strength of the guerrilla forces. Even prior to the El Paraiso attack, according to some sources, U.S. embassy officials were saying that the war would last another five to eight years, a sharp break with earlier assumptions that only two to three years would be required to defeat the guerrillas.[16]

5. The economic crisis, the renewed show of force by the FMLN, the increased organization of business groups and rightwing political forces, and the growing militancy of sectors organized around the UNTS have contributed to a further deterioration of the position of Duarte. Splits within the Christian Democratic party have also weakened the center and increased the polarization of the political situation.

6. The new U.S. Immigration Reform and Control Act, which prohibits the hiring of undocumented immigrants, is expected to reduce the number of Salvadorans migrating to the United States and may force large numbers to return to El Salvador, thus increasing the already high levels of unemployment and underemployment and thereby intensifying the levels of urban unrest. Estimates of the number of Salvadorans in the United States range from 500,000 to 1 million. Salvadoran government and military officials are concerned that the return of a large number of Salvadorans might threaten the government's stability. The law is also expected to reduce remittances from Salvadorans in the United States to their relatives at home, another serious blow to the Salvadoran economy. These payments have been estimated by the U.S. embassy at $350 million to $600 million and by other sources at more than $1 billion, which would make them by far the major source of U.S. dollars, surpassing coffee exports and U.S. aid.[17]

In certain respects the current realignment of forces resembles the pre-1983 configuration: the Duarte government and sectors of the military are united in pushing the U.S. counterinsurgency project; the right wing, including elements in the military, shares the goal of defeating the FMLN but does not wish to share the costs and strongly opposes the Duarte government; and the FMLN-FDR seems to be pursuing a dual strategy of military victory over the armed forces, on the one hand, and a political solution, involving some form of shared power as a precondition for elections, on the other.

Yet there have been significant changes since the earlier period. First, as in the early 1980s, the organization and mobilization of popular sectors, including labor, students, church-related groups and even some professional and business groups are increasing. These groups do not all necessarily identify with the FMLN-FDR, but they share its goals, particularly in the areas of reform and a negotiated solution to the war.[18]

At the same time, the FMLN-FDR is more united today than in the early 1980s when the various guerrilla groups were still fragmented, and the guerrillas have demonstrated their ability to outmaneuver the much better-equipped forces of the government. The situation today thus differs from that in the early 1980s, when the popular movement was highly organized and mobilized but the FMLN-FDR was relatively weak and divided, and from that of the 1983–1984 period, when the FMLN-FDR was scoring significant military victories against the government forces but the popular forces had been decimated by the terrorism of the 1980–1981 period. The conjuncture of popular mobilization and the military strength of the guerrilla forces might result in a new revolutionary moment, were it not for the international geopolitical situation.

All major actors in El Salvador thus face profound dilemmas. The Duarte government and the armed forces confront the continued deterioration of the economy and the projected return of thousands of Salvadorans from the United States; both factors may be expected to add to the growing social unrest and militancy of popular sectors. And it is doubtful that this militancy can be contained without unleashing a new repression, which could end the willingness of the U.S. Congress to provide the economic and military aid necessary for the war effort and probably essential for the survival of the government.

For the FMLN-FDR, a victory over the armed forces, even if militarily feasible, could lead to direct U.S. intervention in the war, while a negotiated solution seems to be blocked by the opposition of the military and the U.S. government, although the Arias plan could create space for a renewal of dialogue. And for the U.S. government, the goal of a military victory over the insurgents today seems more elusive than ever. The United States is thus left with three options: the continued prosecution of an increasingly expensive and destructive war; direct military involvement, entailing high domestic and international costs; or a thorough reassessment of its goals in Central America as a prelude to a change in U.S. policy and support for a negotiated settlement.

Notes

1. Between October 1979 and the end of 1983 nearly 40,000 civilians were killed by the military or security forces or by death squads (in large part composed of active or retired military and security personnel). On the conduct of the war, see chapter by Barry, Vergara and Castro in this volume.

2. Meetings between the Duarte government and the FMLN-FDR were held in La Palma in October 1984 and in Ayagualo in November 1984. The two sides could not reach agreement, however, and no further negotiations were held until the kidnapping of Duarte's daughter in September 1985, when discussions focused on concrete measures such as her release and the release of political prisoners. In June 1986 Duarte again called for dialogue and the FMLN-FDR accepted, but the discussions were called off when the armed forces occupied the town of Sesori, in San Miguel, where the meeting had been scheduled to take place.

3. In January 1986 the armed forces intensified their operations against the civilian support base, beginning with Operation Phoenix, which drove the population from the Guazapa volcano area; this was followed by operations in Chalatenango and Morazán.

4. If, for example, in the past the FMLN needed a thousand pair of boots a month to enable its troops to continue the fight, infrastructure was required to manufacture the boots. If groups of fifty are trying to get boots as the necessity arises, they can be bought. For this purchase money is needed, which is more readily available than infrastructure.

5. Economic data in this section is drawn from Francisco Lazo, "Crisis económica de El Salvador," *CINAS Cuaderno de Trabajo* No. 9, Mexico (January 1987); Departamento de Economía, Universidad Centroamericana, "Dinámica y Crisis de la Economía Salvadoreña," *ECA*, XLI (January–February 1986); "Balance de la Economía Salvadoreña 1985," *Coyuntura Económica*, I, 4–5 (February–March 1986); "Estadísticas

Económicas," *Boletín de Ciencias Económicas y Sociales*, IX, 3 (May–June 1986), and Fundación Salvadoreña para el Desarrollo Económico y Social, "Cómo está nuestra economía? 1985," San Salvador, 1986.

6. The burden of the January 1986 economic package fell most heavily on wage earners and unemployed. Wage increases were limited and outdistanced by price increases; by mid-1986 the prices of basic goods had increased by approximately 60 percent and the prices of medicines were up 150 percent.

7. The name has subsequently been changed to Libertad.

8. FUSADES, "La necesidad de un nuevo modelo económico para El Salvador: Lineamientos generales de una estrategia," El Salvador, 1985; and Herman Rosa and Roberto Suay, "El nuevo modelo norteamericano para Centro América: El caso de El Salvador," *Boletín de Ciencias Económicas y Sociales*, IX, 1 (January–February 1986).

9. See chapter by Edelberto Torres Rivas in this volume.

10. The UNTS was formed by organizations that had traditionally supported the Christian Democrats, such as the UPD (Unión Popular Democrática), CTS (Central de Trabajadores Salvadoreños), and COACES (Confederación de Asociaciones Cooperativas de El Salvador), as well as by opposition unions and federations such as FENASTRAS (Federación Nacional de Trabajadores Salvadoreños) and ANDES (Asociación Nacional de Educadores Salvadoreños). Subsequently the UPD pulled out of UNTS, but member organizations of the UPD remained, and the UNTS continues to be the major opposition labor coalition.

11. The same strategy has also been used by AIFLD (American Institute of Free Labor Development), which has actively promoted a union base for the Christian Democrats. Recently, however, AIFLD and the Christian Democrats have come in conflict regarding control of pro-government unions. See Norman Casper, "El IADSL y la corrupción del movimiento sindical en El Salvador," *ECA*, XLI (March 1986). Another government tactic has been the recognition of parallel unions in factories or workplaces where opposition unions are strong.

12. Information on U.S. aid to El Salvador can be found in United States Agency for International Development, "U.S. AID El Salvador: General Information," El Salvador (1986), and in Jim Leach, George Miller and Mark O. Hatfield, "U.S. Aid to El Salvador: An Evaluation of the Past, A Proposal for the Future," Report to the Arms Control and Foreign Policy Caucus, U.S. Congress, Washington (February 1986).

13. For information on the results of the earthquake, see *Proceso*, 7, 259 (15 October 1986), and 7, 262 (5 November 1986); *Boletín de Ciencias Económicas y Sociales*, IX, 6 (November–December 1986); and *ECA*, XLI, 457–458 (November–December 1986).

14. *Proceso*, 7, 278 (11 March 1987): 4–5; *Central America Bulletin*, 6, 4 (April 1987).

15. On the second economic package and reaction to it see *Proceso*, 7, 270 (14 January 1987); and 7, 272 (28 January 1987); *ECA*, "Marcha atrás del 'segundo paquetazo,'" XLII, 461 (March 1987); and the *Central America Bulletin*, 6, 7 (July 1987). The Supreme Court decision declaring the war tax unconstitutional was based on the grounds that the war was a civil war, among Salvadorans, and did not involve a declaration of war against another nation.

16. *Proceso*, 7, 278 (11 March 1987): 5.

17. Segundo Montes, "La crisis salvadoreña y las consecuencias de una repatriación masiva de refugiados en los Estados Unidos," *Boletín de Ciencias Económicas y Sociales*, X, 1 (January–February 1987).

18. In some circles these newly organized and mobilized groups are referred to as a "third force" separate from both the government and the FMLN-FDR and having the purpose to bring pressure on both to end the war. On the concept of a "third force" see Ignacio Ellacuría, "Caminos de solución para la actual crisis del país,: *ECA*, XLII, 462 (April 1987).

11

The Nicaraguan Experiment: Characteristics of a New Economic Model

Michael E. Conroy and Manuel Pastor, Jr.

In the first half of the 1980s the U.S. debate about Central America was often inflamed by widely varying perceptions about the direction of Nicaraguan social and economic policies. The Reagan administration, for example, repeatedly asserted that Nicaragua had become a clone of Soviet Marxism-Leninism, tempered perhaps by tampering in Cuban laboratories.[1] This impression of Nicaragua was fortified at times by the rhetoric of the Sandinista government. Moreover, the modes of historical analysis and political thought most frequently encountered in contemporary Nicaragua do reflect the profound influence of Marxist thought in pre-1979 intellectual circles.

Most observers, however, including U.S. embassy personnel in Managua when speaking not for attribution, scoff at the notion of Nicaragua as a simple rerun of the Cuban experience. Scholars of the Cuban revolution and those familiar with other socialist and non-socialist developments in the Western Hemisphere have been quick to note the differences between Nicaragua and Cuba, both in declared policy and in actual practice. Those studying the Nicaraguan experience itself point to the non-Marxist origins of and the rationale for many of the economic policies implemented during the first years of the Sandinista regime.[2] Indeed, the importance of private capitalist production in Nicaragua's critical export sector, the evolving nature of Nicaraguan agrarian reform, the stimulus given to private-sector production by the Sandinista government (often at the cost of virulent criticism from its most radical supporters), and the courting of foreign private investment, for example, hardly fit with a simplistic view of the Nicaraguan economic experiment as typically socialist.

Characterizing the nature of revolutionary Nicaragua thus remains a difficult intellectual task. On the one hand, we must acknowledge that the Nicaraguan experience is by definition unique, since both the anti-Somoza insurrection and its aftermath were attributable to unique social and political forces. On the other hand, examining the histories of archetypically socialist countries such as the Soviet Union and the Peoples Republic of China can bring out certain criteria that will allow us to assess the socialist nature of the Nicaraguan transformation. And comparing Nicaragua with other attempts in the Western Hemisphere to turn away from traditional capitalism, particularly the social experiments in Cuba since 1959 and in Jamaica under Michael Manley, can help us locate the Nicaraguan development strategy within a spectrum of other countries' responses to dissatisfaction with traditional capitalist development paths.

In making these comparisons, we do not discuss whether Nicaragua should incorporate the policies employed by actually existing socialist or various transitional societies. Rather, we are simply trying to establish reference points by which to gain insight into the problems and possibilities in present-day Nicaragua. Certain inherent limitations, however, apply to this type of comparative analysis. First, even if the architects of the new Nicaragua had intended to create, in some form, "another Cuba," the geopolitical realities of a bipolar world may have led them to restrain their public pronouncements. Second, Nicaraguan economic policies were forged in a crucible of U.S. aggression that often seemed designed to destroy the emerging economic structure whatever its origins and tendencies. The reaction to this aggression has likely led Nicaragua to adopt certain policies that may not have been part of the Sandinistas' original development strategy, a point we return to below.

In this essay, then, we characterize the evolution of the Nicaraguan experiment, making reference both to other transitional experiences and to the unique characteristics of the Nicaraguan model. We develop a set of criteria by which to characterize a transition as socialist, drawing these criteria from a brief comparison of the experiences of the Soviet Union and the People's Republic of China (especially during their periods of transition) and from an examination of the "third path" of "democratic socialism" attempted in Jamaica in the 1970s. We then contrast the Nicaraguan experience with comparable periods in what might be viewed as the contemporary application in the Western Hemisphere of the archetypal Marxist-Leninist or orthodox socialist model: the Cuban revolution. We close by raising questions about the possibilities for self-sustaining economic progress in Nicaragua and by noting the challenge that the Nicaraguan model presents for U.S. policy.

Some Initial Criteria from Archetypal Socialism:
The Soviet and Chinese Models

Whether because of historical precedence or sheer magnitude, the Soviet Union and China are often taken as the archetypes against which other socialist experiments must be measured. Jameson and Wilber, for instance, propose an implicit typology of socialism in developing countries based on similarities to and dissimilarities from these classic examples.[3] Drawing upon the experiences of China and the Soviet Union, they suggest a set of "central questions which will appear in any socialist development pattern": (1) the nature of the initial seizure of power, (2) the changes wrought on the preexisting society to create preconditions for socialism, (3) the development strategy then enacted, (4) the nature of organizations and institutions subsequently erected, and (5) the specific role of the state. Reviewing the history of the socialist archetypes with respect to these questions, they argue, helps define both a range of policies that one should expect in new socialist societies and a set of central problem areas that must be addressed by any socialist model.[4]

FitzGerald has proposed a separate set of overlapping problems facing small peripheral societies in the process of transition from a historically inherited situation of capitalist underdevelopment. He calls attention to seven concrete problems: articulation of different forms of production, reinsertion into the international division of labor, labor and distribution, price formation and the appropriation of surplus, macroeconomic management and planning, accumulation and economic development, and the defense of the transition itself.[5]

We draw upon these authors, as well as others, to develop several criteria for evaluating the socialist character of the society that has been created (where there has been time for consolidation), the society toward which a nation may be moving, and the transitional policies that may have been implemented to move it in that direction.[6] Like Jameson and Wilber, we begin by setting forth six criteria based upon various characteristics of the socialist transition in the Soviet Union and China. We return to these criteria later when we evaluate the Nicaraguan experience since 1979. We begin with:

1. *Initial policies criterion.* The nature of the immediate changes implemented to bring about a transition toward socialism provides a first test of the intent and direction of ultimate change. Changes are more socialistic to the extent that the new regime immediately and dramatically reduces or eliminates private ownership, expands collective or state ownership, and consolidates that control through changes in the supporting financial and management institutions.

There were similarities in the initial actions of the revolutionary states of the Soviet Union and China which indicated that the new leadership hoped to create the preconditions for socialist transition; these similarities are all the more striking because the conditions the two governments first encountered were dramatically different. In both instances, the initial policy package included rapid elimination of the economic role of foreign capitalists and steps toward the collectivization of landed estates and nationalization of industries. In terms of FitzGerald's concern about how the revolutionary state deals with the coexistence of differing forms of production, we would suggest that, in both China and the Soviet Union, old capitalist forms of production were quickly eliminated, even before alternative socialist forms had been clearly put in place.

2. *Labor process and basic needs criterion.* One way to evaluate the socialist character of state policies is to examine any changes in the organization of

the labor process and in the provision of wage goods and other basic services. For the underdeveloped capitalist economy in the periphery, the key questions include: How does the new society replace the economic pressures and institutionalized violence that accompanied primitive accumulation? How does it provide for improvements in the fulfillment of basic needs? How does it deal with the tension between the propensity for work intensity and production to decline and the expectation of immediate improvements in the standard of living?[7]

Both China and the Soviet Union paid significant early attention to improving education, health, and housing services. The principal focus, however, soon shifted to the processes of growth and accumulation. Both societies have been criticized on the grounds that this shift in focus toward aggregate growth drew attention away from the earlier goals of increasing consumption and enhancing workers' participation in the labor process.

3. *Price-setting and planning criterion.* Controls on prices and the implementation of planning to replace price signals is another feature associated with socialist models. Here we must investigate what new price-setting mechanisms and other institutional characteristics are established for fundamental resource allocations. Are various markets allowed a role, or are they replaced by either decentralized planning mechanisms or central planning? How is the relationship between domestic prices and international prices—especially relevant in small, open, peripheral contemporary economies—managed and maintained?

Although China maintained a higher degree of decentralization in its planning structure, the experiences of both China and the Soviet Union did include centralized price-setting and the planned management of output. As FitzGerald notes, the task of coordinating mixed forms of production during transitional periods may require preservation of market-based transactions, particularly between different modes or forms of production;[8] the minimizing of market-based price signals in the Soviet and Chinese experiences may partly reflect the rapidly emerging dominance of the socialist mode of production.

4. *External policies criterion.* External economic policies, including relationships to international finance and the international division of labor, may serve to distinguish not only among varieties of socialist experiences but also between socialist experiences and state capitalist experiences; nations in the latter category, for example, generally maintain extensive connections with international capitalism. In examining external policies, we should ask: To what extent does the society "delink" itself (in the words of Díaz Alejandro)[9] or otherwise turn inward, rather than outward, in its development strategies? To what extent will international financial assistance be sought and international trade be maintained? How will the nation choose to align itself among international blocs?

Because the character of international institutions and the functioning of the international economy in the 1980s are very different from what they were at the time of the Soviet or the Chinese revolution, these previous experiences may be less relevant for the Nicaraguan case. Indeed, the classic autarchic strategy pursued by China, first after 1949, then more completely after the break from the Soviet Union, may be impossible in Nicaragua due to both its relatively small size and the historic limitations on domestic production created by previous colonialism. Even in contemporary socialist countries, however, the questions of limiting, controlling, and taking advantage of the international division of labor remain important policy concerns.

5. *Broader "role of the state" criterion.* The extent of the government's involvement in internal development strategies—including the degree of the state's power in the economy, the levels of worker self-management, and the space left for the capitalist sector (if it continues to function)—is a particularly knotty dilemma for socialist societies. In evaluating whether a society is socialist, we might ask: How extensive has the role of the state become? What specific roles does it play? What techniques, what goals, what instruments are employed? What institutions function outside the state and how do they function?

The archetypal socialist models of the Soviet Union and China are marked by a significant enhancement of the state's responsibilities for short-run macroeconomic management and long-run development, as well as by a direct state role in production itself. The preeminent role of the state in the Chinese and Soviet experiences has been criticized as bureaucratic authoritarianism by Bahro[10] and as little more than state capitalism by Cleaver.[11] Distinguishing the socialist state and socialist development from the varieties of state capitalism found in contemporary Mexico or Brazil has also been a topic of importance to contemporary socialists. Obviously, an extensive state role is not enough to characterize a development path as socialist; we must also examine, for example, the new roles of working-class organizations as well as the various other criteria we are developing here. Nonetheless, socialism has usually been associated with expansion of state property and state power.

6. *Counterrevolutionary reaction criterion.* The history of the need for defense of the transition itself suggests an additional, ironic criterion: that the degree of socialism (or at least the historical and institutional distance from the prevailing global capitalist alternative) is evidenced by the extent to which the new society needs to be defended against economic and military aggression. It follows, then, that new policies are restricted by, and economic performance is affected by, the need to defend the revolution against counterrevolution.

The October Revolution led to civil war and external aggression, both of which overshadowed the initial development of the early Soviet model. The total defeat of the Kuomintang left China relatively free of serious external military aggression in the formative years of its revolutionary regime, but international economic isolation and aggression dictated some of its early inward orientation. Virtually every Third World nation that has turned toward a more socialistic development strategy has experienced both military and economic pressures to stem or limit the transition. In evaluating a country's choices of policy and social direction, we must not only recognize the need for self-defense but also reflect on the impact of such self-defense on the possibilities for successful development. Nicaragua would seem to be no exception to this general pattern.

Additional Criteria: Class and Democracy

Class Orientation

In establishing the above criteria for evaluating alternative socialist modes of organization we have for the most part followed previous authors. We have, however, excluded Jameson and Wilber's suggestion that the form in which a government took power is important in determining the socialist character of a society. Both the Soviet and the Chinese experiences did involve tumultuous revolutions and extraconstitutional processes. Nonetheless, revolutions, coups, and barracks revolts are also common modes of taking power in capitalist countries. At the same time, the electoral, nonviolent accession of Manley in Jamaica and of Allende in Chile does not disqualify those transitions as socialist; certainly the method of coming to power did little to lessen counterrevolutionary attacks against them.

That power seizure and electoral successes both produced governments we might label as socialist suggests that there is one criterion not dealt with directly by Jameson and Wilber or FitzGerald: *the class criterion.* From their origins in classical Marxist analysis, both the Soviet and the Chinese experiences represent revolutionary change designed to benefit the working class, the peasantry, and allied classes. The choices necessitated by a number of the criteria above—the decision, for example, to expropriate capitalist property or to involve the state in the provision of basic commodities— follow from a focus upon the needs of oppressed peoples within a distinctly class-based and class-divided society. The difference between the extraconstitutional processes of the militarily based "revolutions" in Brazil, Peru, and South Korea and those that characterized China and Cuba, for example, is that the latter revolutions sought to put previously dispossessed social groups in power. Similarly, the distinction between the state's role in socialism and its role in state capitalism in the Third World is largely linked to the groups for whom the state is acting. As shown below, the Nicaraguan experiment, despite other differences from socialist archetypes, is intended to benefit workers and peasants. A unique feature of the first years of Sandinista rule, however, was the way the Nicaraguan revolution attempted to maintain a broad multiclass alliance while pursuing the commitment to certain specific classes. We return to this point below.

Democratic Process: The Jamaican Road

A further criterion for evaluating socialism emerges from the experience of Jamaica under Prime Minister Michael Manley and his People's National

Party (PNP). In his personal retrospective on eight years in power as a "democratic socialist," Manley tells how the search for a political program led the PNP to forge a new developmental strategy between two contemporary possibilities which he saw as diametrically opposed: market capitalism and state-dominated socialism.[12] Such a "third path" was also attempted in Chile under Allende, in Portugal from 1974 to 1976, in Guyana after 1966, and in Tanzania and Angola; we focus on the Jamaican experience as an alternative that may have suggested various policies to the Sandinista Front in Nicaragua partly because it occurred during the formative years of the Sandinista movement and partly because Jamaica, like Nicaragua, had to learn to deal with the reaction of the United States to its experiment.

In developing the argument for a "third path," Manley suggested first that Jamaica in the early 1970s had inherited the fundamental characteristics of classical colonies. In his view, no attempt had ever been made to produce what was needed for Jamaica, only what was needed by someone else outside Jamaica. Moreover, trade involved not the careful exchange of relative surpluses, but rather the importation of all that was needed and the export of all that was produced. Finally, the surplus that might have been used to increase local production was consistently exported as profits.[13]

One solution to Jamaica's problems was to adopt the model of Puerto Rico, a model that stressed the development of a manufacturing sector and relied upon foreign capital and technology. Manley felt, however, that Jamaica had already been applying the Puerto Rico model since the Norman Manley government of the 1950s. Bauxite and aluminum investments, production, and exports grew dramatically, but so did imports of the raw material and intermediate inputs needed for production. Thus, by 1968

> behind the glittering indicators of success lay stark facts. Unemployment was increasing. Social services reflected little improvement. The degree of economic dependence was actually increasing rather than decreasing. Finally, the traditional problem of exporting surplus to foreign owners remained unchanged because new industries were also foreign.[14]

An alternative model open to Jamaica was that of Cuba, a country that had attempted to eliminate the impoverishing neocolonial system by nationalizing all foreign capital, diversifying production to fulfill domestic needs, and stimulating industrialization on the basis of the newly nationalized profits of sugar exports. In Cuba, the fundamental social problems of concern to Manley—employment, health care, and education—had been addressed directly and successfully by the state. While noting these accomplishments, Manley felt uncomfortable with Cuba's political system and lamented the lack of political rights for those "outside of the revolution."[15] He argued instead for: "another path, a third path, a Jamaican way rooted in our political experience and values, capable of providing an economic base to our political independence and capable of some measure of social justice for the people."[16]

Manley's critique of the Cuban experience suggests an additional criterion for evaluating a society in transition: the *democratic process criterion.* Manley's notions of democratic process were, in large part, a reflection of the parliamentary system Jamaica had adopted from the advanced capitalist countries, particularly England, and he failed to recognize grass roots participation in Cuban decision-making processes or to distinguish between political processes that reflected the initial direction of the revolution and the social controls forced on Cuba by external aggression. Nonetheless, Manley was critical of the Cuban experience in that his notion of democratic process required not only that the citizenry actively participate in crucial decisions about the transition but also that some political space be allowed for a viable opposition. Whether his criterion reflects a luxury available primarily to governments that come to power by electoral means and within relatively well-established traditional electoral systems is less important than the fact that there exist many others for whom this democratic process criterion is also important.

When Manley's PNP was swept into office in 1972, the new government's policies were substantially less dramatic than might have been expected from what was billed as a deliberate attempt to create some form of "democratic socialism." Rather than expropriate the foreign-dominated bauxite companies, Manley created a financial surplus for the state by sharply increasing the severance taxes on their production. While the state itself grew only to the extent that it absorbed bankrupt firms and expanded fundamental services,[17] Manley's government extended its economic role by introducing price controls on wage goods, increasing subsidies in order to make many basic goods more widely available, and implementing import controls to save available foreign exchange for use on essential commodities. Health and education programs were also enlarged, often with the aid of Cuban teachers and medical personnel.

As time went on, however, opposition to the new policies by foreign investors and lenders, the International Monetary Fund (IMF), and the foreign-dominated raw materials industries caused a series of financial crises in the external sector. These exchange problems, and the intervention of the IMF, led to the repeal of many of the bauxite export taxes and some of the import and price controls. Less able to provide for the basic needs of his constituency, Manley lost his political support. In 1980, the collective influence of the opposition press, deteriorating domestic and international economic conditions, and overt support by the U.S. government for his electoral opponent, Edward Seaga, brought the entire experiment to an end.

The Jamaican experience, and the equally significant experience of Allende in Chile, suggested that meeting the democratic process criterion (at least as specified by Manley) might undermine the ability to bring about real structural transformation of the economy, partly because the criterion allowed counter-revolutionary or antisocialist elements wide latitude to sabotage economic and social change. For the Sandinistas, this possibility must have increased interest in the more dramatic and less pluralistic paths followed by the Soviet Union, China, and, in this hemisphere, Cuba.

Nicaragua and the Experience of Cuba

We now use the criteria developed from the Chinese and Soviet experiences as well as from the Jamaican "third path" to contrast the emerging Nicaraguan society and economy with that of Cuba, the country with which Nicaragua is most often compared in the popular press. Insofar as possible, we attempt to contrast the first seven years of post-insurrection Nicaragua (1979–1986) with a similar time span in Cuba. As we shall see, the differences between the two countries are sometimes striking.

Initial Policies

After the revolutionary triumph in 1959, Cuba quickly nationalized virtually all foreign capital and all foreign landholdings; export agriculture, especially sugar production, was the main target in a deliberate attempt to finance social programs from the surplus generated in that foreign-oriented sector. By the mid-1960s two waves of agrarian reform had washed across Cuba, and two-thirds of agriculture had been transformed into state-run farms or state-controlled cooperatives. The vast majority of production and nearly all employment were state-controlled, with most basic commodities distributed through a complex rationing system. As Cuba sought to institute East European–style centralized planning, markets played a very small role in determining prices, production levels, labor allocation, and a host of other fundamental economic variables.[18]

In Nicaragua, in contrast, seven years after the insurrection major multinational firms continue to function, both independently and in mixed enterprises with the government. Most prominent among them are Exxon, Royal Dutch Shell, and Texaco (petroleum refining and production of derivatives for sale throughout Central America); British-American Tobacco (cigarette manufacture for local consumption and export to Europe); and Pan American (hotels and motels). The list also includes nearly a hundred other major multinationals that provide substantial quantities of new computer equipment (IBM/Mexico), private and public accounting services (Price, Waterhouse), and training in public administration (Harvard University).

In addition, export agriculture in Nicaragua has remained predominantly in private hands (to the dismay of some early Soviet commentators as well as some observers on the Nicaraguan left).[19] Instead of nationalization and collectivization of all export production, Nicaragua chose to nationalize the trading of exports, negotiating prices of inputs and harvests with capitalist producers in a contentious process that was often mistaken outside Nicaragua for simple private sector complaints about the revolutionary government. This approach reflected a conscious attempt to stimulate accumulation by using surpluses realized in international trade. The strategy was accompanied, however, by a variety of political problems, particularly when the need to placate the capitalist agricultural sector with special treatment and maintain downward pressures on agricultural wages clashed with the interests of the worker and peasant base of the Sandinista Front (FSLN).

Agrarian reform in revolutionary Nicaragua was also dramatically different from that in Cuba. By the mid-1980s, nearly a third of the total land affected had been distributed to cooperatives and individuals with private, irrevocable titles, and by 1985 the vast majority of expropriated land was being distributed to small producers and cooperatives rather than being converted into state farms. Moreover, the participation of the Nicaraguan peasantry in the design and implementation of agrarian reform was unusually active by comparison with the role of peasants in other socialist (and nonsocialist) experiences, a feature consistent with the democracy criterion suggested by Manley.[20] A final difference with archetypically socialist land reforms was the role reserved for large private estates, a role explicitly guaranteed by provisions in the 1981 Agrarian Reform Law stating that effectively used land could not be expropriated, no matter how large the holdings. Although peasant unrest in 1985 did lead the Sandinista government to expropriate land near Masaya (including some that belonged to an important leader of the internal civilian opposition) and authorize in January 1986 the further expropriation of land "for public use or social interest," the large capitalist landholders retained an importance in the accumulation process unusual for a "socialist" agrarian reform.

The Labor Process and Basic Needs

By the mid-1960s the Cuban labor market had been radically transformed. Most job assignments were made through government agencies as part of a process supposedly designed to rationalize the use of a work force whose employment was guaranteed. The onus of responsibility for finding employment had thus been shifted from the individual worker to the state, and open unemployment had been substantially reduced.

In the Nicaragua of the mid-1980s open unemployment was in excess of 20 percent in urban areas. The state had made no attempt to take direct responsibility for providing employment to a majority of the population. Labor markets had not been restricted and it remained the individual worker's responsibility to find a job capable of providing for his or her sustenance.

Nicaragua had, however, developed a series of programs that reflected a commitment to fulfill people's basic needs. The well-documented literacy crusade, a series of health mobilizations, establishment of the universal right to free health care, and rapid expansion of educational opportunities and enrollments all bear witness to this commitment, especially since these policies were established in conditions of considerable economic duress.[21] This, of course, mirrors Cuba's own rapid expansion of health care and education in the earliest years of the revolutionary regime.

While Nicaragua avoided excessive intervention in labor markets, it did intervene in product markets by establishing some price controls and rationing systems. Initiated in early 1980, the rationing was designed (1) to protect the standard of living of the impoverished majority as the country underwent the severe macroeconomic adjustment required by the devastation that followed the insurrection and by the world economic crisis of 1980–1983, and (2) to serve as a redistributive measure to raise the effective standard of living of the poor majority. Although rationed products were generally also available at unsubsidized prices in the marketplace and in food stores, by the mid-1980s Nicaragua was suffering severe shortages of many goods abundantly available to middle- and high-income groups in the rest of Central America and in most other small countries: gasoline, cooking oil, many types of medicine, paper, and a wide variety of other Western imported goods, especially luxury goods. The shortage of imported goods in particular arose from a deliberate government decision to use limited hard currency to import items more necessary for continued production or for meeting basic needs; whereas this policy may have suggested insensitivity to those whose consumption patterns included more imported goods, it does not imply chaos or the simple malfunctioning of the economy. On the contrary, the whole rationing apparatus reflected the political decision to have the state "manage scarcity" rather than "letting scarcity manage itself" through an unfettered price mechanism that would benefit higher income groups. This strategy played to the Sandinista low-income political base and indicated an attempt to ensure that basic needs be met.

Price Setting and Planning

Centralized price determination and an attempt to implement overall central planning were clear characteristics of the Cuban experience. By the mid-1960s banking had been nationalized and external trade had come under the control of the central government. By the end of the decade the role of the private sector had been reduced to agricultural production on small family farms and to limited provision of informal services in the urban areas. Retailing, wholesaling, manufacturing, and major construction had also become the exclusive province of the state.

Despite its rationing system, Nicaragua in the mid-1980s relied far more than Cuba on market-determined pricing and privately controlled production. Like Cuba, Nicaragua nationalized its banking systems and rationed internal credit in order to stimulate preferred production. State control of banking, however, is not a characteristic unique to socialist development models. The problems of private capital markets in small, open economies are well known, and it is widely acknowledged that the creative use of credit is one of the most powerful development tools even in market-based economies. In the 1970s and early 1980s, for example, the banking system was nationalized in Mexico, El Salvador, Costa Rica, and in about twenty-five other market-oriented Third World countries. Nicaragua's control of imports and exports also is not unique to socialist models. In the 1980s, for example, the Salvadoran state had (partly at the insistence of the United States) taken public control of the country's most important export product, coffee, in order to stem capital flight.

Government control of the banking system and international trade, as well as the expansion of government distribution systems, did narrow the realm within which Nicaraguan private producers could function. Those who were previously engaged in import-export businesses were particularly affected. On the one hand, because the government absorbed more of the risk of price fluctuations for both imports and exports, producers were better protected from the vicissitudes of international markets. On the other, they faced more government regulations, such as minimum wage requirements and higher occupational safety and health standards. The context within which profit-making decisions are made in Nicaragua had been deliberately altered, and many businesspeople who were successful before 1979 decided that they could not operate under the new conditions. Nonetheless, in contrast with the extensively socialized economy of Cuba, the Nicaraguan economy remained predominantly private.

External Policies

Cuba did not have the option of autarchy enjoyed by such socialist giants as China and the Soviet Union. Its natural resource limitations, the colonial heritage of export monoculture, and low levels of industrialization meant that Cuba had to retain some niche in the international division of labor. Whatever its original intentions, however, the Cuban government was forced to turn to the socialist bloc for trading partners after the punitive embargo imposed in 1961 by the United States and subsequently agreed to by a majority of Latin American governments. Cuba also depended on socialist countries for development finance, partly because its abrogation of external debt to capitalist countries and institutions made borrowing in international credit markets impossible.[22]

At the outset, Nicaragua had a better opportunity than Cuba to reduce dependence on international trade, partly because Nicaraguan agricultural production possibilities are richer and more varied than those of Cuba and thus agricultural self-sufficiency was more easily within Nicaragua's reach. Rather than attempting a quick and perhaps costly shift to self-sufficiency, however, Nicaragua sought to diversify dependence—that is, to reduce reliance on a single trading partner, the United States—while continuing to benefit from its comparative advantage in certain exports. To reach this goal, Nicaragua tried to expand and diversify its participation in the international capitalist system of trade and finance while simultaneously using state control and appropriation of most of the surplus or "profits" generated to improve the consequences of international integration. Although Nicaragua also developed extensive trade and credit relations with the socialist bloc countries, only approximately 25 percent of all financial assistance (other than military) between 1979 and the beginning of 1985 had come from those countries; a considerably smaller proportion of Nicaragua's total trade was with the same countries.[23] In May 1985, however, the United States imposed an embargo on trade with Nicaragua; this action will likely make it more difficult for the Sandinistas to avoid the excessive financial and trade reliance on the socialist bloc which is typical of Cuba.

In contrast with Cuba's approach to the debts incurred by the prerevolutionary regime, the Nicaraguan government committed itself to servicing its international debt, expecting that this policy would leave open the channels of international financial assistance which have been available both to other transitional societies (such as Tanzania) and to established socialist societies (such as Poland).[24] The World Bank, applauding Nicaragua for its "responsible" decision, initially proposed that substantial amounts of aid be provided.[25] After 1981, however, intervention from the United States representatives at the World Bank, the Export-Import Bank, the International Monetary Fund, and the Inter-American Development Bank blocked most multilateral loans and grants. This overt politicization of the lending process has been criticized even by U.S. allies.[26]

The Role of the State

The comparison of Cuba and Nicaragua also reveals basic differences in the role and functioning of the state and state planning in the economy. As noted earlier, in the mid-1980s market signals continued to play an important role in contemporary Nicaragua. Farmers' decisions with respect to crops, fertilizers, herbicide and insecticide combinations, and the employment of labor were, for example, largely market-determined. The government's attempts to alter the composition of production were mostly limited to moral suasion, the establishment of minimum conditions for the labor force, a variety of price and credit incentives, and the setting of intermediate import prices. Indeed, one market sector uncontrolled by the state, the so-called informal sector, actually expanded in the first years of Sandinista rule as government attempts to hold down money wages in order to protect price and profit levels in the private capitalist sector led many wage workers to shift to the self-employment typical of informal activities in the hope of increasing their real incomes.[27]

As for planning, in the mid-1980s it remained a primitive art in Nicaragua, hindered by the absence of even the most fundamental baseline data, by the lack of instruments for controlling the predominantly private economy, and by a shortage of skilled planners. The planning that was undertaken came much closer to the project-specific planning promoted by the World Bank than to the systematic approaches of Eastern Europe or China (or to the planning system that finally began to function in Cuba in the 1970s). Planning documents, discussions with planners, and government statements, showed little evidence that planning comparable to the Soviet or contemporary Cuban models was contemplated. The economic role of the state in Nicaragua was mostly limited to implementing fiscal and monetary policy, managing state farms, and conducting a host of specialized programs to deal with concrete problems.

Counterrevolutionary Reaction
and the Defense of the Revolution

Seven years after their respective revolutions, Cuba and Nicaragua both were subjected to direct military attacks by counterrevolutionary exiles organized and financed by the CIA. The two nations had also developed relatively large, efficient, well-equipped armies with the support of the Soviet Union. And both had seen the burden of military expenditures adversely affect their domestic economies.

In the mid 1980s it became clear that the *contra* war had had a significant impact on Nicaragua's economic progress and evolution. By 1985 direct damage to economic targets, especially in the coffee growing northern highlands, had cost Nicaragua more than $300 million (a figure that has certainly grown since then) and 50 percent of current government expenditures were destined for defense.[28] Many of the most successful social programs, implemented in 1979 and 1980, had been slowed or halted by the economic demands of the war. Fewer new schools and clinics were constructed while agricultural and industrial production suffered because available hard currency was being used to support the war effort. Moreover, the requirements of military mobilization had created chronic shortages of manual labor.

The contra war, however, appeared to have had some positive effects in terms of internal support for government economic policies. It is true that in the absence of U.S. intervention, many private capitalists would have been obligated to adjust to the new realities of a Sandinista Nicaragua; U.S. support of counterrevolution encouraged these individuals to resist change and engage in economic sabotage rather than find new avenues for profit-making in the transformed economic landscape. At the same time, the external origins and financing of the contras were so clearly seen by most Nicaraguans that even those dissatisfied with some aspects of the revolutionary process tended to rally behind the government. There is anecdotal evidence that many private-sector producers and other Nicaraguans would have demanded more of the government if there had been no war. There was probably more acceptance of rationing and shortages, and more support for austerity, than might have existed if no external aggression had been directed against Nicaragua. At the same time, it is clear that a less painful way to retain political support would have been to accomplish those developmental tasks being derailed by the war.

The Role of Class

It is in the fundamental class orientation of the revolution that Nicaragua draws closest to both Cuba in particular and the socialist archetypes in general. One feature that distinguishes the growth of the state in Nicaragua from similarly extensive state expansion in Brazil is the support the Brazilian state gave to elites in what might be termed a "capitalist accumulation project." In contrast, Nicaraguan state policy has been designed to meet the basic needs of the principal constituents of the Sandinista Front: the working class and the peasantry.

Although the Sandinista Front did intend the new development path to benefit primarily workers and peasants, it argued that its accumulation project represented a broadly conceived "logic of the majority." This broad vision, a unique feature of the Nicaraguan model, allowed the front to draw support from a wide variety of classes. The multiclass character of the developmental strategy, as well as the continuing roles for markets and private property described above, even led some to the left of the Sandinistas to fear that Nicaragua would evolve into a state-supported capitalist economy with a strong, hegemonic party born of the revolutionary process—that is, another Mexico.

Political Participation

We turn now to the criterion of special concern to Michael Manley: democratic processes. Evaluating democracy and the adequacy of political participation is always a thorny and hotly disputed process. Without doubt, Cuba represents a transition model that has not implemented traditional Western electoral processes. There is evidence that grass roots participation in fundamental decision making in Cuba exists to an extent generally ignored by many of that nation's critics. Yet, the lack of an opposition press and of other vehicles for voicing dissent, the centralization of most social and economic decision making, and the absence of competing political parties leaves Cuba open to the sort of criticisms Manley and others might voice.

In Nicaragua, on the other hand, continuous and contentious expressions of opposition marked most of the early years of the revolution. Among the mass organizations that were critical of the government, some to its right and some to its left, were anti-Sandinista private-sector, labor union, and church-based groups. The newspaper with the largest paid circulation, *La Prensa*, was virulently anti-Sandinista; before June 1986, it had never been blocked from publishing for more than a few days at a time, albeit often with partial censorship. The level of censorship varied in response to several factors: the onset and deepening of the counterrevolutionary war, worsening social and economic conditions, and a tendency of the paper's owners and editors to test the limits of censorship with deliberately provocative articles.[29]

Along with the attempt to maintain a degree of political space for opposition forces, Nicaragua moved to ensure popular participation in government decision making. By the mid-1980s this effort had passed through a number of phases. In the immediate aftermath of the insurrection, a wide variety of nationally oriented mass organizations had been formed. In addition, all major constituencies were initially represented in the Council of State, a body that was, in fact, largely dominated by worker and peasant groups throughout its short history.[30]

By 1984 elections had been held for a new legislative body and for the presidency. Although the elections have been publicly criticized (with little detail) by the U.S. Department of State, numerous international observer groups have concluded that the electoral process was fair and legitimate.[31] When the new National Assembly began to operate in 1985, thirty-four of ninety-six seats were held by representatives of six opposition political parties, and the Sandinista political base of workers and peasants actually had less explicit and proportional representation than it had enjoyed under the transitional council.

In October 1985 the Sandinista government imposed a state of emergency on the nation, thus restricting civil liberties. Although some analysts argue that the scope of restrictions was exaggerated in the media, and that the decision was based on legitimate fears about the formation of a new internal front in the ongoing counterrevolutionary war, the state of emergency dealt a blow to Nicaragua's international image.[32] The image was further damaged when, in June 1986, on the heels of a U.S. congressional vote to increase aid to the contras, the Sandinista government abandoned its flexibility in applying the state-of-emergency rules and closed down *La Prensa*. Under the Arias plan, however, *La Prensa* once again resumed publishing and internal restrictions have been relaxed. In general, despite various problems, it remains difficult to dismiss Nicaragua's commitment to pluralism as mere window dressing, particularly in view of the external and internal constraints on Nicaraguan democratic structures posed by intervention and counter-revolution.

The Challenge of the Nicaraguan Experiment

By the mid-1980s Nicaragua had indeed moved in the direction of some form of socialism. At the same time, the evolving economic and social experiment models in Nicaragua exhibited many important differences from the archetypal models of the Soviet Union and the People's Republic of China, the "third path" of Jamaica, or the experience of revolutionary Cuba. The major role played by the private sector in critical agricultural exports, the use of market processes for wholesale and retail distribution of goods, the active role of labor unions and peasantry in the design and implementation of the most important policies affecting their own welfare, and the relatively high levels of political pluralism and public dialogue all combined to make the Nicaraguan experience a distinct transitional experiment.

It is not clear, however, whether the Nicaraguan policies embody too many contradictions to permit the consolidation of a stable and viable model of development. Will the present mode of accumulation, based on the state as locus of accumulation and driven by continued exports of unprocessed agricultural products, generate the surplus needed to underwrite programs for the fulfillment of basic needs? Will the attempt to preserve the private sector in crucial roles prove compatible with national needs for expanded production and improvements in the living standards of the poorest groups? Will the capitalist class ultimately be able to accept the state's leading role in investment? Can the Sandinista Front retain sufficient political strength to permit resolution of the ongoing class conflict in its favor? Will Nicaraguan society move toward the more centralized socialism found in Cuba or perhaps toward a more capitalist model, such as that in Puerto Rico? Can the turn toward the latter be achieved under the continued hegemony of the Sandinista Front?

While these internal conflicts and contradictions are certainly problematic enough, the stability and viability of the Nicaraguan model is also partly dependent on the reaction of international actors such as the United States. Unfortunately for Nicaragua, the U.S. has thus far reacted with great alarm. As a result, the Sandinista government has been confronted by a U.S. economic embargo, constant U.S. military maneuvers in neighboring Honduras, and a counterrevolutionary military force trained and funded by the United States. If the United States-funded counterrevolutionary war continues through the decade, shortages and production difficulties may lead Nicaragua to move policies away from the present experiment with a mixed economy and closer to the more orthodox socialist experiences of Cuba, China, and the Soviet Union. If forced upon Nicaragua, this direction could still result in significant improvements over the economic system inherited from the Somoza dynasty; it would not, however, seem to be what the architects of the Nicaraguan model originally had in mind.

In the early and mid-1980s the challenge for U.S. policy was to recognize that Nicaragua was developing an alternative to both the Soviet and Cuban models as well as to the prototypical free-enterprise system. The Reagan administration met this challenge by labeling the Sandinistas Marxist-Leninist and launching a political, military, and economic aggression against Nicaragua which is easily interpreted as a deliberate attempt to sabotge the Sandinista experiment. Yet even if U.S. objectives in the Third World include the preservation of private sector participation and maintenance of international systems of trade and finance, Nicaragua offers a potentially exciting development model in which rapid accumulation is consistent with fundamentally democratic processes. For the rest of the decade, the continuing question is whether the United States, perhaps under a new administration, will leave simplistic stereotypes to one side and allow the Nicaraguan experiment to run its own course.

Notes

This paper has benefited significantly from the research assistance of Gustavo Marquez, from the comments of Linda Fuller of the book's editorial board, and from the constructively critical support of James Rebitzer, Harry Cleaver, and Rhonda Williams at the University of Texas. Thanks also to Betsy Cohn and the Central American Historical Institute for research help and to Luisa Reyes for typing drafts and redrafts.

1. U.S. Department of State, *The Soviet-Cuban Connection in Central America and the Caribbean,* Bureau of Public Affairs (Márch 1985).

2. See, for example, M. E. Conroy, "False Polarisation? Differing Perspectives on the Economic Strategies of Post-Revolutionary Nicaragua," *Third World Quarterly* 6 (October 1984) 4:993–1032.

3. Kenneth P. Jameson and Charles K. Wilber, "Socialism and Development: An Editors' Introduction," *World Development,* Special Issue on Socialism and Development, 9 (1981) 9/10:803–811.

4. Ibid., p. 804.

5. E. V. K. FitzGerald, "Notes on the Analysis of the Small Underdeveloped Economy in Transition," in *Transition and Development: Problems of Third World*

224 *Michael E. Conroy and Manuel Pastor, Jr.*

Socialism, ed. Richard R. Fagen, Carmen Diana Deere, and José Luis Coraggio (New York: Monthly Review Press, 1986), pp. 28–53.

6. The criteria we develop are also an alternative to the schema proposed by Michal Kalecki. See his "Observations on Social and Economic Aspects of Intermediate Regimes," in his *Essays on Developing Countries* (Atlantic Highlands, NJ: Humanities Press, 1976), and his *Selected Essays on the Economic Growth of the Socialist and the Mixed Economy* (Cambridge: Cambridge University Press, 1972).

7. FitzGerald, "Small Underdeveloped Economy."

8. Ibid., pp. 15–17.

9. Carlos Díaz Alejandro, "Delinking North and South: Unshackled or Unhinged?" in *Rich and Poor Nations in the World Economy,* ed. Albert Fishlow, et al. (New York: McGraw-Hill, 1978).

10. Rudolf Bahro, *The Alternative in Eastern Europe,* trans. David Fernbach (London: Verso Editions, 1981).

11. Harry Cleaver, *Reading Capital Politically* (Austin: University of Texas Press, 1978).

12. Michael Manley, *Jamaica: Struggle in the Periphery* (New York: W. W. Norton & Co., 1982).

13. Ibid., p. 25.

14. Ibid., p. 37.

15. Ibid., p. 38.

16. Ibid.

17. See Kenneth P. Jameson, "Socialist Cuba and the Intermediate Regimes of Jamaica and Guyana," *World Development* 9 (1981) 9/10:871–888.

18. See Hugh Thomas, *The Cuban Revolution* (New York: Harper & Row, 1977); Jameson, "Socialist Cuba"; Carmelo Mesa-Lago, ed., *Revolutionary Change in Cuba* (Pittsburgh: University of Pittsburgh Press, 1971); and Claes Brudenius, *Revolutionary Cuba: The Challenge of Economic Growth with Equity* (Boulder, CO: Westview Press, 1984).

19. See "Nicaragua: The Sorry Path of Sandinism," *Communist Program* 6 (September 1984); Oscar René Vargas, "Nicaragua y Revolución II," *Coyocoacan* (April–June 1981): pp. 59–104; and Henri Weber, "Nicaragua: The Sandinist Revolution," in F. Ambursley and R. Cohen, eds., *Crisis in the Caribbean* (New York: Monthly Review Press, 1983).

20. Carmen Diana Deere, "Agrarian Reform and the Peasantry in the Transition to Socialism in the Third World," Helen Kellogg Institute for International Studies, University of Notre Dame, Working Paper #31, December 1984.

21. See Valerie Miller, *Between Struggle and Hope: The Nicaraguan Literacy Crusade* (Boulder, CO: Westview Special Studies on Latin America and the Caribbean, 1985); and John Booth, *The End and the Beginning: The Nicaraguan Revolution,* 2nd ed. (Boulder, CO: Westview Press, 1985).

22. For a recent reinterpretation of the international financial needs of and financial alternatives for transitional countries, see Barbara Stallings, "External Finance and the Transition to Socialism in Small Peripheral Countries," in *Transition and Development: Problems of Third World Socialism,* ed. Richard R. Fagen, Carmen Diana Deere, and José Luis Coraggio (New York: Monthly Review Press, 1986), pp. 54–78.

23. See M. E. Conroy, "External Dependence, External Assistance, and Economic Aggression against Nicaragua," *Latin American Perspectives,* Issue 45, 12 (Spring 1985) 2:39–67; Ruben Berrios, "Economic Relations between Nicaragua and the Socialist Countries," *Journal of Interamerican Studies and World Affairs* 27 (Fall 1985) 3:111–139; and M. E. Conroy, "Patterns of Changing External Trade in Revolutionary

Nicaragua: Voluntary and Involuntary Trade Diversification," in Rose J. Spaulding, ed., *The Political Economy of Nicaragua* (New York: Allen and Unwin, 1986).

24. See Stallings, "External Finance."

25. World Bank, *Nicaragua: The Challenge of Reconstruction*, Report 3524-N1, 8 September 1981.

26. Cf. Daniel Siegel and Tom Spaulding, with Peter Kornbluh, *Outcast among Allies: The International Costs of Reagan's War against Nicaragua*, Institute for Policy Studies Issue Paper (Washington: Institute for Policy Studies, November 1985).

27. The shift from wage work to the informal sector was encouraged by the fact that access to Nicaragua's ample package of social services was not tied to a worker's place of employment. Thus one reason to stay in wage work—to retain access to social services—had been effectively removed. This policy was changed in early 1986.

28. E. V. K. FitzGerald, "Una evaluación del costo económico de la agresión del gobierno estadounidense contra el pueblo de Nicaragua," paper presented at the Latin American Studies Association Congress, Albuquerque, April 1985. A recent Nicaraguan estimate puts the destruction of goods and losses in production owing to the contra war at almost $600 million for the period 1982–1986. See Instituto Nacional de Estadísticos y Censos, "Agresión: Costos y Daños."

29. See John Spicer Nichols, "The Media," in *Nicaragua: The First Five Years*, ed. Thomas W. Walker (New York: Praeger, 1985), chap. 8, pp. 183–201.

30. See Luis Serra, "The Sandinist Mass Organizations," in *Nicaragua in Revolution*, ed. Thomas W. Walker (New York: Praeger, 1982), chap. 5, pp. 95–114; see also Serra, "The Grass-Roots Organizations," in *Nicaragua: The First Five Years*, ed. Walker, chap. 3.

31. See, for example, *The Electoral Process in Nicaragua: Domestic and International Influences*, Report of the Latin American Studies Association Delegation to Observe the Nicaraguan General Elections of November 4, 1984 (Austin: Latin American Studies Association, 19 December 1984); *The Elections in Nicaragua, November 1984*, Report of the Irish Inter-Party Parliamentary Delegation; *Report of a British Parliamentary Delegation to Nicaragua to Observe the Presidential and National Assembly Elections, 4 November 1984*. All these reports are available in photocopy from the Central America Resource Center, P.O. Box 2327, Austin, TX 78705.

32. Cf. David R. Dye, "The National Emergency in Nicaragua: A Provisional Interpretation," *LASA-NICA Scholars News* (January 1986) 9:1–4.

12

A Multitude of Voices: Religion and the Central American Crisis

Margaret E. Crahan

The Catholic church in Central America has traditionally been viewed as a powerful institution that speaks with one voice, reflecting a coherent worldview shared by the vast majority of its leaders and members. Recent events in the region, however, suggest that the Catholic church as an institution, and also as a community of believers, does not have a monolithic view of the current crises in El Salvador, Guatemala, Honduras, and Nicaragua.[1] Rather, a multitude of positions are being taken, some of them contradicting one another and thus leading to internal disputes and tensions. Thus the Catholic church is not united behind a single strategy for resolving the current crises. In addition, the level of intraecclesial conflict within each country varies substantially.

This essay analyzes the different roles currently being played by the Catholic church in El Salvador, Guatemala, Honduras, and Nicaragua in order to establish its capacity to help resolve the conflicts currently plaguing Central America. The role of the church in each of the four countries is examined to establish its positions and its influence, as well as the principal issues being debated. Included is an analysis of the relative strength and unity of the church leadership, as well as its capacity to mobilize the grass-roots membership. The degree to which the latter accepts the decisions of the hierarchy or diverges from them is also examined. Relations between civil and ecclesiastical elites are evaluated in order to establish the likelihood that the churches can influence secular leaders, in government or in the opposition, to resolve the present conflicts. These analyses reveal the multiplicity of positions within the Catholic church in Central America, how they affect its actions, and possible future directions the church will take.

Historical Background

Historically, the Catholic church in Central America has played a unique role. From the outset of European colonization in the sixteenth century the church has had an institutional presence ofttimes superior to that of the state. Traditionally the church, as an institution, aligned itself with political, economic, and social elites, whereas sectors of the church identified themselves with the poor and the exploited. The resulting tension between moral imperatives and institutional goals has been a constant in the evolution of the Catholic church in Latin America.

As pressures from the poor majority for socioeconomic change escalated in post–World War II Latin America, church leaders became increasingly preoccupied with the necessity for and the direction of such changes. By the 1950s the Catholic church was acutely aware of the erosion both of its membership and of its influence, as more and more of the lower and middle classes joined secular political parties, labor organizations, student groups, and other associations. In addition, the post–World War II period witnessed an influx of Protestant missionaries, particularly from the United States. As they offered more direct spiritual, psychological, and material surcease from socioeconomic problems, some Protestant denominations, particularly the more fundamentalist ones, experienced rapid growth, especially in rural areas and urban slums where the Catholic Church had not concentrated its personnel. Such competition was a major preoccupation of the Latin American bishops who traveled to Rome in the early 1960s for the Second Vatican Council (1962–1965).

At the Council the Latin-American bishops voiced their growing concern over the level of poverty, exploitation, and repression in their countries and the consequent threat to peace and stability. They were also fearful of the inroads that radical revolutionary movements and Protestant churches were making, particularly among the middle class, students, and organized labor. Efforts dating back to the 1920s and 1930s to incorporate them firmly into the church through organizations like Catholic Action, Christian Democratic parties, Young Catholic Workers, and Young Catholic Students appeared by the 1960s to be insufficient to meet the new challenges. Such problems, combined with a growing concern within the church over the decline of its moral leadership, prompted the bishops gathered in Rome to consider thoroughgoing reforms in the hope of making the church more effective in exercising moral leadership and retaining the loyalty of its members.

As a consequence, Vatican II undertook the task of making far-reaching theological, pastoral, liturgical, and organizational changes. Salvation was not to be construed as pertaining simply to an afterlife; rather it was to include the creation of the Kingdom of God on earth. That is, the believer was obliged to struggle for just societies conducive to social concord and hence to peace. The objective was to reduce conflict by increasing respect for the full spectrum of human rights—political, economic, social, religious, and cultural. The implications of such a position for the Catholic church in countries like those in Central America were far-reaching. Even the simple enunciation of this point of view challenged conservative elites in countries such as El Salvador, Guatemala, and Honduras, as well as the personalistic dictatorship of the Somozas in Nicaragua.

The reaffirmation of Vatican II by the Latin-American bishops at Medellín, Colombia, in 1968 and the announcement of a preferential option for the poor stimulated widespread experimentation by religious institutions and church people. The new concern for the poor encouraged the dissemination of a theology of liberation which argued that Catholics must join the struggle for socioeconomic justice if they were to be true to the Gospel message. The upshot was that increased political activism on behalf of the poor and the oppressed was not only legitimized but encouraged. In addition, liberation theology opened the way for Catholics to dialogue and build alliances with groups advocating substantial structural change, including Marxists. Through these theological and ideological developments the church became more directly involved in political and ideological struggles throughout Central America. Administrative, pastoral, and liturgical reforms were also undertaken that would have far-reaching consequences for the Catholic church and the societies in which it was predominant.

Chief among the reforms was the decentralization of decision making within the church, with more authority being vested in national bishops' conferences and organizations of priests, brothers, nuns, and lay activists. Entrusted with a larger role in the church's hierarchical structure, bishops' conferences became active in attempting to give the church more presence in the daily lives of its members. As the majority of these were poor, the new policy meant a sharper focus on social welfare activities and the analysis and denunciation of socioeconomic injustice and human rights violations. National conferences of clergy and religious sometimes undertook studies that frequently documented gross violations of human rights. Lay activists, particularly those drawn from the expanding middle class, students, and the agrarian sector, became more deeply involved in religious work as the Catholic church became more attentive to the concerns of these segments of society.

As a result of these new directions, the Catholic church's image as a defender of the status quo diminished while its image as a supporter of profound, even radical, change grew. Consequently governmental repression of clerics, religious, and lay activists who were increasingly accused of being Marxists or communists, became more common. This policy was pursued in order to exploit the deeply rooted anti-Marxist feeling within Latin America and the church and in order to justify disappearances, assassinations, and torture. The repression, however, tended to reduce political differences among church people, at least until it slackened.

Besides priests, brothers, and nuns, other targets of right wing terror were members of Christian base communities (CEBs) and lay preachers, known as Delegates of the Word. Encouraged by the reforms of Vatican II and Medellín, the CEBs signaled an attempt to revitalize pastoral life within the church by providing a more participatory experience. Their establishment was also a response to the chronic shortage of priests throughout Latin America in that it placed leadership responsibilities in the hands of laypersons. In the late 1960s and throughout the 1970s, these communities spread into rural areas and urban slums where the church had not previously concentrated its personnel. Often utilizing the methodology of liberation theology (analyzing reality, reflecting, acting), these groups offered some communities the first opportunity to devise common responses to common problems. Hence they increased demands for political and economic reforms which sometimes led to the organization of workers and other activities regarded as suspect by conservative elements of society. Networking was facilitated not only by the CEBs, but also by Delegates of the Word, who spread throughout rural Central America.

The CEBs did not, however, adopt a uniform stance concerning change in society or in the church. Some focused on spiritual regeneration, others on political activism. In general, CEBs reflected the full spectrum of thinking, both theological and political. Nevertheless, whatever their individual orientation, they did contribute to the revitalization of the church, making it more accessible. Overall, such developments helped raise the political consciousness, not only of the poor and the oppressed, but also of church personnel, thus generating further pressures on Catholic leaders to become involved in political and ideological struggles.

The capacity of the Catholic church to respond was limited not only by the historical weight of hierarchical structures and traditions, but also by its desire to maintain the universality of its appeal. Hence, although the bishops enunciated a preferential option for the poor at Medellín in 1968 and reaffirmed it at the bishops' conference at Puebla, Mexico, in 1979, they did not accept class warfare as inevitable; they continued to call for reconciliation of all the contending forces within society. This position alienated some elements of the church, albeit a minority, which insisted on the necessity of armed struggle to effect the changes they felt necessary to achieve just societies. The difference of opinion was made clear in evaluations of liberation theology by the Vatican in 1984 and 1986. The chief criticism was that some versions of liberation theology promoted a conflictual vision of society, thereby encouraging the Marxist view that class warfare was inevitable.[2]

It should be noted that the divisions that exist cannot be characterized simply as hierarchy versus grass roots; rather, they cut across status, class, and generations. In fact, the majority of church people are not identified with either the most conservative or the most radical elements within the church. In general, they continue to support change, preferably by nonviolent means, and to advocate the struggle for peace in the midst of warfare. Neither the conservative nor the radical church leadership, however, has the capacity to mobilize the majority of the faithful behind a single strategy to resolve the present conflicts. Hence the debate continues, and the church is increasingly not a monolithic institution but rather the source of a multitude of sometimes conflicting voices, all of them claiming moral leadership. The weight of specific issues being debated varies from country to country, as is seen in examining the situations in El Salvador, Guatemala, Honduras, and Nicaragua.

El Salvador

Economic growth in Central America in the 1950s and 1960s stimulated the expansion of the middle class and of organized labor. The impact of this development on historical political parties and alignments was substantial. According to Francisco Villagran Kramer, formerly the vice president of Guatemala,

> The traditional division between liberals and conservatives began to give way with the emergence of ideological parties of various tendencies. Social-Democratic tendencies began to take hold among liberal sectors, and political elements once linked to the church began to form Christian-Democratic parties. The traditional conservative parties reacted to the trend by taking strong anti-Communist positions, and the military foresaw the need to establish closer working links with the conservatives in order to safeguard the political system.[3]

As part of the political realignment the Catholic church became less closely identified with traditional elites while liberal and progressive church people were becoming more numerous and outspoken. Their frankness caused them to be attacked by right-wing elements, both within and without the church.

Foreign missionaries were also suspect. The 1960s witnessed an influx of priests and religious from Europe and North America, most of whom were shocked by the level of exploitation and repression they found in El Salvador. More liberally educated, and accustomed to societies with higher levels of political participation than the majority of Salvadoran clergy, the newcomers tended to be activist. With their access to international networks and resources they made a considerable impact on the church and on Salvadoran society. By disseminating information about Salvadoran conditions abroad they generated international attention and pressure, particularly in response to the more egregious violations of human rights. The problems of the rural population were a major concern as the increasing concentration of landownership was dispossessing peasants and raising the level of rural unemployment.[4]

These conditions intensified the debate over the need for agrarian reform. At a 1970 national congress on land reform, Father José Inocencio Alas, a diocesan priest who had been active in organizing Christian base communities and working with peasants in the Suchitoto area, was a church representative. His statements in support of agrarian reform apparently precipitated his detention by the government. Although not always in agreement with Alas's progressive positions, Monsignor Arturo Rivera y Damas, representing the archdiocese of San Salvador, staged a sit-in at the office of the minister of defense and refused to leave until Alas was released. Such detentions, as well as the torture and murder of priests, nuns, and active lay-persons increased over the next few years, reaching a high point in 1980–81. From 5 January 1980 to 27 February 1981 church institutions and personnel suffered approximately 300 attacks by paramilitary groups, most of them composed of police or soldiers.[5]

Among those attacked was the archbishop of San Salvador, Monsignor Oscar Arnulfo Romero. The escalation of repression in the late 1970s in El Salvador affected the prelate so severely that he ultimately came to defend insurrection, stating in November 1978, "When a dictatorship seriously violates human rights and attacks the common good of the nation, when it becomes unbearable and closes all channels of dialogue, of understanding, of rationality, when this happens, the church speaks of the legitimate right of insurrectional violence."[6] Romero's denunciations of human rights violations, attracting national and international attention, contributed to the 15 October 1979 overthrow of the government of General Carlos Humberto Romero. His stand also led to his assassination while he was saying mass on 24 March 1980. Although the assassination generated even more support for Romero's prophetic position, it also made Salvadoran church people more cautious. Some CEBs were disbanded and others went underground while priests, religious, and laypersons began to curtail their activities.

Archbishop Romero's denunciations of human rights violations by the Salvadoran army and police forces, along with the work of organizations such as the archdiocesan legal aid office (Socorro Jurídico) led some observers to conclude that the Catholic church stood in opposition to the government. Instead, bishops, clergy, religious, and laity reflected the full spectrum of political opinion and ideological differentiation in the country. The hierarchy was split, as Bishops José Eduardo Alvarez (San Miguel), Pedro Arnaldo Aparicio (San Vicente), and Marco René Revello (Santa Ana) took more conservative positions than Bishops Arturo Rivera y Damas and Gregorio Rosa Chávez (San Salvador). The former supported evolutionary change within both the church and society and were deeply suspicious of those who challenged secular and ecclesiastical authorities. They were generally critical of Archbishop Romero's strong stances, and they are somewhat uncomfortable with the current attempts of Archbishop Arturo Rivera y Damas to mediate between the government and the opposition (the Democratic Revolutionary Front [FDR] and the Farabundo Martí Front for National Liberation [FMLN]).

In the aftermath of Archbishop Romero's assassination, Rivera y Damas stated that he himself had "moved toward a neutral, central position, convinced that I have a broad perspective and can play a prophetic role."[7] He has placed primary emphasis on promoting peace talks and humanizing the war by negotiating truces, exchanges of prisoners, and release of political kidnap victims, including the daughter of President José Napoleón Duarte. The archbishop has had more success with his humanitarian efforts than with peacemaking. In both enterprises he has been assisted by long-standing friendships with the leaders of both the Duarte wing of the Christian Democratic party, and the political wing of the armed opposition, the FDR.

Taking advantage of the growing public demand for peace and Duarte's desire to consolidate public support for his presidency after his inauguration in June 1984, Rivera y Damas spearheaded efforts to arrange talks. Meetings at La Palma on 15 October and at Ayagualo on 30 November, however, brought no agreement on an agenda; from 1984 to 1987 no substantial progress was made toward negotiations. According to Rivera y Damas the stalemate revealed the lack of political will on both sides, in spite of the fact that by his estimate 80 percent of all Salvadorans favor dialogue.[8] The archbishop has also alleged interference by the United States and the Soviet Union.[9]

On 8 August 1985 the Salvadoran conference of bishops issued a pastoral letter calling for a renewal of talks between the government and the FDR/FMLN as the only means of preventing destruction of the country. The prelates recognized the Duarte government as "a constitutional government in power as the result of a democratic process endorsed by massive attendance at the polls in four successive elections that have been a repeated referendum in favor of democracy."[10] In reply the FDR/FMLN argued that the elections had been held in the midst of war and repression and were strongly influenced by U.S. financing. In addition, the bishops' criticisms on the FMLN's continuing resort to violence and its dependence on ideologies that the prelates styled as opposed to human dignity were rejected by the FDR/FMLN. The latter claimed that such accusations were contrary to the neutrality that mediators should maintain.[11]

The possibility of dialogue was not again brought up until 1 June 1986, when President Duarte publicly called for talks with the FDR/FMLN and asked Archbishop Rivera y Damas to mediate. The president's stated objective was to convince the opposition to cease armed struggle and participate in electoral politics. Duarte's call came in the face of mounting opposition to economic austerity measures, implemented in January 1986 which devalued the currency, limited imports, and imposed wage and price controls. A poll conducted by the government indicated that Duarte's support had fallen to 24 percent and that workers had increasingly taken to the streets in antigovernment demonstrations. Conservatives, including businessmen, were also critical of the austerity plan.[12] The FDR/FMLN, while accepting the talks in principle, characterized Duarte's move as a tactical maneuver intended to jeopardize any dialogue. They also objected that the proposed talks would be limited to pressuring the opposition to lay down its arms and participate in the electoral process.[13] Prior to the projected meeting the Salvadoran army entered and occupied the town of Sesori where it was scheduled to take place. As a result of the military occupation, as well as of the conflicting agendas of the Duarte government and the FDR/FMLN, the 1986 initiative bore no fruit. In October 1987, as part of a regional peace plan, new talks were begun, but the two sides remained deeply divided.

Church leaders have had somewhat more success in humanizing the conflict by negotiating truces at Christmas and Easter, as well as during the 1983 visit of Pope John Paul II, arranging the release of prisoners of war and political kidnap victims, and reducing gross violations of human rights by publicly denouncing them. International pressure, including some from the United States, has also helped diminish rights violations. In late 1985 Archbishop Rivera y Damas asserted that no further progress was possible without structural reforms, support for education, and more U.S. economic aid and less military aid.[14]

After the massive earthquake on 10 October 1986, the Salvadoran bishops renewed the call for peace talks:

> If this earthquake cannot help overcome the difficulties which prevent the dialogue from being taken seriously, the question remains: what will it take and what future awaits the country? Neither political calculations, nor prestige, nor security, nor reference to constitutional guarantees attributed to the Armed Forces, not military vetoes, nor the desires of the United States should impede the dialogue.[15]

This statement confirms that all the bishops had come to regard negotiations as the only solution to the Salvadoran crisis. No longer are Rivera y Damas and Rosa Chávez the only prelates supporting peace talks.

The desire of the vast majority of Salvadorans for peace has reinforced the episcopacy's calls for dialogue. The contradictory agendas of the United States-backed Duarte government and the FDR/FMLN, however, have thus far prevented any substantial progress. Thus Rivera y Damas and the Catholic leadership bear the burden of continuing to press for peace talks while the contending forces show little political will to compromise. The Catholic church lacks the power to force the government and the FDR/FMLN to the negotiating table, partly because the church is not sufficiently united behind a specific strategy. The hierarchy still faces a formidable task in trying to accomplish goals beyond humanization of the conflict.

Guatemala

The agenda of the Catholic church in Guatemala is similar to its agenda in El Salvador: increased socioeconomic justice and stricter observance of human rights in order to achieve peace and stability. The chief impediments to realization of these goals are, according to the church, poverty and exploitation in a predominantly agricultural country. Although Guatemala has more land and a smaller population than El Salvador, the concentration of landholding has resulted in a high rate of unemployment. In 1983 it was estimated that 2 percent of landowners controlled 72 percent of the arable land in a country where agricultural laborers constituted 65 percent of the work force and earned approximately $3.20 a day.[16] The increase in land concentration in the 1960s and 1970s encouraged emigration to the cities and abroad and stimulated the organization of peasant associations. The latter development was also encouraged by Catholic sponsored social welfare programs, leadership training, and Christian base communities.

The Catholic church has proceeded with a degree of caution partly because of its fear of encouraging radicalism, and thereby of heightening the repression that has existed in Guatemala since the 1950s.[17] Nevertheless, beginning in the 1970s the Catholic church and some Protestant denominations, through their public denunciations, focused national and international attention on the level of human rights violations in the country. Since 1984, with the advent of a new archbishop, Próspero Penados del Barrio, the Catholic church has intensified its support of democratic elements in the hopes of diminishing the strength of the armed forces and of the extreme right and left. Yet the effort has been somewhat tentative, given the degree of repression that continues in Guatemala and the Catholic church's desire not to encourage the conservative sectors of society to support Protestant expansion.

In pursuing its human rights policy the Catholic church has displayed more receptivity to political and socioeconomic change than it did in 1954 when it supported the Central Intelligence Agency-backed overthrow of the civilian reformist government of Jacobo Arbenz. In the aftermath of the coup the church expanded its pastoral work to include combating alleged radical inroads. To that end new dioceses and parishes were established, particularly in rural areas and urban slums, and political parties such as the Christian Democrats, Guatemalan Social Concord, and Social Action were encouraged. The objectives of these groups were, however, surpassed by the goals enunciated at Vatican II and Medellín, which stimulated an influential minority of Guatemalan church people to take a much more activist role in promoting socioeconomic change. National conferences of priests and religious focused on devising new pastoral strategies that would allow them to implement a preferential option for the poor. These included increasing the number of lay preachers and catechists and organizing Christian base communities. Emphasis was also placed on raising the consciousness of youth through organizations like the Young Catholic Students, Young Catholic Workers, and the Crater Group. By and large the hierarchy moved more slowly since it was preoccupied with the possibility of "falling into a Marxist analysis and thereby supporting the positions of the guerrillas."[18]

By the early 1970s a growing number of active church people, becoming disenchanted with reformist developmentalism as the primary means of reducing endemic poverty, were more receptive to the idea of radical change. Their shift in direction was reflected in the programs of the Center for Integral Development in Huehuetenango, the Institutes for Training in Quetzaltenango and El Petén, and the San Benito Center in Cobán, whose activities tended to politicize the rural laity, as well as the clergy and religious who worked with them. Government repression reinforced this trend. In January 1975 bishops, clergy, and religious denounced the assassination of four Delegates of the Word in the diocese of Vera Paz, rejecting the government's claims that they were subversives.[19] At the same time other groups within the church criticized programs aimed at organizing the poor and raising their political consciousness. Archbishop Mario Casariego, who supported this position, approved the expulsion by the government of foreign missionaries characterized as troublemakers.

The 1976 earthquake, which caused more than 20,000 deaths, pushed the Catholic church even more deeply into social welfare activities. It also prompted the issuance of a pastoral letter entitled "United in Hope" which called upon Catholics to respond not only to the devastation wreaked by the natural disaster but also to that caused by structural injustices.[20] Increased governmental activism caused church people to disappear in even larger numbers. In the period 1978–1982 twelve priests and one nun were killed, and innumerable laypersons met the same fate. More than 100 priests and religious were expelled from the country or were forced to leave because their lives were threatened.[21]

Not all the church people who were assassinated had been progressives. In February 1981 four priests were sent by the church to the province of Quiché to renew work there. One of them, a member of the Sacred Heart order, expressed little fear because he was known to be conservative. Two weeks after his arrival he was shot and killed. A U.S. missionary, Brother James Miller, who left Nicaragua after the Sandinistas came to power because he was opposed to their leftist policies, was killed in 1982 in Huehuetenango, a few months after the slaying of a Mennonite missionary, John David Troyer.[22]

Revulsion against such assassinations, in addition to army massacres in rural areas, contributed to the March 1982 coup which brought to power retired General Efraín Ríos Montt, who was regarded as a reformer. Elements within the army, preoccupied by the discrediting of the military and the loss of international aid caused by the repression and corruption of the García regime, intervened in the national elections and installed Ríos Montt. A fundamentalist evangelical, Ríos Montt appointed two elders of his church, The Word, to high government posts.[23] The General's evangelical beliefs and contacts were brought into play to promote rural pacification, as well as to obtain economic and diplomatic support from the United States. Pat Robertson of the Christian Broadcasting Network, Jerry Falwell of the Moral Majority, the Campus Crusade for Christ, Gospel Outreach, and World Vision provided financial assistance, amounting to several million dollars. They also lobbied for a resumption of U.S. military aid to Guatemala on the grounds that Guatemala was the last bastion against the spread of communism in Central America.[24]

Ríos Montt's ouster in August 1983 by General Oscar Mejía Victores reportedly stemmed in part from growing resentment over fundamentalist influences in the Ríos Montt government. The evangelicals' close identification with the United States also caused consternation. Ríos Montt's brother, Mario Enrique, the Catholic bishop of Escuintla, warned that "Protestants and Marxists are both against us—Protestantism is the arm of conservative capitalism, Marxism is the arm of atheist Communism."[25] The prelate was expressing a general belief common not only in Guatemala, but also in the rest of Central America.

Today many Catholics in Guatemala have lost faith in the capacity of capitalism, as it has developed in Latin America, to alleviate socioeconomic injustice. At the same time the majority do not believe that communist systems guarantee the full spectrum of human rights—political, economic, social, religious, and cultural. Some Catholics look to a species of socialism, but there is little unanimity concerning its content. As a consequence, while the Catholic church in Guatemala continues to denounce socioeconomic injustice and the repression behind it, church people have not agreed on any common strategy. Given the continuance of human rights violations by the armed forces, even after the inauguration of the Christian Democratic government of Vinincio Cerezo in January 1986, the church is increasingly concerned that its goal of greater socioeconomic justice cannot be achieved by peaceful means.

Penados, the new archbishop, sees more risks in supporting the status quo than in promoting change, even if the latter means offering opportunities to revolutionary groups, including Marxists.[26] This stance, which the Nicaraguan bishops took in June 1979, shortly before the overthrow of Somoza, also has some support in El Salvador. It has less support in Honduras, where the evolution of the church has been limited by the scarcity of resources in both personnel and money.

Honduras

The Catholic church in Honduras is institutionally the weakest and least politicized in Central America, largely because of its lack of resources in a country that has the lowest per capita income in the Western Hemisphere, except for Haiti. At the time of the Medellín conference, Honduras had only 200 priests, of whom 27 were Hondurans.[27] The church therefore had to depend heavily on foreign missionaries and laypersons to carry out its activities. The introduction of Delegates of the Word in the 1960s allowed the Catholic church to become more active in areas where it previously had had little or no presence. Many of the lay preachers were peasants who incorporated their daily concerns into their religious work, thereby raising consciousness within the church about rural poverty and exploitation. By 1983 Delegates of the Word outnumbered priests approximately 40 to 1 (i.e., 10,000 to 255).[28] A consequence has been that while the Honduran hierarchy has been relatively cautious politically, the church has increasingly become the institutional base for lay activists, particularly from among the rural and urban poor. As a result, the church has focused more on the promotion of socioeconomic change. It was therefore increasingly identified by the public with the poor majority and has shown more opposition to conservative elites.

Before Medellín the Catholic church in Honduras had experimented with some of the same strategies used throughout Latin America to combat loss of influence and reincorporate its traditional cadres, especially the urban bourgeoisie. In Honduras this group was historically quite small and was less open to socioeconomic reforms than other Latin American countries. Honduran Catholics did, however, share the strong anticommunism of their neighbors. In 1959, in the wake of Castro's triumph in Cuba, there was a national anticommunist crusade. Such sentiment has remained fairly strong among Honduran Catholics of all classes.

In the 1960s there was increasing concern over the failure of the poor to benefit substantially from economic development. In 1961 the auxiliary bishop of Tegucigalpa, Monsignor Evilio Domínguez, in a pastoral letter entitled "The Parish, the Pastor, and Pastoral Work," called upon church personnel to focus on the needs of the poor. That same year, as part of an effort to assist the impoverished rural masses, sixteen radio schools were established to provide basic education and spiritual guidance. Some peasant communities were aided in organizing cooperatives and other self-help organizations.[29] A mid-1975 demonstration in Olancho in support of agrarian reform was violently disrupted by landowners and the army, and fourteen people, including two priests, were killed. Although denouncing the massacre and excommunicating those responsible for it, the hierarchy evidenced concern that the increasing activism of Catholic clergy, religious, and laity would only lead to further repression. Consequently the bishops attempted to rein in the most progressive sectors of the church and reasserted their control over a variety of religious organizations. As one commentator styled it, the church headed for the catacombs.[30]

Caution on the part of the institutional church was also encouraged by strong competition from conservative Protestant groups. Currently, the members of the approximately 2,000 Protestant congregations in Honduras constitute 8 percent of the total population (4,300,000). Of these, about 60 percent are pentecostals, principally from the Assemblies of God, the Church of God, and the Prince of Peace church. Concentrating on the rural and urban poor, these churches stress the value of a close-knit supportive community that attempts to provide for all one's spiritual, psychological, and material needs. Politics is generally regarded as corrupting, and cooperatives, peasant organizations, and labor unions are rejected as communist. The fundamentalists regard sin as exclusively individual, rather than as both individual and structural, as Medellín did. They also describe salvation as individual, rejecting the Catholic and mainline Protestant tendency to regard it as being realized through both individual and communal efforts to achieve the Kingdom of God on earth and in the hereafter. They also place heavy emphasis on one's personal relationship to God, which is reinforced in revival campaigns led by such international evangelical celebrities as Jimmy Swaggart.[31]

Protestants and Catholics who support more radical options run the risk of being expelled from Honduras or losing their lives.[32] The Honduran bishops, fearing that any increase in activism will make the Catholic church a target for strong repression, prefer to rein in the most progressive elements. To date they have been successful in this effort, but increasing violence in Honduras has made it more difficult for them to maintain their position.

Nicaragua

The leadership of the Catholic church in Nicaragua took a clear-cut political stand on 2 June 1979, when the bishops asserted in a pastoral letter that the long-standing and substantial violations of human rights perpetrated by the Somoza government made it moral and licit to participate in the nationwide insurrection to overthrow him.[33] At that time it was estimated that approximately 85 percent of all priests, religious, and laypersons in the country were opposed to Somoza.[34] The bishops' letter did not represent an abrupt about-face but was rather an outgrowth of increasing disaffection within the church, at all levels, over the corruption in and repression by the regime.

As early as 1972 the hierarchy had publicly expressed wide-ranging criticisms of socioeconomic and political conditions in the country and had urged the "transformation of structures."[35] Particular emphasis was placed on guaranteeing broad-based political participation and an independent judiciary. Drawing on Catholic social doctrine dating to the late nineteenth century, the prelates challenged the exploitation of labor and the repression that it necessitated. Failure to meet basic human rights, it was implied, undercut the legitimacy of the government, although the bishops did not go as far as they did when they justified insurrection in 1979.

When the massive earthquake of 1972 destroyed most of downtown Managua, many clerics, religious, and lay people previously engaged in teaching in elite private schools began to work in the tent cities that sprang up around the capital. There they experienced firsthand the corruption of the Somoza regime, as foreign relief assistance was diverted into the pockets of government officials. In the large squatter settlement OPEN 3 and in other settlements the inhabitants began to organize for mutual self-help. Church people, who sometimes participated in these efforts, became more politicized. Networks of church-related groups and individuals facilitated communal action and communication. Secular political groups, including the Sandinista Front for National Liberation (FSLN), were also active and cooperated with church groups. A few individuals, including priests, joined the FSLN or encouraged Nicaraguan youths to do so. By 1978, when the insurrection had gained momentum, church people and ecclesial organizations not only provided humanitarian and other assistance to the guerrillas, but also helped to legitimize their cause, both within and outside Nicaragua. The 2 June 1979 pastoral letter complemented such activities and served to promulgate the image of the church as united behind the Sandinista movement and the government it created after the overthrow of Somoza.

The unity was more apparent than real. Although the bishops, by and large, supported the insurrection, they were concerned about the nature and the direction of the new Government of National Reconstruction. Within two weeks of its creation, the church hierarchy counseled the government to beware of all foreign "isms" and to devise political and social structures rooted in Nicaraguan, not foreign, realities. The new institutions should be free of state idolatries, and the Sandinistas should avoid the "massification" of society in its mobilization of the populace. More important, belief in God should not be excluded from the task of national reconstruction.[36]

Such cautionary words were little noticed in the prevailing euphoria and the predictable chaos that followed destruction of the Somoza dynasty. The appointment of a number of priests to ministerial level posts—including Miguel d'Escoto as foreign minister, Edgard Parrales as minister of social welfare, Ernesto Cardenal as minister of culture, Fernando Cardenal as director of a national literacy campaign, and Xabier Gorostiaga as head of national economic planning—had more impact. There were no major protests from their superiors in the church, partly because such participation was regarded as a way of gaining direct influence over the course of the new government.[37]

By the autumn of 1979, however, criticism was beginning to emerge, primarily from the archbishopric of Managua, the Superior Council of Private Enterprise (COSEP), and the newspaper La Prensa. These critics alleged unwarranted concentration of power in the hands of the Sandinistas, economic mismanagement, and restrictions on political pluralism. On 17 November the Nicaraguan episcopacy, though reaffirming its support of the government, expressed concern that the newly created mass organizations and the national literacy campaign were being used to inculcate atheism, which in turn would lead Nicaraguans to abandon their faith. Strong support for freedom of expression to correct governmental errors was asserted. The prelates felt that the Catholic church had a unique responsibility to criticize emerging political and economic structures, while still recognizing the government's commitment to meet basic socioeconomic needs and rectify the injustices of the Somoza era. The only way the Sandinistas could fully accomplish this double purpose, the bishops asserted, was to empower the people through a pluralistic and participatory political system.[38] The implication was that the Sandinistas were not moving in that direction.

The Sandinistas addressed the hierarchy's concerns in a position paper issued in October 1980. In it they recognized the church as playing a major role in Nicaraguan society and as having contributed significantly to the insurrection and to the task of national reconstruction. The document also expressed the belief that there was no inherent contradiction in being both a Christian and a revolutionary. In fact, membership in the FSLN was open to all Nicaraguans, irrespective of their religious beliefs, so long as they did not attempt to proselytize within the organization. The FSLN, while affirming its respect for Nicaraguan Catholic religious traditions, reserved the right to ensure that religious celebrations were not used for political or commercial purposes. This caveat was the Sandinistas' response to attempts to utilize processions and other religious activities to express antigovernment sentiment.[39] The bishops strongly rejected this attempt to assert civil authority over the church.

The Sandinistas rebuffed suggestions that they were attempting to divide the Catholic church. Any differences that existed, they claimed, flowed from conflicting opinions within the church and by 1980 it was clear that such divisions did exist. Although the bishops were the most visible religious critics of the Sandinistas, opposition to and support for the government came from all sectors of the church. This reflected the situation in Nicaragua generally.

The Catholic church in Nicaragua is frequently described as being split along class and generational lines, with the bishops and bourgeois laity being antigovernment and the rural and urban poor being progovernment, but the situation is much more complicated. For example, Catholics in Estelí strongly supported the insurrection but today there is considerable difference of opinion among them about the government and there exists an ongoing debate over how to integrate one's Christian and revolutionary commitment.[40] This pattern, seen elsewhere in Nicaragua, responds not only to preexisting divisions within the church but also to the political and ideological struggle currently being waged in Nicaragua.

The principal issues in contention between pro- and antigovernment sectors of the church are the nature of political pluralism, the role of criticism and critics in a revolutionary society, the best way to engender participation in political and economic decision making, the legitimacy of the Sandinista popular army, freedom of expression and religion, and the role of Marxism. The historical weight of the Catholic church's identification with Western liberalism is seen in the insistence of some church people that democracy cannot survive in a system where one party is dominant. A fair number of Catholics, representing all classes, would seem to prefer a Christian Democratic or Social Democratic option. Under present conditions, the issue is the Sandinistas or the *contras* and given that choice, most church people seem to opt for the government presently in power.[41]

The debate over the role of the Catholic church as critic of the government has focused on the statements of Cardinal Miguel Obando y Bravo, his vicar Monsignor Bismarck Carballo, and Bishop Pablo Antonio Vega, of Juigalpa. Because of the severity of their criticisms, the latter two were forced to leave Nicaragua in 1986. Vega, who was expelled on 4 July, was accused by the Sandinistas of having publicly urged support for the overthrow of the government. To document the charge, the Sandinistas cited a press conference Vega held in Managua on 2 July, when he asserted that "armed insurrection is the right of the people" and that a U.S. invasion would be the fault "of those who support only one bloc," that is, the Soviet Union.[42] President Daniel Ortega justified Vega's expulsion on the grounds that "freedom of religion does not mean that one can conspire against the [Sandinista] revolution with the people of the counterrevolution, with President Reagan's people, with the people of the CIA."[43] In 1987, the government permitted Vega and Bismarck Caballo to return to Nicaragua.

The most divisive church-state issue has been the role of Marxism in the consolidation of the Nicaraguan revolution. The bishops have claimed that Marxism, as a foreign and atheistic ideology, is antinationalistic because Nicaragua is a Catholic country. They argue that the ideological base of the revolution should reflect the Christianity of the majority of the people. They fear that unless the Sandinistas abandon Marxism, an antireligious one-party state with a state controlled economy is in the offing. As the Sandinistas are unlikely to renounce their ideology, implicit in the bishops' arguments is the suggestion that they must be removed from power.[44] There is, however, no agreement as to the means to accomplish this objective. A review of public and private statements made by the bishops reveals that, although they have called for a dialogue of reconciliation to include all groups, even the contras, they have reached no consensus as to its content. Furthermore, the prelates differ on the role the Sandinistas, as well as ex-Somocistas, should play in any future government. These differences also exist among the Nicaraguan population.

In Nicaragua as in El Salvador, there is a strong desire for a cease fire and peace but no agreement as to how to reach these goals. Sharp differences also persist among Catholics on the question of negotiations with the contras, although some church people accept the idea of amnesty for rebel fighters. Virtually every parish and every CEB reflects differences of opinion concerning the format of and the parties to peace talks. Given the difficult relations between church and state, the likelihood that the hierarchy could serve as an effective mediator is slight. Attempts to resolve civil-ecclesiastical difficulties through negotiations have themselves achieved little success.[45]

Much has been written about the so-called popular church in Nicaragua, which allegedly is strongly supportive of the revolutionary government. What is referred to by the phrase is essentially a sector of the church comprising some Christian base communities, parishes, student groups, and a goodly number of foreign clergy and religious, most of them concentrated in Managua, León, and Estelí. The idea that the popular church is composed largely of radicalized peasants is not supported by the data. Interviews with church people across the political spectrum in 1981, 1984, 1985, and 1986 revealed remarkable unanimity concerning the strength and composition of the popular church. Respondents agreed that such an entity does not formally exist and prorevolutionary Catholics have taken pains to deny any intention of operating outside the institutional church.[46] Furthermore, estimates of the actual strength of this sector are strikingly similar, whether they emanate from the right, the left, or the center. Most sources suggest that 15 to 20 percent of Nicaraguan Catholics regard themselves as Christian revolutionaries and as strong supporters of the government. About the same percentage are described as fearful of revolutionary change and opposed to the government. The majority are characterized as uncomfortable with both sides and dismayed by conflict within the church as well as by tensions between civil and ecclesiastical officials. Under these conditions it is unlikely that church leaders on either the right or the left could mobilize the mass of the faithful behind a single agenda.

Both Catholic and Protestant churches have been the focus of intense political and ideological struggle in Nicaragua. Although largely approving the overthrow of the Somoza dynasty because of its systematic violations of political, civil, economic, social, religious, and cultural rights, the churches were not offering a carte blanche to whatever new political leadership might emerge. The Marxism of some of the new political elites has alienated a number of church people, a not surprising reaction in view of the strong hold of anti-Marxism and liberalism on Nicaraguan Christians. The situation is further complicated by the presence of priests in the government and by the vocal prorevolutionary minority within the churches. The high degree of political polarization in Nicaraguan society in general has exacerbated differences between church people, so that the Catholic church seems to be at war with itself. It is noteworthy that so far no mass exodus from the church has occurred and that no schismatic movement has developed. Rather, leaders of all the contending factions have repeatedly asserted their loyalty to the Catholic church and their faith in its capacity to transcend the present divisions.

Conclusion

Pope John Paul II most visibly involved himself in the Central American crisis during his visit in March 1983, when he repeatedly appealed to Central Americans to abide by the teachings of the Catholic church on socioeconomic justice and human rights. Only in that fashion, he argued, could peace be restored. The pope was particularly insistent that long-term resolution of the conflict could be found neither in right-wing authoritarianism nor in left-wing totalitarianism. Throughout, he exhorted the faithful to work for just societies by nonviolent means and to avoid accepting class struggle as a necessity. In addition, John Paul reasserted the church's policy of prohibiting clerics from holding political office or otherwise directly participating in politics.[47] The keynote of his trip was reconciliation and recommitment to the nonviolent pursuit of justice.

During the 1983 visit and thereafter, the pope revealed serious concern about what he regards as the tendency of liberation theology to disseminate Marxist concepts of class conflict. Despite his belief that increasing economic disparities between rich and poor nations and between the rich and poor within nations are at the root of conflicts such as those in Central America, he rejects class struggle and armed conflict as a solution.[48] Instead, he offers his own theology of social liberation, which emphasizes individual conversion to the cause of justice, rather than revolutionary movements. Social liberation is "to be realized knowing that the primary liberation which man must obtain is liberation from sin, from social evil that rests in his heart, and which is the cause of 'social sin' and oppressive structures.[49]

To accomplish this objective the pope has called for an intense spiritual mobilization of all Catholics, and of all men and women of goodwill, in Central America. Emphasis should be placed on the "conversion" of the leaders of the contending forces to reconciliation, that is, on negotiations to achieve peace settlements that will lead to the establishment of a government representing virtually all political positions. The pope does not believe, as argued by some Catholics, that the inclusion of the full spectrum of ideologies makes agreement on how to effect socioeconomic change very difficult.

Hence, the Vatican position on Nicaragua has been to support the April 1984 call of the bishops for a national dialogue between the government and the opposition, including the contras. More recently, Rome has encouraged dialogue between church and state and is less supportive of the confrontational tactics of Cardinal Miguel Obando y Bravo and Bishop Pablo Vega. The situation in Nicaragua is so profoundly polarized, and the Catholic church so fragmented internally, that it is unlikely that the church could be accepted as sufficiently neutral and nonpartisan to mobilize broad-based support for an all-encompassing national dialogue.

In El Salvador, Rome's discomfort with the role of Archbishop Romero and the progressive sector has diminished, largely because Monsignor Rivera y Damas has moved the archbishopric of San Salvador to a more centrist position. He has managed to do so even while maintaining working relations with both government and opposition leaders. Rivera y Damas has also won increasing support from other bishops for his strategies. His procedures have made possible sporadic talks between the Duarte government and the FDR/FMLN and have achieved some progress in humanizing the warfare. Without a major shift in the positions of the Duarte and U.S. governments, as well as of the FDR/FMLN, however, a negotiated solution to the present crisis is unlikely. The Catholic church does not have sufficient strength to force a change in those stances, even though the majority of Salvadorans quite clearly support peace.

Since 1984 the Vatican has been strongly supportive of the repositioning of the Catholic church in Guatemala under the leadership of Archbishop Penados. There the church's visible support of human rights and civilian government has strengthened liberal elements within the church, who no longer need fear that church authorities might cooperate with the government in expelling them. The pope also shares the hierarchy's concern over the substantial inroads of Protestant churches. As a consequence, Rome has encouraged Catholics to redouble their evangelizing efforts in Guatemala, emphasizing Catholic religious and social values as offering the best chance for peaceful change. Special appeals have been made in defense of Indian rights and of church efforts to promote them.[50] Nevertheless, continued repression in Guatemala has caused the Catholic church to move cautiously, particularly with respect to rural mobilization. Hence, although the church has become more supportive of change and less tolerant of the status quo, its overall impact is limited.

The same is true in Honduras, where the internal weaknesses of the Catholic church and increased militarization and violence have encouraged caution. Heavily dependent on foreign personnel and financing, the Honduran church is comfortable with Pope John Paul's vision of the theology of social liberation. As a result, emphasis has in recent years been placed on evangelizing in order to convince individuals of the need for socioeconomic justice through peaceful reforms. Although a minority of church members do favor a more activist approach, they have been unable to galvanize the majority of the faithful. Yet, the increasing militarization of the country has created tensions that contribute to the growth of the activist sector, raising the possibility of more conflict between church people and civil-military authorities, as well as more divisions within the Catholic church.

Lacking the numerical predominance of Catholics, as well as their institutional strength, Protestants in Central America have not emerged as a major actor in the present crisis. Such a development is unlikely anyway, given the divisions among and within denominations. The major Protestant denominations reflect some of the same splits among conservatives, moderates, liberals, progressives, and revolutionaries which afflict the Catholic church. The fundamentalists are generally conservative, pro-United States, and anticommunist. Debates between them and mainstream Protestants over the best response to socioeconomic problems have been sharp. To date there is no indication that these groups will play a major role in the resolution of the current crisis in Central America.

At best the churches in Central America have helped to alleviate the suffering caused by endemic poverty and the current warfare. Involvement in such efforts continues to have a politicizing effect on church people, forming strong progressive minorities, particularly among clerics and religious, within the Catholic church and the leading Protestant denominations. There is, however, no agreement within these churches over the best way to implement their stated commitments to peace, justice, and human rights. The lack of consensus among church groups reflects the same lack in the population as a whole. Because churches are committed to the universality of their message, that is, the incorporation of all people, it is highly unlikely that they could ever agree on specific strategies to achieve peace through socioeconomic change. It is equally unlikely that the Catholic church, as an institution, could serve as a vehicle for resolving conflict, largely because of the differing political and ideological preferences of church people. Furthermore, the churches manifest no substantial agreement as to the actual structure of a more just society. As a consequence, the task of building a new society rests in the hands of the national and international political leadership, who, together with the churches, continue to speak with a multitude of often conflicting voices.

Notes

1. Costa Rica is not dealt with in this essay as it is not suffering the level of conflict experienced by El Salvador, Guatemala, Honduras, and Nicaragua. Panama is usually not categorized as part of Central America. This chapter is focused primarily on the Catholic church and only incidentally on Protestant churches because of the lack of space and the predominance of Catholicism in the countries under consideration. For example, Catholics constitute approximately 90.9 percent of the population of El Salvador, 83.3 percent in Guatemala, 96 percent in Honduras, and 90.7 percent in Nicaragua (*Statistical Abstract of Latin America* [1985], vol. 24).

2. The Congregation for the Doctrine of the Faith, "Instruction on Certain Aspects of the 'Theology of Liberation'" (September 1984), and "Instruction on Christian Freedom and Liberation" (April 1986).

3. Francisco Villagran Kramer, "The Background to the Current Political Crisis in Central America," in Richard E. Feinberg, ed., *Central America: International Dimensions of the Crisis* (New York: Holmes & Meier, 1982), pp. 19–20.

4. From 1960 to 1975 the number of landless peasants in El Salvador rose from 12 percent to 41 percent and unemployment ranged up to 50 percent for eight months of the year (Donald E. Schulz, "Ten Theories in Search of Central American Reality," in Donald E. Schulz and Douglas H. Graham, eds., *Revolution and Counterrevolution in Central America and the Caribbean* [Boulder: Westview Press, 1984], p. 5).

5. Tommie Sue Montgomery, "The Church in the Salvadoran Revolution," *Latin American Perspectives* 10, 1(Winter 1983):81.

6. Monsignor Oscar Romero as quoted in Alan Riding, "The Cross and the Sword in Latin America," in Marvin E. Gettleman et al., eds., *El Salvador: Central America in the New Cold War* (New York: Grove Press, 1981), p. 196.

7. Monsignor Arturo Rivera y Damas, speech in Washington, 6 April 1981.

8. Foreign Broadcast Information Service (FBIS), "Archbishop Rivera y Damas Holds News Conference," *Latin America: Daily Report*, 6, 186 (25 September 1985), pp. P3–5.

9. FBIS, "Rivera y Damas on U.S., USSR 'Interference'," *Latin America: Daily Report*, 6, 223 (19 November 1985), p. P2.

10. "Salvadoran Rebels Repeat Call for Dialogue, Criticize Bishops' Claims," *Latinamerica Press*, 17, 35 (26 September 1985), pp. 3–4. For original of the pastoral letter see Conferencía Episcopal de El Salvador, "Reconciliación y Paz" (San Salvador), 8 August 1985, p. 14.

11. "Salvadoran Rebels," pp. 3–4.

12. Marjorie Miller, "Duarte Calls for Revival of Talks with Guerrillas: Salvadoran Asks Church to Set 3rd Session," *Washington Post*, 2 June 1986, pp. A1, A21.

13. "FDR/FMLN Communiqué on the State of the Dialogue," El Salvador, 27 June 1986, pp. 1–2.

14. FBIS, "Church Forum Discusses Armed Conflict," *Latin America: Daily Report*, 6, 226 (22 November 1985), p. P13.

15. "Pastoral Message of the Salvadorean Bishops," *LADOC*, 17, 4 (March/April 1987):27–28.

16. Oscar Rolando Sierra Pop, "The Church and Social Conflict in Guatemala," *Social Compass* 30, 2–3 (1983):318.

17. Estimates of the number of disappearances in Guatemala between 1977 and 1987 range from 45,000 to 70,000. The vast majority of these are ascribed by international human rights organizations to the police and armed forces. See American Association for the Advancement of Science, *Guatemala: Case Reports, 1980–1985* (Washington: AAAS, 1986); Americas Watch, *Creating a Desolation and Calling It Peace: May 1983 Supplement to the Report on Human Rights in Guatemala* (New York: Americas Watch, n.d.); Americas Watch, *Guatemala: A Nation of Prisoners* (New York: Americas Watch, 1984); Americas Watch and British Parliamentary Human Rights Group, *Human Rights in Guatemala during President Cerezo's First Year* (New York: Americas Watch, 1987); Amnesty International, *Guatemala: A Government Program of Political Murder* (London: Amnesty International Publications, 1981); Amnesty International, *Memorandum to the Government of Guatemala Following an AI Mission to the Country in April 1985* (New York: Amnesty International USA, 1986); Comisión

de Derechos Humanos de Guatemala, *Informe preliminar a la Organización de las Naciones Unidas, sobre la situación de los derechos humanos y libertades fundamentales en Guatemala* (July–October 1983), (Mexico City: CDHG, 1983); Inter-American Commission on Human Rights, *Report on the Situation of Human Rights in the Republic of Guatemala* (Washington: Organization of American States, 1981); Comisión Interamericana de Derechos Humanos, *Tercer informe sobre la situación de los derechos humanos en la República de Guatemala* (Washington: Organization of American States, 1985); International Human Rights Law Group and the Washington Office on Latin America, *The 1985 Guatemalan Elections: Will the Military Relinquish Power?* (Washington: WOLA/IHRLG, 1985).

18. Sierra Pop, "Church and Social Conflict," p. 328.

19. Ibid., p. 335.

20. Ibid., p. 344.

21. Mike De Mott, "Guatemalan Church: Persecuted, Suffering and in Danger," *Latinamerica Press*, 17, 9 (14 March 1985), p. 5.

22. Warren Hoge, "Guatemalan Clerics Targets of Violence," *New York Times*, 5 May 1981, p. A5; "Kill U.S. Cleric in Guatemala," *New York Daily News*, 16 February 1982, p. C-6.

23. Francisco Bianchi was named secretary of public relations and Alvaro Contreras as Ríos Montt's personal assistant. Together with the officers who staged the coup they were the most influential of Ríos Montt's advisors. See Marlise Simons, "Latin America's New Gospel," *New York Times Magazine*, 7 November 1982, p. 115.

24. Donna Eberwine, "To Ríos Montt, with Love Lift," *Nation*, 26 February 1983, pp. 238–40. The government of Ríos Montt proved no less repressive than its predecessor; while assassinations of political and labor leaders declined, thousands of Indians were killed and many more displaced during the rural pacification program. (Editors' note: See article by Gabriel Aguilera Peralta in this volume.)

25. Monsignor Mario Enrique Ríos Montt, as quoted in Simons, "Latin America's New Gospel," p. 116.

26. Próspero Penados del Barrio, "Padre Popi: 'Church Can Do Very Little,'" *Latinamerica Press*, 17, 43 (21 November 1985), p. 6.

27. By 1973 the number of priests in Honduras had increased to 211, of whom 170 were foreigners. There was 1 priest for every 10,327 inhabitants, as compared with 1 for every 5,215 Nicaraguans and 1 for every 3,738 Costa Ricans. By 1983 there were 255 priests in the country, or 1 for every 15,111 Hondurans. See William Barbieri, "The Catholic Church in Honduras," in *Honduras: A Look at the Reality* (Hyattsville, MD: Quixote Center, 1984), p. 11; Pablo Richard and Guillermo Meléndez, eds., *La iglesia de los pobres en América Central: Un analisis socio-político y teológico de la iglesia centroamericana (1960–1982)* (San José, Costa Rica: Departamento Ecuménico de Investigaciones, 1982), p. 322; Alan Riding, "Honduran Lay Preachers Hear the Pope," *New York Times*, 9 March 1983, p. 4.

28. "Religious Voices: Delegates of the Word," in *Honduras: A Look at the Reality*, p. 11.

29. Richard and Melendez, *La iglesia*, p. 322.

30. Martin Francis, "The Catacomb Honduran Church Now Faces a New Gladiator: U.S. Militarization," *Honduras Update*, 3, 12 (September 1985), p. 4.

31. Ivan Santiago G., "U.S.-backed Pentecostals win Honduran converts: Massive campaigns bring rapid growth," *Latinamerica Press*, 18, 14 (17 April 1986), pp. 6–7; Barbieri, "Right-Wing Sects," in *Honduras: A Look at the Reality*, p. 11.

32. William D. Montalbano, "Mystery in Honduras—Fate of Padre Lupe: U.S. Relatives Hunt Clues to Priest Last Seen with Rebels," *Los Angeles Times*, 10 October

1983, pp. 1, 6; James [Guadalupe] Carney, *To Be a Revolutionary: An Autobiography* (San Francisco: Harper & Row, 1985); "Honduras: U.S. Jesuit Detained, Questioned," *Latinamerica Press*, 17, 32 (5 September 1985), pp. 1–2; "An American Catholic Priest Was Released without Charges," *Los Angeles Times*, 22 August 1985, p. I-2.

33. Conferencía Episcopal de Nicaragua (CEN), *Presencia Cristiana en la Revolución: Dos Mensajes—Momento Insurreccional 2 de junio 1979; Iniciando la Reconstrucción, 30 de julio 1979* (Managua: Cristianos en el Mundo, Comisión, Justicia y Paz, Documento, 1979), pp. 4–8.

34. Sergio Mendez Arceo (Bishop of Cuernavaca, Mexico), "Introduction to Pastoral Letter of the Episcopal Conference of Nicaragua," 17 November 1979, Managua, p. 2.

35. CEN, "El campo de la acción política de la Iglesia," 19 March 1972, Managua, p. 8.

36. CEN, *Presencia . . . 30 de julio de 1979*, p. 14.

37. By May 1980 the attitude in Rome and among Nicaraguans in the church hierarchy toward priests in politics had become more negative. In that month the Vatican issued a worldwide directive prohibiting priests and religious from directly participating in politics. In mid-1981 the clerics holding office in Nicaragua worked out a compromise with the bishops, whereby they would remain in office but could not use their clerical status to support the government. Acceptance of the compromise on the part of the episcopacy was owing to its desire not to alienate the progressive sector within the church or to increase tensions with the state. By late 1984, however, the Vatican canonically censored Miguel d'Escoto, Ernesto and Fernando Cardenal, and Edgard Parrales for continuing in office. The clerics in reply insisted that their responsibility to promote the welfare of the Nicaraguan people through their holding office overrode their obligation to submit to their religious superiors. See Christopher Dickey, "Nicaraguan Priests to Stay in Office under Compromise," *Washington Post*, 17 July 1981, p. A24.

38. CEN, Pastoral Letter, 17 November 1979, Managua, p. 2.

39. Dirección Nacional del Frente Sandinista de Liberación Nacional, Comunicado Oficial de la Dirección Nacional del F.S.L.N. sobre la Religión (San José, Costa Rica: Departamento Ecuménico de Investigaciones, 1980), p. 10.

40. Elizabeth Quay Hutchinson, "¡Entre Cristianismo y revolución, no hay contradicción! Catholic Activism in the Insurrections of Estelí, Nicaragua," senior thesis, Harvard and Radcliffe Colleges, March 1986.

41. Rosa Maria Pochet and Abelino Martínez, *Nicaragua-Iglesia: manipulación o profecía* (San José, Costa Rica: Departamento Ecuménico de Investigaciones, 1987), pp. 168–179.

42. Marjorie Miller, "Nicaragua Widens Controls on Political Meetings," *Los Angeles Times*, 4 July 1986, p. I-5.

43. Marjorie Miller, "Ortega Defends Exile of Church Leaders," *Los Angeles Times* 6 July 1986, p. I-14.

44. CEN, "Carta del Episcopado Nicaraguense a las Conferencías Episcopales del Mundo," 17 July 1986, Managua; CEN, "Comunicado," 29 August 1983, Managua; CEN, "Pastoral Letter on Reconciliation," 22 April 1984, Managua; Jesuits of Nicaragua, "A Word of Christian Freedom and Love," 5 May 1984, Managua.

45. CEN, "Mensaje," 18 February 1982, Managua; interview with spokesperson for Nicaraguan Episcopal Conference, Managua, 10 December 1986.

46. Comunidades Eclesiasticales [sic] de base, Managua, "Managuan BECs Defend Their Church Identity," *LADOC*, 12, 6 (May–June 1982):5–6.

47. Edward Cody, "Guatemalan Executions Shock Pope," *Washington Post*, 4 March 1983, pp. A1, A22.

48. "Pope Assails Foreign Intrusion in Latin America," *Los Angeles Times*, 14 October 1984, p. I-4.

49. Don A. Schanche, "Pope Offers His Own Plan of Latin Social Liberation," *Los Angeles Times*, 12 October 1984, pp. I-1, 20.

50. Richard J. Meislin, "Pope Issues Plea for Indian Rights in Guatemala Visit: Persecution Is Charged," *New York Times*, 8 March 1983, pp. 1, 4.

Central America and the United States: A Chronology of Events from 1979 to 1987

1979

July 19. Nicaragua: Victory of FSLN (Sandinista Forces for National Liberation, or Sandinistas) over National Guard ends Somoza dynasty. Government Junta of National Reconstruction established.

October 15. El Salvador: Coup against Gen. Carlos Humberto Romero, President of El Salvador, by progressive elements in the armed forces. They establish a revolutionary junta composed of two military officers and three civilians from center and moderate left parties.

1980

January 3. El Salvador: Civilian members of the Junta and most of the cabinet resign on the grounds that the military continues to exercise control, continuing repression and blocking reforms. A new junta is formed on January 9 composed of military officers and members of the Christian Democratic party.

March 3. El Salvador: Second junta falls and third created, with participation of Christian Democrat José Napoleón Duarte, resulting in split in Christian Democratic party; dissident group forms the Social Christian Movement. New junta institutes an agrarian reform and other reforms.

March 24. El Salvador: Assassination of Archbishop Oscar Arnulfo Romero.

April 2. The United States approves $5.7 million in military aid to El Salvador.

April 18. El Salvador: Formation of Democratic Revolutionary Front (FDR), composed of opposition political parties and mass organizations, including unions, peasant associations, professional and student associations. Supports the revolutionary movement.

August 23. Nicaragua: Elections announced for 1985.

October. Guatemala: Alliance formed of guerrilla organizations (ORPA, EGP, FAR, and the leadership nucleus of the Guatemalan Workers' party).

November. El Salvador: Guerrilla organizations join forces in Farabundo Martí Front for National Liberation (FMLN).

November 27. El Salvador: Six leaders of the FDR assassinated by security forces and paramilitary agents.

December 2. El Salvador: Four U.S. church women assassinated by the National Guard.

December 4. U.S. military and economic aid to El Salvador suspended.

December 13. El Salvador: Third junta dissolved; Christian Democrat José Napoleón Duarte becomes Acting President. U.S. economic aid resumed.

251

1981

January 5. El Salvador: Assassination of José Viera, president of Salvadoran agrarian reform institute and two U.S. AFL-CIO representatives, Michael Hammer and Mark Pearlman, in El Salvador.

January 11. El Salvador: Beginning of major FMLN offensive.

January 14. U.S. military aid to El Salvador, cut off after assassination of U.S. churchwomen, is resumed.

February 23. U.S. State Department issues White Paper stating that Soviet Union, East Europe, Cuba and Nicaragua are involved in aiding Salvadoran revolutionary groups. $15 million remaining of $75 million aid package to Nicaragua is cut off.

April–May. U.S. Congress adopts certification requirements specifying conditions for military aid to Salvadoran government.

May 16. El Salvador: Duarte government calls for Constituent Assembly elections in 1982.

August 28. Joint communique by Mexico and France recognizing the FDR-FMLN as a "representative political force."

October 7–9. Honduras: Joint U.S.-Honduran naval and air maneuvers.

November 29. Roberto Suazo Córdova of the Liberal Party elected president of Honduras and takes office on January 27.

November. Guatemala: Army carries out major counterinsurgency offensive in Chimaltenango province.

November 23. President Reagan authorizes a $19.9 million CIA-directed plan to aid paramilitary operations against Nicaragua, allegedly to interdict arms flow to Salvadoran rebels.

1982

January. Foreign Ministers of Costa Rica, El Salvador and Honduras announce the formation of the Central American Democratic Community, excluding Guatemala and Nicaragua.

February 20. Mexican president José López Portillo proposes agreements in El Salvador, Nicaragua, and between the United States and Cuba.

February 7. Guatemala: The EGP, ORPA, FAR, and the leadership nucleus of the PGT form the Guatemalan National Revolutionary Unity (URNG). Subsequently it is endorsed by the Guatemalan Committee of Patriotic Unity, formed by exiled leaders in mid-February.

February 24. President Reagan announces Caribbean Basin Initiative.

March 7. Guatemala: Official presidential candiate, General Angel Aníbal Guevara, wins elections.

March 23. Guatemala: Military coup brings Gen. Efraín Ríos Montt to power, initially as head of three-person junta. In June Ríos Montt becomes sole leader of Guatemala. Counterinsurgency attacks against villages in Quiché, Alta Verapaz, Chimaltenango, San Marcos, and Baja Verapaz are stepped up. In July, Ríos Montt declares a state of siege.

March 25. Nicaragua: Sandinista government declares state of emergency.

March 28. El Salvador: Constituent Assembly elections in El Salvador give rightwing parties control of Assembly. Under U.S. pressure, the Army high command appoints businessman Alvaro Magaña as acting president, but Roberto D'Aubuisson, reputed death squad leader and founding member of the National

Republican Alliance (ARENA) becomes President of the Assembly. In May the Assembly calls a halt to the agrarian reform.

July 26–August 5. Honduras: Joint U.S.-Honduran military maneuvers near the northeast border of Nicaragua.

September 15. Mexico and Venezuela propose talks between the United States and Nicaragua and between Nicaragua and Honduras.

October 4. U.S. organized Forum for peace and democracy held in San José, Costa Rica, with official representatives from Honduras, Costa Rica, El Salvador, Belize, Jamaica, and the Dominican Republic.

December 21. Boland amendment passed by U.S. House of Representatives by a vote of 411–0, prohibiting the U.S. Department of Defense (DOD) and Central Intelligence Agency (CIA) from providing military equipment, training or advice for the purpose of overthrowing the Nicaraguan government.

1983

January 7. President Reagan lifts embargo on arms sales to Guatemala, approving sale of $6.3 million in helicopter parts and military equipment.

January 8–9. Meeting of foreign ministers of Mexico, Venezuela, Colombia and Panama on island of Contadora, Panama, where they issue a call for dialogue and negotiation among the Central American countries.

February 1–6. Honduras: Joint U.S.-Honduran military maneuvers (Big Pine I), involving 1,600 U.S. troops and 4,600 Honduran troops.

March 2–9. Visit of Pope John Paul II to Central America.

April 20–21. Joint meeting of Contadora foreign ministers and those of five Central American countries to agree on general rules for negotiation. At subsequent meeting in May they create a technical group to gather information and study procedures for reaching a regional agreement.

April 28. Reagan administration names special envoy Philip Habib to explore political settlement for Central America.

July 16–17. Meeting of four presidents of Contadora countries in Cancún, Mexico, where they issue the Declaration of Cancún establishing six principles as a basis for agreement among the Central American countries and send letter to President Reagan soliciting U.S. cooperation in search for peaceful settlement in the region.

July 21. President Reagan names bipartisan commission, headed by Henry Kissinger, to recommend solutions for Central America.

July 26. President Reagan announces major military and naval maneuvers in Central America (Big Pine II) involving 19 ships with 16,456 troops as well as 4,000 ground troops, which take place from 5 August 1983 to 5 February 1984.

July 28. House passes "Boland-Zablocki" bill to end support for the covert war in Nicaragua.

August 8. Guatemala: Ríos Montt overthrown in military coup; succeeded by General Mejía Víctores.

September–October. Intensification of contra war against Nicaragua with bombing of international airport, oil facilities, and major ports.

September 7–9. Central American governments agree to 21 points of Bases para la Paz en Centroamérica proposed by Contadora.

October 25. U.S. invasion of Grenada, first use of active U.S. combat forces in Latin America since 1965 invasion of Dominican Republic.

1984

January 10. Report of Bipartisan Commission on Central America (Kissinger Commission) released, calling for $8 billion in aid to the region over a five year period. Although members of the Commission dissent on specific issues, the report essentially endorses the goals of the Reagan administration in Central America.

February. CIA mines Nicaragua's harbors. Several ships of Nicaragua and five other nations damaged in next few months. U.S. vetoes proposed U.N. Security Council resolution condemning the mining.

February 21. Nicaragua: Plans announced for elections on November 4.

March 19–29. Honduras: Joint U.S.-Honduran emergency deployment readiness exercise. U.S.-Honduras military exercises continue almost uninterruptedly throughout 1984 and subsequent years.

March 24. El Salvador: Presidential elections held, followed by run-off in May between Christian Democrat José Napoleón Duarte and ARENA candidate Roberto D'Aubuisson. Duarte wins and takes office on June 1. Impressed with Duarte's credentials, the U.S. Congress approves an escalation of U.S. military aid to El Salvador. Results in new phase of war, including aerial bombardment of countryside and expansion of Salvadoran army from 12,000 to 50,000 troops.

March 31. Honduras: General Gustavo Alvarez Martínez, chief of Armed Forces who cooperated closely with U.S. counterinsurgency policy in Central America, is forced to resign. He is succeeded by Air Force General Walter López Reyes.

April. Nicaragua brings suit against the United States in the World Court for mining its harbors and other acts of sabotage.

June. U.S. and Nicaragua begin talks at Manzanillo, Mexico.

June 9–10. First Contadora peace proposal submitted to Central American governments.

June 25. Joint House-Senate conference rejects Reagan request for $21 million in supplemental aid to the contras.

July 1. Guatemala: Elections for a constituent assembly to write a new constitution and draft an electoral law for presidential elections in 1985.

August 8. Nicaragua: Election campaign begins; state of emergency decreed March 1982 is lifted.

September. U.S. Congress learns of CIA training manual for the contras, "Psychological Operations in Guerrilla Warfare," which includes instructions for "neutralizing Sandinistas" and "creating martyrs" for the contra cause.

September 21. Nicaragua agrees to sign Contadora peace treaty, but it is rejected by U.S. State Department and by Costa Rica, El Salvador, and Honduras.

October 3. Boland amendment extended by House and Senate Intelligence committees for another year and tightened to prohibit DOD, CIA, and any other agency engaged in intelligence activities from providing support for military or paramilitary operations in Nicaragua.

October 15. El Salvador: First meeting between Duarte government and FMLN-FDR held in La Palma, Chalatenango, followed by a second meeting on November 30 at Ayagualo, La Libertad.

November 4. Nicaragua: Elections for president and vice president and Constituent Assembly held, with Sandinistas winning a majority. Daniel Ortega and Sergio Ramírez become president and vice president, respectively.

November 6. Reagan reelected. Announces that Nicaragua may be importing Soviet MIG-21 jet fighters (subsequently found to be a false alarm).

1985

January. Reagan administration suspends bilateral talks between Nicaragua and the United States.

February 11–May 3. Honduras: Pig Pine III exercises, involving up to 4,500 U.S. troops.

February. Reagan speech calling contras "freedom fighters," and comparing them to founding fathers.

March 31. El Salvador: Christian Democrats victorious in assembly and municipal elections, gaining control of assembly which has been in hands of rightwing parties, and 200 of 262 municipalities.

April 11. Memorandum from Lt. Col. Oliver North to Robert McFarlane, head of National Security Council, noting that from the expiration of U.S. assistance in July 1984 until April 9, 1985 the FDN had received $24.5 million, of which over $17 million "has been expended for arms, munitions, combat operations and support activities." He proposed efforts to obtain further funds from private donors. During this time North was also involved in efforts to obtain funds from foreign governments.

April 23. Senate votes humanitarian assistance to the contras.

April 23–24. U.S. House of Representatives rejects administration's $14 million contra aid request.

April–May. Nicaragua: President Daniel Ortega visits Western and Eastern Europe and the Soviet Union in search of economic and military support.

May 1. Reagan declares a national emergency and imposes economic sanctions against Nicaragua on the grounds that the actions of the Nicaraguan government constitute "an unusual and extraordinary threat to the national security and foreign policy of the United States."

June 12. U.S. Congress (House) approves $27 million in non-military aid to the contras.

June 19. El Salvador: Four U.S. marines and several others killed in attack by FMLN forces at restaurant in San Salvador.

July. Formation of Support group (sometimes referred to as Lima group) of four South American countries (Argentina, Brazil, Peru and Uruguay) to strengthen work of Contadora.

August 29. Guatemala: Beginning of week of massive demonstrations in Guatemala City for the first time in five years, protesting inflation and increased bus fares and calling for higher wages and for price freezes.

September. Contadora presents second Act for Peace and Cooperation in Central America. Rejected by Nicaragua on grounds of concessions to the United States.

October 15. Nicaragua: Government re-institutes state of emergency, requesting press and media to submit all material to censorship prior to publication or broadcast.

October 24. Guatemala: Elections for presidency, followed by a run-off election on December 8 won by Christian Democrat Vinicio Cerezo, who takes office on January 14.

October 24. El Salvador: FMLN releases Ines Guadalupe Duarte Durán, daughter of President Duarte, and 33 mayors and municipal officers, in return for the release of 22 political prisoners and permission for 96 wounded guerrillas to leave the country to receive medical help abroad.

November 24. Honduras: Liberal party candidate José Azcona Hoyo is elected president and is inaugurated January 27.

December. Boland prohibition against military aid to contras enacted; permits classified amounts of aid for communications, training and advice.

1986

January. El Salvador: Military maneuvers to push FMLN out of strategic locations, beginning with Operation Phoenix in the Guazapa volcano area, with subsequent operations in Chalatenango, Morazán, western Cabañas, and Usulután. FMLN mounts counterattacks.

January 23. Contadora and Support groups issue Message of Caraballeda in Venezuela calling for renewal of negotiations among Central American countries and of U.S.-Nicaragua talks.

January 23. El Salvador: President Duarte presents austerity package, including devaluation of the colón.

February 2. Costa Rica: Elections for president and for National Assembly won by National Liberation Party with 52 percent of the votes in the presidential elections and approximately 48 percent in the assembly elections. Dr. Oscar Arias elected president, takes office in May.

February 5. El Salvador: New labor confederation, Unidad Nacional de los Trabajadores Salvadoreños (UNTS), formed by unions, labor confederations, peasant organizations and cooperatives, including many formerly linked with the Christian Democratic party as well as those of the opposition.

May 1. Guatemala: Small (5,000 to 10,000) demonstration, calling for wage adjustments to offset inflation and moratorium on foreign debt payment, marks first May Day demonstration by unions in six years.

June 1. El Salvador: President Duarte proposes third round of peace talks with FDR-FMLN.

June 7. Third revised Contadora act presented by Contadora and Support groups, subsequently rejected by Costa Rica, El Salvador, and Honduras.

June 19. El Salvador: FMLN attack on military base in San Miguel. 250 military and 20 FMLN killed or wounded.

June. El Salvador: Inauguration of United to Reconstruct, a program for repopulation of key communities under Army supervision.

June 25. U.S. House of Representatives votes 221-209 to provide $100 million in contra aid (Edwards-Skelton bill), also removes restrictions on CIA and Pentagon training and provides $300 million in economic grants to Guatemala, El Salvador and Honduras.

June 26. Nicaragua: Government closes opposition newspaper *La Prensa.*

June 27. World Court finds that U.S. actions against Nicaragua have violated international law in training, arming and directing contra forces in military operations against Nicaragua; mining Nicaragua's harbors; flying military aircraft over Nicaragua; and several other points.

June 27. Nicaragua: Father Bismarck Carballo prohibited from re-entering Nicaragua; subsequently, on July 4, Bishop Pablo Antonio Vega was escorted out of the country.

September 19. El Salvador: Third round of talks scheduled between President Duarte and FMLN-FDR fails to materialize after Salvadoran army occupies prospective site, village of Sesori in eastern El Salvador.

October 9. Nicaragua: Plane flying military supplies to contras shot down. Three crew members die in crash; survivor Eugene Hasenfus captured by Sandinistas.

October 10. El Salvador: Massive earthquake in San Salvador in which 1,500 are killed, thousands more injured, and 250,000 to 300,000 left homeless. The damages are estimated at $1.5 to $2 billion.

November 6. New U.S. Immigration Reform and Control Act (Simpson-Rodino bill) grants amnesty to undocumented aliens who entered U.S. before January 1, 1982 but imposes sanctions on employers who hire undocumented immigrants.

November 25. U.S. Attorney General Edwin Meese reports that funds from arms sales to Iran have been secretly diverted to contras. National Security Advisor Vice Admiral John Poindexter resigns and Lt. Col. Oliver North is removed from National Security Council due to involement in Iran-contra crisis. Tower commission appointed by President Reagan to investigate.

December 22. El Salvador: New economic package approved by Christian Democratic controlled assembly involving income and property taxes affecting chiefly high and middle income groups.

December. Federal District Court Judge Lawrence E. Walsh named special prosecutor in Iran-contra affair. Special House and Senate investigating committees set up.

1987

January. Nicaragua: New constitution goes into effect.

January–April. U.S. holds Big Pine '87 maneuvers in Honduras, within seven miles of Nicaraguan border, followed in May by Solid Shield '87, largest military exercise held in Honduras in five years.

February 16. Split in Nicaraguan opposition group, United Nicaraguan Opposition (UNO), results in resignation of Adolfo Calero, followed by resignation of Arturo Cruz on March 9. In May, UNO is replaced by new umbrella group, Nicaraguan Resistance.

February 16. President Arias of Costa Rica presents peace proposal calling for cease fire in Guatemala, El Salvador, and Nicaragua; talks with unarmed opposition; cutoff of outside aid to insurgent forces; amnesty for insurgents; full observance of civil rights and democratic processes; and revival of a Central American parliament. Plan is subsequently endorsed by U.S. Senate.

February 26. Tower Commission report released including information on National Security Council involvement in sale of arms to Iran and soliciting funds from private and government sources for Nicaraguan contras.

March 9. U.S. Supreme Court decision affirms criterion of well-founded fear of persecution as grounds for asylum.

March 31. El Salvador: Attack of FMLN against El Paraiso military barracks in Chalatenango, following series of successful attacks in 1986-87. Results in reassessment of strength of FMLN.

June–July. Open hearings by Select Committees of U.S. House of Representatives and U.S. Senate on administration involvement in sale of arms to Iran, diversion of funds to contras, efforts to raise money for contras from foreign governments and private sources, and subsequent cover-up.

August 7. Central American governments sign Arias peace plan, bypassing proposed peace plan by Reagan and Rep. Wright. In subsequent months, Central American governments take measures to implement the plan. In the case of Nicaragua, these include the reopening of *La Prensa* and permission for Father Caballo and Bishop Vega to return to the country.

September 10. Reagan administration announces intention to seek $270 million in aid to contras over the next 18 months. Subsequently, aid request is postponed; Congress approves continuation of non-lethal aid ($3.5 million in October, $3.2 million in November).

October 13. President Arias of Costa Rica receives Nobel Peace Prize.

About the Editors and Contributors

Adolfo Aguilar Zinser is a senior associate at the Carnegie Endowment for International Peace and researcher in CIDE (Centro de Investigaciones y Docencia Económica), Mexico, where he is a coordinator of a series of reports on Mexico's relations with Central America. He has published numerous articles on Mexico, U.S.-Mexican relations and Central America.

Gabriel Aguilera Peralta is a researcher at the Facultad Latinoamérica de Ciencias Sociales (FLACSO), San José, Costa Rica, and former director of the Instituto Centroamericano de Documentación e Investigación Social (ICADIS). He has written extensively on the military, counterinsurgency and violence in Guatemala and Central America.

Cynthia Arnson is a foreign policy legislative assistant in the U.S. House of Representatives, specializing in Central America, and a Ph.D. candidate at the Johns Hopkins School of Advanced International Studies. She has written extensively on U.S. policy in Central America, with emphasis on El Salvador.

Deborah Barry is coordinator for North American Relations, CRIES (Coordinadora Regional de Investigaciones Económicas y Sociales), Managua, where she is conducting a study on U.S. military policy in Central America. Previously she worked in the Ministries of Agriculture and Planning.

José Rodolfo Castro is former director of the Department of Political Science, Universidad de El Salvador, and of the Department of Sociology, Universidad Centroaméricana, Managua. He is currently coordinator of the project Conflicts and Alternatives for Peace in Central America for CRIES.

Michael E. Conroy is associate professor of economics and associate director of the Institute for Latin American Studies, University of Texas. He is founder of the Central America Resource Center which he co-directed between 1983 and 1985, and has written several articles on the Nicaraguan economy.

Margaret E. Crahan is Henry R. Luce professor at Occidental College, Los Angeles. She has written on Spanish colonial administration, church-state relations, twentieth century Cuba, and African cultural heritage in the Caribbean, including *Human Rights and Basic Needs in the Americas* and *Africa and the Caribbean*.

Patricia Weiss Fagen is associate of the Refugee Policy Group, Washington, D.C., and associate professor of history at San Jose State University, California. She is the author of *Exiles and Citizens: Spanish Republicans in Mexico* and of numerous articles on Latin American history and politics, human rights, and U.S. refugee and asylum policy.

Jeffry A. Frieden is assistant professor of political science, University of California, Los Angeles. He is author of *Banking on the World: The Politics of American International*

Finance (Harper, 1987) and of several articles on the politics of international monetary and financial issues.

Linda Fuller is assistant professor of sociology, University of Southern California, Los Angeles. She is the author of several articles on labor in Cuba and is completing a book on workers' control in post-revolutionary Cuba.

Xabier Gorostiaga is regional coordinator of CRIES (Coordinadora Regional de Investigaciones Económicas y Sociales). He is former director of the Nicaraguan Institute for Economic and Social Research (INIES) and of National Planning in the Nicaraguan Planning Ministry (1979–1981).

Nora Hamilton is associate professor of political science at the University of Southern California, Los Angeles. She is author of *The Limits of State Autonomy: Post Revolutionary Mexico* and of articles on Mexico and Central America, and co-editor of *Modern Mexico: State, Economy and Social Conflict.*

Terry Karl is assistant professor of government, Stanford University. She is the author of numerous articles on Central American and Venezuelan politics and on U.S.–Central American relations and is currently working on a book: *The Impact of Oil Booms on Oil-Exporting Countries: Democracy over a Barrel in Venezuela.*

Peter Marchetti, a Jesuit and sociologist, is director of research and graduate programs at the Universidad Centroamericana in Managua, and former advisor to the Ministry of Agrarian Reform and Agricultural Development.

Manuel Pastor, Jr., is assistant professor of economics at Occidental College, Los Angeles. He is author of *The International Monetary Fund and Latin America: Economic Stabilization and Class Conflict* (Westview, 1987) and recipient of a Fulbright Research Grant to study stabilization programs in Bolivia and Peru.

Kenneth E. Sharpe is associate professor of political science at Swarthmore College. He is the author of *The State vs. the Transnational Corporations: The Political Economy of the Mexican Auto Industry* and is co-editor of *Confronting Revolution: Security through Diplomacy in Central America.*

Ricardo Stein is deputy executive director of the Fundación Salvadoreña de Desarrollo y Vivienda Mínima, San Salvador. Formerly he was director of the Centro Universitario de Documentación e Información at the Universidad Centroamericana José Simeón Cañas and editor of the weekly newsletter *Proceso.*

Edelberto Torres Rivas is secretary general of the Facultad Latinoamérica de Ciencias Sociales (FLACSO), San José, Costa Rica and author of numerous studies on Central America with emphasis on the regional economies and migration.

Raúl Vergara, an economist, is a former captain of the Chilean Air Force and member of the Executive Secretariat of the Organización de Militares por la Democracia en América Latina y el Caribe (OMIDELAC). He is advisor for the CRIES project Conflict and Alternatives for Peace in Central America.

Index

Act of Peace and Cooperation for Central America (1984), 105
Additive development (desarrollo aditivo), 122
Afghanistan, 4, 80
  U.S. refugee policy, 7, 11, 61–63, 66, 72
Africa, U.S. refugee policy, 62
Agrarian reform, 139, 146, 162
  Cuba, 215
  El Salvador, 177–179, 182–183, 186, 193, 231
  Guatemala, 163
  Honduras, 238
  Nicaragua, 207, 215–216
Agrarian Reform Law of Nicaragua (1981), 216
Agreement on the Central American System of Integration Industries (1958), 144
Agreement on the Tariff and Customs System, 148
Aguacate, Honduras, 26
Ahuas Taras II, 107
AID. See U.S. Agency for International Development
Alas, José Inocencio, 231
Alfonsín, Raúl, 120
Algeria, 154
Allende, Salvador, 37, 212–214
Alliance for Progress, 32
Alta Verapaz, Guatemala, 160
Alvarez, José Eduardo, 232
Alvarez, Gustavo, 44
Amado, Juan José, 101
Angola, 4, 20, 37, 80, 213
Aparicio, Pedro Arnaldo, 232
Aquino, Corazón, 79
Arbenz Guzmán, Jacobo, 167, 235
ARENA. See National Republican Alliance
Argentina, 62, 85, 106, 111

Arias peace plan (1987), 1, 11, 113, 203, 222
Asia, U.S. refugee policy, 62
Assemblies of God, 238
Asylum, 61–70. See also Refugees and displaced persons
Ayagualo, El Salvador, 184, 233

Bahro, Rudolf, 211
Barnes, Michael, 26
Belize, 68, 101
Betancur, Belisario, 102
BHRHA. See U.S. Bureau of Human Rights and Humanitarian Affairs
Big Pine II, 107
Bishop, Maurice, 107
BLI. See Irregular Warfare Battalions
Boland, Edward, 44–45
  amendment, 25–26, 31
Boner, Bill, 43
Borge, Tomás, 90
Brazil, 3, 106, 111, 211–212, 220
Brezhnev doctrine (1968), 79
British-American Tobacco, 215
Bureau of Human Rights and Humanitarian Affairs. See U.S. Bureau of Human Rights and Humanitarian Affairs
Burton, Dan, 50
Bush, George, 42

CACM. See Central American Common Market
Cambodia, 17, 80
Campíns, Luis Herrera, 100, 102
Campus Crusade for Christ, 236
Cancún, Mexico, 104
Capitalism, 120, 123, 125, 207–209, 211, 213
  and the Catholic Church, 236–237
Caraballeda declaration, 106